Contributions to Economics

The series *Contributions to Economics* provides an outlet for innovative research in all areas of economics. Books published in the series are primarily monographs and multiple author works that present new research results on a clearly defined topic, but contributed volumes and conference proceedings are also considered. All books are published in print and ebook and disseminated and promoted globally. The series and the volumes published in it are indexed by Scopus and ISI (selected volumes).

Wanglin Ma · Dil B. Rahut · Tetsushi Sonobe
Editors

Beyond Income

Subjective Well-Being and Rural Transformation in Asia

ADBInstitute

Springer

Editors
Wanglin Ma
Lincoln University
Christchurch, Canterbury, New Zealand

Dil B. Rahut
Asian Development Bank Institute (ADBI)
Tokyo, Japan

Tetsushi Sonobe
National Graduate Institute for Policy
Studies (GRIPS)
Tokyo, Japan

ISSN 1431-1933 ISSN 2197-7178 (electronic)
Contributions to Economics
ISBN 978-981-92-4956-5 ISBN 978-981-92-4957-2 (eBook)
https://doi.org/10.1007/978-981-92-4957-2

This Springer imprint is published by the registered company Springer Nature Singapore Pte Ltd.
The registered company address is: 152 Beach Road, #21-01/04 Gateway East, Singapore 189721, Singapore

Preface

Rural Asia is undergoing a profound and multifaceted transformation. Over the past several decades, rapid economic growth, structural change, and technological progress have reshaped rural livelihoods across the region. While rising incomes and expanding opportunities remain central objectives of development policy, they do not always capture how people experience and evaluate their lives. Rural households often face complex trade-offs as economies evolve. Migration can bring higher incomes but also social separation; technological progress may improve productivity while creating new uncertainties, and modernization can enhance living standards while altering traditional social structures. As a result, development outcomes must increasingly be assessed not only in terms of material progress but also through the lens of human well-being.

In recent years, the concept of subjective well-being, i.e., how individuals perceive and evaluate their lives, has emerged as a valuable complement to traditional economic measures of welfare. Indicators such as happiness, life satisfaction, loneliness, depression, and worry provide important insights into the lived experiences of individuals and communities. For rural populations in Asia, whose livelihoods remain closely linked to agriculture, environmental conditions, and social networks, these dimensions of subjective well-being are particularly significant.

This book, *Beyond Income: Subjective Well-Being and Rural Transformation in Asia*, offers a timely and important contribution to the growing literature that seeks to integrate subjective well-being into development analysis. Bringing together a set of carefully researched chapters, the book explores how different dimensions of rural transformation, ranging from agricultural productivity and labor migration to energy transitions, sanitation improvements, ageing, and early-life experiences, shape the well-being of rural populations.

By combining insights from agricultural economics, development economics, public health, and social policy, the book's evidence shows that subjective well-being is shaped not only by income but also by factors such as health conditions, environmental quality, social relationships, and psychological experiences accumulated over the life course. Also, the book underscores that policies aimed at improving rural welfare must adopt a multidimensional approach. Investments in agricultural productivity, rural infrastructure, clean energy, and sanitation can generate substantial benefits for people's quality of life. At the same time, attention must be given to mental health, social inclusion, and the long-term impacts of early-life conditions. By bringing these issues together, the book provides valuable insights for policymakers seeking to design more holistic and inclusive rural development strategies.

As Asian countries continue to pursue economic growth and modernization, it is essential to ensure that progress translates into genuine improvements in people's lives. The perspectives presented in this book remind us that development is ultimately about enhancing human well-being in all its dimensions.

Christchurch, New Zealand — Wanglin Ma
Tokyo, Japan — Dil B. Rahut
Tokyo, Japan — Tetsushi Sonobe

Acknowledgements

The editors gratefully acknowledge the reviewers who carefully reviewed the chapters before their acceptance, and former staff member Adam Majoe of the Asian Development Bank Institute (ADBI) for coordinating the editing and production process. They also thank Dr Raja Rajendra Timilsina, Dr Ngawang Dendup, Prof. Song Soo Lim, Mami Nomoto, and Chiisye Toki of ADBI for their invaluable support in organizing the international conference "*Innovations for Sustainable Agriculture and Rural Development*", held on 22–24 September 2025. The papers in this book were presented during the Part 2 Session, themed on "*Enhancing the Subjective Well-Being of Rural Residents: Pathways, Impacts, and Policies*", on Day 3 of the conference. Other people who contributed to the conference were also greatly acknowledged.

Introduction and Summary

Across developing Asia, rural transformation has reshaped livelihoods, production systems, and social structures at an unprecedented pace. Rapid economic growth, structural transformation, urbanization, and technological change have lifted millions of people out of poverty. Agricultural modernization, improved infrastructure, and expanding off-farm employment opportunities have increased incomes and broadened opportunities for rural households. Yet rising income alone does not necessarily translate into a better quality of life. In many rural communities, economic progress has been accompanied by new social pressures, environmental challenges, and psychological stresses that affect how people experience and evaluate their lives.

These realities have prompted a growing recognition that development must be assessed not only through objective indicators such as income, productivity, and consumption, but also through measures of subjective well-being—how individuals perceive and evaluate their lives in terms of happiness, life satisfaction, mental health, and future expectations. Subjective well-being captures dimensions of welfare that traditional economic metrics often overlook, including psychological security, social belonging, autonomy, and perceptions of opportunity. In rural Asia, where livelihoods remain closely tied to agriculture, community networks, and environmental conditions, these subjective dimensions of welfare are particularly important.

Recent research has increasingly highlighted that rural transformation influences individuals' subjective well-being through multiple pathways. Changes in agricultural productivity, employment structures, energy use, sanitation infrastructure, and social institutions shape not only material living standards but also people's mental and emotional experiences. For example, improvements in rural infrastructure can enhance comfort and health, while labor migration may increase income but simultaneously generate loneliness or family separation. Similarly, technological progress and modernization can expand opportunities but may also create new uncertainties and expectations. As a result, understanding the human dimension of rural development requires examining how structural changes shape people's lived experiences beyond income alone.

This book aims to deepen understanding of the relationship between rural transformation and subjective well-being in Asia. By integrating insights from agricultural economics, development economics, and social sciences, the book explores how economic, social, and environmental changes influence rural people's perceptions of their quality of life. The chapters provide empirical evidence from multiple Asian contexts and examine how different aspects of rural transformation—from farm production and labor markets to energy transitions, sanitation infrastructure, mental health, and early-life experiences—shape subjective well-being outcomes.

The book consists of seven chapters that collectively explore the drivers and consequences of subjective well-being in rural Asia. Each chapter examines a distinct dimension of rural transformation and its implications for human welfare.

Chapter 1, *The Satisfaction Paradox in Developing Asia: How Subjective Well-Being Shapes Socio-Political Empowerment among Rural Women: Evidence from 12 Asian Economies*, investigates the complex relationship between subjective well-being and women's socio-political empowerment in developing Asia. Using World Values Survey data from twelve Asian economies, the chapter examines whether higher levels of happiness and life satisfaction translate into greater empowerment among rural women. The results reveal a "satisfaction paradox": while happiness can strengthen aspirations for autonomy and equality, other dimensions of well-being—such as perceived freedom and financial satisfaction—may reduce motivation for systemic change. The analysis also uncovers substantial heterogeneity across education, income, employment status, and marital status. By highlighting the potential disconnect between subjective well-being and empowerment, the chapter challenges conventional development narratives that equate higher life satisfaction with improved agency and equality, and calls for policy interventions that consciously link well-being improvements to empowerment outcomes.

Chapter 2, *Happy Farmers, Efficient Farms: Insights from Potato Production in India*, explores how farmers' subjective well-being influences agricultural productivity. Using primary survey data from 793 potato-producing households in Uttar Pradesh, India, the chapter applies stochastic frontier analysis and a conditional mixed-process model to examine whether happier farmers achieve higher technical efficiency. The findings reveal that greater happiness is significantly associated with improved technical efficiency and higher crop yields, with the effects being particularly pronounced among better-educated farmers. These results suggest that psychological well-being can shape farmers' motivation, decision-making, and openness to improved farming practices. By integrating behavioral dimensions into the study of agricultural productivity, the chapter highlights the importance of considering farmers' well-being alongside traditional economic and technological interventions to promote sustainable agricultural development.

Chapter 3, *Types of Off-Farm Employment and Multidimensional Subjective Well-Being among Wheat Farmers: Evidence from China*, examines how different types of off-farm employment affect the subjective well-being of rural households. Using household survey data from wheat-producing regions in China, the chapter distinguishes between three employment categories: farming only, local off-farm employment, and migrant off-farm employment. Employing a multivalued treatment effects model, the study evaluates their impacts on multiple well-being indicators, including happiness, life satisfaction, anxiety, loneliness, and depression. The findings reveal significant heterogeneity: while migrant off-farm employment improves happiness and life satisfaction and reduces negative subjective well-being outcomes, local off-farm employment may have the opposite effect. By demonstrating that employment quality and location matter for well-being outcomes, the chapter provides insights into the social and psychological consequences of rural labor transformation and offers policy recommendations for improving rural livelihoods under China's rural revitalization strategy.

Chapter 4, *Clean Energy Use for Heating and Rural Subjective Well-Being in China: Implications for Energy Transition*, investigates the well-being impacts of household energy transitions in rural China. Using household survey data and applying endogenous switching regression and multivalued treatment effects models, the chapter evaluates how the use of clean heating energy affects residents' happiness and life satisfaction. The results indicate that transitioning to clean heating energy significantly improves subjective well-being, particularly when households fully switch to clean fuels rather than partially adopting them. The positive effects operate primarily through improved health outcomes and more comfortable indoor temperatures. By highlighting the broader welfare implications of energy transitions, the chapter contributes to policy debates on rural decarbonization and underscores the importance of promoting complete transitions to clean energy systems.

Chapter 5, *Improved Sanitation through Flush Toilet Use and Rural Subjective Well-Being in China*, investigates the role of improved sanitation infrastructure in enhancing rural quality of life. Using household data from multiple regions in China, the study evaluates the impact of flush toilet use on subjective well-being, as measured by happiness, life satisfaction, and future confidence. The empirical results suggest that access to flush toilets significantly improves all three dimensions of subjective well-being, with stronger effects among younger, poorer, and less-educated rural residents. By linking sanitation infrastructure to both health and psychological well-being outcomes, the chapter demonstrates how investments in rural living environments can generate broader social benefits. The findings support ongoing efforts to promote sanitation improvements as part of rural development strategies.

Chapter 6, *Mental Health and Life Satisfaction in Later Life: Evidence from Bangladesh*, examines the determinants of mental well-being among older adults in Bangladesh. Drawing on primary survey data from 400 individuals aged 60 and above, the chapter analyzes multiple dimensions of well-being, including life satisfaction, quality of life, and depressive symptoms, using validated psychological scales and ordered probit models. The findings highlight depressive symptoms as the strongest negative correlate of both life satisfaction and quality of life, while education, social engagement, and supportive family relationships are positively associated with well-being. By providing empirical evidence from a rapidly aging developing-country context, the chapter contributes to the literature on aging and mental health. It emphasizes the need for integrated policies that combine accessible mental health services with initiatives that foster lifelong learning and community engagement.

Chapter 7, *The Long-Term Impact of Adverse Childhood Experiences on Subjective Well-Being: Longitudinal Evidence from Rural China*, explores how childhood adversity shapes well-being outcomes later in life. Using longitudinal data from the China Health and Retirement Longitudinal Study (CHARLS), the chapter analyzes the long-term effects of adverse childhood experiences on life satisfaction and depressive symptoms among middle-aged and older adults in rural China. The results reveal that adverse childhood experiences significantly reduce subjective well-being in later life, primarily through pathways such as poorer health, unhealthy behaviors, and reduced social participation. These effects are particularly pronounced among individuals with higher levels of education and those living in eastern China. The chapter underscores the lasting consequences of childhood adversity and highlights the importance of early-life interventions and mental health support systems to improve long-term well-being outcomes.

Contents

1 The Satisfaction Paradox in Developing Asia: How Subjective Well-Being Shapes Socio-Political Empowerment Among Rural Women: Evidence from 12 Asian Economies 1
Avik Ghosh and Suman Sourav
1.1 Introduction 1
1.2 Literature Review 4
1.3 Data and Variables 8
1.4 Empirical Strategy 15
1.5 Results and Discussion 17
1.6 Conclusions, Policy Implications, and Limitations 31
Appendix 33
References 38

2 Happy Farmers, Efficient Farms: Insights from Potato Production in India 43
Lixue Qu, Wanglin Ma, and Nozomi Kawarazuka
2.1 Introduction 43
2.2 Potato Production in India 46
2.3 Estimation Strategies 47
2.4 Data and Descriptive Statistics 50
2.5 Results and Discussion 51
2.6 Conclusion and Policy Implications 61
Appendix 62
References 64

3 Types of Off-Farm Employment and Multidimensional Subjective Well-Being Among Wheat Farmers: Evidence from China 69
Ziqi Wang, Wanglin Ma, and Alan Renwick
3.1 Introduction 69
3.2 Background and Literature Review 71
3.3 Conceptual Framework 76
3.4 Methodology 78
3.5 Empirical Results 85
3.6 Conclusion and Policy Recommendations 91
References 92

4 Clean Energy Use for Heating and Rural Subjective Well-Being in China: Implications for Energy Transition 97
Xiance Sang, Xiaofeng Luo, Hongyun Zheng, and Wanglin Ma
4.1 Introduction 97
4.2 Conceptual Framework and Empirical Strategies 99
4.3 Data Collection, Variables, and Descriptive Statistics 104
4.4 Empirical Results 106
4.5 Conclusions and Policy Implications 113
Appendix 114
References 116

5 Improved Sanitation Through Flush Toilet Use and Rural Subjective Well-Being in China 121
Junpeng Li, Wanglin Ma, Dil B. Rahut, and Quan He
5.1 Introduction 121
5.2 Conceptual Framework 124
5.3 Data, Variable Definitions, and Descriptive Statistics 125
5.4 Empirical Methods 130
5.5 Results 131
5.6 Conclusions and Implications 135
References 136

6 Mental Health and Life Satisfaction in Later Life: Evidence from Bangladesh 141
Alessia Destefanis, Dil B. Rahut, Tetsushi Sonobe, and Shafiun N. Shimul
6.1 Introduction 141
6.2 Literature Review and Conceptual Framework 143
6.3 Survey Design and Data 146
6.4 Measuring Well-Being: Tools, Indicators, Specification 149
6.5 Empirical Findings 157
6.6 Conclusions and Policy Implications 162
Appendix 164
References 168

7 The Long-Term Impact of Adverse Childhood Experiences on Subjective Well-Being: Longitudinal Evidence from Rural China 171
Peng Nie and Xili Lin
7.1 Introduction 171
7.2 Prior Literature and Underlying Mechanisms 173
7.3 Data and Method 176
7.4 Results 181
7.5 Conclusion and Implications 192
Appendix 194
References 198

Editors and Contributors

About the Editors

Wanglin Ma is a Full Professor of Applied Economics at the Department of Global Value Chains and Trade, Faculty of Agribusiness and Commerce, Lincoln University, New Zealand. His research spans agricultural and development economics, with a strong emphasis on identifying strategies that enhance farm performance, strengthen the sustainability of the agrifood systems, improve household welfare and farmers' subjective well-being, and promote sustainable rural and agricultural development. He earned his PhD in Agricultural Economics from the University of Kiel, Germany, and has authored more than 160 articles in leading international journals.

Dil B. Rahut is Vice Chair of Research at the Asian Development Bank Institute (ADBI). He was a Sr. Global Program Manager for the International Maize and Wheat Improvement Centre's (CIMMYT). He also worked in the Research and Statistics Department of the Royal Monetary Authority of Bhutan, the WorldFish Centre as a senior fellow and Japan chair at the Indian Council for Research in International Economic Relations, chief of research, planning, and monitoring at the Bank of Bhutan Ltd, and assistant professor of development economics at South Asian University. He has a Ph.D. in development economics from the University of Bonn's Center for Development Research, Germany. He has over 260 peer-reviewed publications in Scopus-indexed journals and several books focusing on development issues.

Tetsushi Sonobe is a professor of economics at the National Graduate Institute for Policy Studies (GRIPS), a public policy school in Tokyo, and the president of the Japanese Association for Development Economics (JADE). Previously, he was Dean and CEO of the Asian Development Bank Institute (ADBI), Vice President of GRIPS, and professor at GRIPS and Tokyo Metropolitan University. In 2023, he served as the chairperson of T7, the think-tank engagement group of the G7.

Contributors

Alessia Destefanis Paris School of Economics (PSE) & Université Paris 1 Panthéon-Sorbonne, Paris, France

Avik Ghosh Reserve Bank of India, Kanpur, India

Quan He Department of Global Value Chains and Trade, Faculty of Agribusiness and Commerce, Lincoln University, Christchurch, New Zealand

Nozomi Kawarazuka Department of Regenerative Agriculture, International Potato Center, Hanoi, Vietnam

Junpeng Li Business School, Huaiyin Normal University, Huai'an, China

Xili Lin School of Economics and Finance, Xi'an Jiaotong University, Xi'an, China

Xiaofeng Luo College of Economics and Management, Huazhong Agricultural University, Wuhan, China

Peng Nie School of Economics and Finance, Xi'an Jiaotong University, Xi'an, China;
Institute for Health Care & Public Management, Stuttgart, Germany;
IZA@LISER, Belval, Luxembourg

Lixue Qu Department of Global Value Chains and Trade, Faculty of Agribusiness and Commerce, Lincoln University, Christchurch, New Zealand

Alan Renwick Department of Global Value Chains and Trade, Faculty of Agribusiness and Commerce, Lincoln University, Christchurch, New Zealand

Xiance Sang College of Economics and Management, Zhejiang A&F University, Hangzhou, China

Shafiun N. Shimul Institute of Health Economics, University of Dhaka, Dhaka, Bangladesh

Suman Sourav Indian Institute of Science, Bengaluru, Karnataka, India

Ziqi Wang Department of Global Value Chains and Trade, Faculty of Agribusiness and Commerce, Lincoln University, Christchurch, New Zealand

Hongyun Zheng College of Economics and Management, Huazhong Agricultural University, Wuhan, China

Chapter 1
Subjective Well-being and Rural Development in Asia: Concepts, Measurement, and Policy Relevance

Avik Ghosh and Suman Sourav

1.1 Introduction

Rural women in South Asia constitute a pivotal yet frequently underrecognized segment of society, playing a central role in shaping household well-being, agricultural productivity, and community resilience, yet remaining marginalized in socioeconomic decision-making and political participation (Kabeer 2012). Despite persistent exposure to poverty, climate vulnerability, and systemic gender discrimination, these women sustain national economies and social cohesion. Rural women in South Asia face an interconnected web of systemic challenges that perpetuate cycles of inequality across generations (Hasan 2023). They experience severe economic marginalization, with only 32% workforce participation compared to 77% for men in 2023, earning 30–50% less for similar agricultural work (World Bank 2024). Healthcare access remains problematic (Terefe et al. 2025), educational barriers persist, and digital exclusion leaves women 31% less likely to access mobile internet in 2023 (WEF 2024). Gender-based violence affects one in three South Asian women (IFC 2020), whereas climate change disproportionately impacts women farmers (World Bank 2024). These realities raise a fundamental question: can rising "happiness" and life satisfaction among rural women be taken as evidence of genuine empowerment, or might such satisfaction sometimes coexist with- and even entrench- low agency and acceptance of unequal norms? This paper starts from the premise, rooted in the capability and empowerment literatures, that subjective well-being (SWB) is not a neutral proxy for freedom or power: under conditions of structural constraint, women may adapt their aspirations and report high satisfaction while remaining

A. Ghosh (✉)
Reserve Bank of India, Kanpur, India
e-mail: avikghosh@rbi.org.in; avikghosh20@iitk.ac.in

S. Sourav
Indian Institute of Science, Bengaluru, Karnataka, India
e-mail: sumansourav@iisc.ac.in

W. Ma et al. (eds.), *Beyond Income*, Contributions to Economics,
https://doi.org/10.1007/978-981-92-4957-2_1

politically and socially disempowered (Sen 1999; Kabeer 2012; Nussbaum 2000; Graham 2009).

Measures such as GDP, literacy, or life expectancy remain important, but they tell us little about how people actually live, especially women in rural Asia, whose realities are often obscured by aggregate indicators (Stiglitz et al. 2009). Subjective well-being (SWB), which captures how people evaluate their lives, has gained widespread acceptance among academics and in policy discourse (Diener et al. 2018). Subjective well-being refers to individuals' self-assessed evaluations of their overall happiness and life satisfaction, reflecting their cognitive and affective appraisal of life as a whole (Diener et al. 2018; Helliwell et al. 2021). Surveys such as the World Values Survey (Inglehart et al. 2022) and the Asian Barometer Survey (Chang et al. 2011) demonstrate their utility by highlighting dimensions of satisfaction that standard statistics often overlook. These dimensions could finally give voice to millions of rural women facing similar, yet invisible, struggles across South Asia. A deeper dive into the nuances of these survey results underscores contrasting views about the South Asian Countries, where rural women, despite living with deep gender hierarchies, limited economic freedom, and barriers to formal institutions, report high satisfaction with their lives (Inglehart et al. 2022). This so-called "Satisfaction Paradox" makes it difficult for academicians and policymakers to consider subjective well-being at face value in welfare policy-making. Across Southeast Asia, rural women remain central to agricultural production, informal labour, and household management; yet, their access to political voice and institutional representation remains limited. Chattopadhyay and Duflo (2004) demonstrated that reserved seats increased women's representation in village councils; however, this did not automatically dismantle patriarchal decision-making structures. Understanding this dynamic is critical for designing interventions that genuinely advance women's empowerment, rather than mistaking adaptive contentment[1] for substantive progress.

There are at least three reasons why higher SWB might be associated with lower emancipative orientations among structurally constrained women. First, the adaptation literature shows that people often adjust expectations to persistent deprivation, reporting high satisfaction once they "make peace" with limited opportunity sets (Clark et al. 2008; Diener et al. 2018). Second, feminist accounts of empowerment emphasise that women may internalise restrictive gender norms and prioritise harmony, security and fulfilment of prescribed roles over overt contestation (Njiru et al. 2026), so that contentment reflects coping rather than expanded voice (Kabeer 2012; Cornwall and Rivas 2015). Third, research on aspirations argues that when opportunity horizons are narrow, well-being gains can reinforce acceptance of the status quo; only when education, resources and exposure broaden the "capacity to aspire" does higher SWB translate into greater demands for autonomy and equality (Appadurai 2004; Genicot and Ray 2017; Graham 2009). These mechanisms jointly support our central hypothesis that some dimensions of SWB may be negatively

[1] Adaptive contentment occurs when people lower their expectations and feel satisfied with poor conditions because they have gotten used to having limited opportunities (Sen 1999).

associated with indicators of emancipative and sceptical empowerment among rural women.

Despite a rapidly growing literature on subjective well-being and women's empowerment, three important research gaps remain. First, most existing studies examine SWB or empowerment in isolation, without jointly modelling how different dimensions of well-being align with, or cut across, multidimensional socio-political empowerment indicators for rural women in developing Asia. Second, cross-country comparative evidence on rural women in Asian developing economies remains scarce, with many contributions focusing on single countries, urban samples, or national aggregates. Third, little is known about how the relationship between SWB and empowerment varies across the distribution of empowerment and key socio-demographic strata such as education, employment, income, and marital status. To address these gaps, this paper pursues three interrelated research objectives: (i) to document structural patterns and socio-economic determinants of the Socio-Political Empowerment and Values Indicators among rural women in twelve developing Asian economies; (ii) to assess how multiple SWB dimensions (happiness, life satisfaction, perceived freedom and satisfaction with household finances) are associated with these empowerment indicators; and (iii) to examine whether these associations exhibit distributive heterogeneity across empowerment quantiles and socio-demographic groups. In line with the mechanisms outlined above, we hypothesise a "satisfaction–empowerment paradox": happiness may be positively associated with some empowerment dimensions. In contrast, life satisfaction and perceived freedom may be negatively associated with emancipative and critical orientations, particularly among more constrained groups.

Empirically, the study reveals that subjective feelings of happiness consistently drive aspirations for empowerment, fueling women's desires for greater autonomy and equality. In contrast, other dimensions of well-being, such as perceived freedom, life satisfaction, and financial contentment, exhibit more complex effects, often undermining motivation for systemic change or directing aspirations toward specific domains, such as education, rather than broader social reforms. The analysis also highlights demographic and regional heterogeneity: women with higher education and income levels, as well as those who are unmarried, tend to translate well-being gains into stronger empowerment orientations more readily than their less-educated, lower-income, or married counterparts. Regional comparisons reveal that cultural and institutional contexts significantly influence these dynamics, with some countries demonstrating stronger links between improvements in well-being and empowerment. In contrast, others exhibit more pronounced signs of the "satisfaction paradox." These findings underscore the importance of designing policies that raise subjective well-being and deliberately channel its varied dimensions toward substantive empowerment outcomes.

By untangling the "satisfaction paradox" alongside the socio-political empowerment and values indicators framework, this study guides policymakers in discerning when high well-being signals genuine empowerment and when it masks quiet acceptance. On the theory side, the study weaves subjective well-being into the broader conversation on capabilities and empowerment. On the empirical side, it tests these ideas with World Values Survey data from developing Asia. Moreover, on the practical side, it introduces straightforward metrics that can steer gender-aware policy design. Building on these objectives, we articulate the following research questions to guide the empirical analysis: (a) What structural determinants shape variations in the Socio-Political Empowerment and Values Indicators among rural women in developing Asian countries? (b) How does subjective well-being, measured through multiple life satisfaction and well-being dimensions, influence the SPEVI outcomes for rural women? Furthermore, (c) to what extent does the relationship between SWB and SPEVI exhibit distributive heterogeneity across different socio-economic, demographic, and cultural factors?

The remainder of the paper is organised as follows. Section 1.2 presents the literature review. Section 1.3 describes the data and variables. Section 1.4 outlines the empirical strategy. Section 1.5 reports the results and discussion. Section 1.6 concludes with recommendations.

1.2 Literature Review

Section 1.2 first reviews the theoretical foundations of women's empowerment and the empirical literature on the SWB-empowerment nexus, then synthesises the satisfaction paradox/adaptive preferences mechanism to explain potential decoupling, and finally uses this synthesis to motivate a clearly separated conceptual framework and hypotheses guiding the empirical analysis of this study.

1.2.1 Theoretical Foundations and Conceptual Anchoring

Women's empowerment has evolved from being treated as an "outcome" of development to being theorised as a process that expands substantive freedoms and renegotiates power relations. The capability approach positions empowerment as the expansion of real opportunities to choose and act (Development as Freedom), while the resources–agency–achievements triad foregrounds empowerment as the conversion of resources into effective agency under structural constraints (Kabeer 2012). Complementary feminist frameworks sharpen the pathways through which such conversions occur: the staged progression from welfare to control in Longwe's framework (Longwe 1991), the layered distinction between personal, relational, and collective power in Rowlands (1997), and the role of critical awareness in destabilising oppressive norms in Freire's (1970) notion of critical consciousness. Cornwall and Rivas (2015) further caution against depoliticised empowerment metrics by emphasising empowerment as relational and contested rather than purely individual.

These theoretical strands map directly onto the logic of the SPEVI indicators used in this study. AUTONOMY resonates with capabilities and personal empowerment, while WOMJOB/WOMPOL/WOMEDU align with how resources and achievements condition agency in labour markets, political institutions, and education systems (Sen 1999; Kabeer 2012; Rowlands 1997; Longwe 1991). The "values" and "critical orientation" dimensions—EQUALITY, RELATIVISM, and SCEPTICISM—are best interpreted through the political and consciousness-raising traditions that treat empowerment as resistance to embedded hierarchies (Freire 1970; Cornwall and Rivas 2015). In this framing, SPEVI is not merely a collection of attitudinal outcomes; it is a multidimensional proxy for the capability-agency-values architecture that underpins empowerment as both freedom-enhancing and system-challenging.

A final conceptual bridge comes from human empowerment theory: as emancipative values diffuse, individuals increasingly prioritise autonomy and equality, strengthening demands for voice and accountability (Inglehart and Welzel 2005; Olivos et al. 2026). This is consistent with capabilities-based justice, which rejects "thin" welfare gains if they do not translate into genuine freedoms (Nussbaum 2000). The construction of emancipative orientations in SPEVI therefore aligns with established multidimensional measurement traditions, where empowerment is explicitly treated as plural (Alkire et al. 2013) and embedded in macro-cultural trajectories of value change (Welzel 2013), with WVS-based operationalisation rooted in the broader cross-national infrastructure of value measurement (Haerpfer et al. 2022; Olivos et al. 2026).

1.2.2 Subjective Well-Being and Development

Subjective well-being (SWB) has emerged as a central dimension of development, reflecting a paradigmatic shift away from treating economic growth as the primary proxy for societal progress (Bortolotti et al. 2026). While GDP and national income capture material prosperity, they do not adequately reflect the multidimensional nature of human flourishing (Acemoglu 2019). SWB, by contrast, captures both cognitive evaluations of life satisfaction and affective states such as happiness, offering a broader measure of quality of life (Diener et al. 2018). This reorientation is reinforced by global evidence, including the World Happiness Report (Helliwell et al. 2021), which positions well-being as a policy objective. Theoretically, it aligns with Sen's (1999) capability approach, where development is defined by expanding substantive freedoms rather than simply raising incomes. Yet SWB measures remain contested: self-reports may embed cultural bias, aspiration adaptation, and context-specific interpretations (Graham 2009; Easterlin 2013; Hirai 2025). For women, reported well-being may also reflect internalised norms of endurance and sacrifice rather than genuine empowerment (Jayachandran 2019). Accordingly, the SWB–empowerment relationship remains theoretically underdeveloped. Recent empirical work has begun to address this nexus more systematically, showing that empowerment can raise welfare and SWB, but that effects vary by context and empowerment dimension (Fielding and Lepine 2016; Annan et al. 2021; Balasubramanian et al. 2024). Cross-national studies on women's political empowerment similarly indicate that institutional quality and gender regimes mediate the translation of rights and agency into reported happiness (Malah 2021; Manda 2023; Hortas-Rico and Rodríguez-Crespo 2025). This paper extends these debates to rural Asia by modelling how distinct SWB components align with, or cut across, multidimensional socio-political empowerment indicators.

1.2.3 The Satisfaction Paradox and Adaptive Preferences

The "satisfaction paradox" refers to the puzzling finding that individuals may report relatively high subjective well-being or life satisfaction despite experiencing structural deprivation, poverty, or constrained opportunities (Graham 2009; Sen 1999; Clark et al. 2008). The core explanation centres on adaptation, social norms, and relative comparisons that shape evaluations of life quality even under material scarcity. This aligns with the concept of adaptive preferences—first articulated by Sen (1999) and developed by Khader (2011)—whereby people adjust aspirations downward in response to limited feasible choices, expressing satisfaction with conditions that remain objectively unjust. In gendered contexts, women with little exposure to political participation may not interpret exclusion as deprivation, normalising marginalisation as culturally "natural".

This critique also resonates with Nussbaum's (2000) capabilities framework, which cautions against treating subjective reports as sufficient indicators of well-being precisely because adaptive preferences can mask deprivation. Khader (2011) further argues that, in patriarchal settings, women's expressed satisfaction may reflect social conditioning that dampens resistance rather than genuine flourishing. Empirical evidence similarly suggests that women can report high happiness and satisfaction even amid severe inequality, implying that SWB may capture compliance or accommodation rather than empowerment (Graham 2009; Hirai 2025). This creates a policy risk: taking SWB at face value may legitimise unequal arrangements and weaken the perceived urgency of empowerment interventions (Mantsi et al. 2025). Recent work nuances this further by showing that "paradoxical" life satisfaction can coexist with heightened depression risks and persistent disadvantage (Becchetti and Conzo 2022; Blanchflower and Bryson 2024). Feminist scholarship also urges careful use of adaptive-preference language, noting that apparent consent may reflect complex complicity (Abrar-ul-Haq et al. 2025) and constrained agency rather than simple false consciousness (Knowles 2021; Pennings and Symons 2024). Building on these insights, we interpret high SWB among structurally disadvantaged rural women as a potential signal of decoupling between satisfaction and socio-political empowerment.

1.2.4 Empirical Insights from Rural Asia and Research Gaps

Evidence from South and Southeast Asia offers concrete illustrations of how empowerment reforms and subjective evaluations can diverge. In India, political reservations increased women's descriptive representation, but evidence suggests that patriarchal decision-making structures can persist, limiting the conversion of representation into substantive influence (Chattopadhyay and Duflo 2004). In such settings, women may report life satisfaction while simultaneously holding weaker autonomy or egalitarian bargaining positions- consistent with the idea that satisfaction and empowerment do not necessarily move together (Ara 2025; Ambler et al. 2026). Supporting this interpretation, recent evidence from India and Pakistan highlights that women may express contentment with domestic roles even where autonomy in household and reproductive decisions remains limited (Kumar et al. 2024).

Parallel dynamics appear across the region. Microfinance participation in Bangladesh can strengthen economic resilience without consistently transforming political empowerment, while satisfaction and acceptance of household hierarchies may remain intact (Kabeer 2012). In Nepal, marital satisfaction can be high even where women face limited property rights, suggesting adaptation to structural inequities (Allendorf 2007). In Indonesia, life satisfaction may be strongly tied to family harmony and religious virtue even as civic participation remains marginal (Yuniati et al. 2022). More recent studies similarly note that patriarchal structures can compress aspiration horizons and normalise inequality in ways that sustain reported satisfaction (Kar and Tiwari 2020; Ambler et al. 2026), and that in India, life satisfaction may reflect family cohesion more than individual autonomy (Ara 2026). A broader critique argues that using SWB without embedding it within empowerment measurement risks obscuring the persistence of structural inequality (Samman et al. 2016; Samartzidis et al. 2025).

Taken together, the rural Asia literature implies two methodological imperatives. First, SWB must be read alongside multidimensional empowerment/value measures, rather than being treated as a substitute for them; second, the SWB- empowerment association is likely heterogeneous across domains and socio-political strata. This motivates approaches that integrate subjective measures with empowerment indicators and contextual analysis attentive to norms and institutions (Alkire et al. 2013). The contribution of this paper is therefore to move beyond binary claims of whether SWB improves empowerment or SWB masks disempowerment. We do this by estimating how distinct SWB components align with multiple SPEVI dimensions in a cross-country rural Asian setting- addressing the scope and measurement limitations highlighted in prior work.

1.3 Data and Variables

This study utilises data from Wave 7 (2017–2022) of the World Values Survey (WVS), a comprehensive, longitudinal investigation of human beliefs and values conducted globally since 1981 (Haerpfer et al. 2022; Inglehart et al. 2022). The WVS is one of the most extensive cross-national surveys of human values and social attitudes (Båge et al. 2025), covering representative samples from nearly 100 societies that together account for almost 90% of the world's population (Welzel 2013; Inglehart and Welzel 2005). Wave 7, conducted between 2017 and 2022, employed standardized questionnaires administered through face-to-face interviews, ensuring cross-cultural comparability and methodological consistency across participating nations (Haerpfer et al. 2022).

Our analysis focuses exclusively on the development of Asian economies covered by the WVS Wave 7, comprising twelve nations: Bangladesh, Indonesia, India, Kazakhstan, Kyrgyzstan, Myanmar, Pakistan, the Philippines, Thailand, Tajikistan, Uzbekistan, and Vietnam. This selection aligns with our research objectives of examining socio-political empowerment patterns within similar developmental contexts while maintaining sufficient cultural and economic diversity to explore heterogeneous effects. These countries represent varying stages of economic development, political systems, and cultural contexts within the Asian region. The study focuses on marginalized populations, particularly women, with a special emphasis on rural contexts, given their heightened vulnerability to socio-economic and political exclusion, as extensively documented in the introduction and literature review sections. Rural women in developing Asian countries face compounded disadvantages stemming from patriarchal structures, limited access to resources, and reduced political participation opportunities. Our analytical sample consisted of 18,928 observations across the 12 selected countries, of which 11,555 were from rural areas and 5,958 were rural women respondents.,[2] providing adequate statistical power for robust empirical analysis while maintaining representativeness across diverse cultural and economic contexts.

Country-specific sample sizes vary moderately across the 12 countries, reflecting the World Values Survey's design of drawing nationally representative samples of at least 1,000 adults per country rather than allocating observations strictly in proportion to population size. To enhance transparency, Appendix Table A.1 reports, for each country, the total number of respondents, the number of rural respondents, the number of rural women respondents, and the share of rural women in the national sample. Since all regression models include country fixed effects and cluster-standard errors at the country level, these modest cross-country differences in sample size are unlikely

[2] The World Values Survey (WVS) Wave 7 identifies settlement type using a harmonised "size of town" item and coding scheme across all participating countries. We define "rural" respondents as those living in villages, small towns, or countryside/farm locations, based on this common instrument. Although the underlying spatial structure differs across countries, the use of the same question and response categories ensures that the rural subsamples are defined in a conceptually comparable way, allowing pooled analysis of rural women across the twelve Asian countries.

to bias the estimated relationships between subjective well-being and socio-political empowerment.

The dependent variables comprise eight carefully selected indicators under the Socio-Political Empowerment and Values Indicators (SPEVI) framework. These indicators capture multidimensional aspects of women's empowerment by drawing on established WVS questions that assess political participation, social autonomy, decision-making authority, and value orientations toward gender equality (Solotaroff and Pande 2014). The selection of these eight indicators reflects the contemporary understanding of empowerment as encompassing both instrumental capabilities and intrinsic agency, consistent with recent theoretical developments in gender economics literature (Sen 1999). The SPEVI framework includes the Welzel emancipative values index (RESEMAVAL), the autonomy sub-index (AUTONOMY), the gender equality indicators for employment (WOMJOB), politics (WOMPOL), and education (WOMEDU), the equality sub-index (EQUALITY), the relativism sub-index (RELATIVISM), and the scepticism index (SCEPTICISM). Each indicator[3] represents distinct but interconnected dimensions of empowerment, enabling a comprehensive assessment of women's socio-political status across varied cultural contexts, in line with established approaches to empowerment measurement (Miedema et al. 2018).

Subjective well-being is operationalized through five WVS questions (Q46–Q50) that capture different dimensions of happiness and life satisfaction (Diener et al. 2018, Helliwell et al. 2021). These questions assess overall life satisfaction, happiness levels, perceptions of life control, and general well-being evaluations using standardized scales that have demonstrated cross-cultural validity. These are the independent variables in this study. The selection of these particular questions reflects established psychometric literature, which confirms their reliability and validity across diverse cultural contexts, particularly in developing country settings (Minkov and Bond 2017). As demonstrated in recent cross-national studies, the five SWB questions utilize established measurement scales that enable robust cross-cultural comparisons while maintaining sensitivity to cultural variations in the conceptualization of well-being. To establish the empirical foundation for our analysis, we conduct independent-samples t-tests comparing the eight SPEVI indicators for rural men and women across our sample countries. Table 1.1 presents these results, revealing statistically significant differences across seven indicators at conventional significance levels. All SPEVI variables are coded so that higher values reflect more emancipative or gender-egalitarian attitudes, and are normalised to lie on the 0–1 interval; dichotomous items are coded 0/1, while multi-category items are mapped to equally spaced points between 0 and 1 (for example, 0–0.5–1 or 0–0.33–0.66–1) to preserve the underlying ordinal structure and ensure comparability across indicators.

[3] In our empirical analysis, we do not collapse these eight Socio-Political Empowerment and Values Indicators (SPEVI) into a single composite empowerment index. Instead, we treat them as analytically distinct but theoretically related outcomes within the broader human-empowerment and emancipative-values framework. This avoids imposing strong assumptions that heterogeneous domains such as autonomy, gender equality and scepticism are strictly commensurable on a single scale, while still allowing us to study a coherent empowerment space.

Table 1.1 T-test results for gender differences in SPEVI indicators

Variable	Name	Description	Range	Mean male	Mean female	T-statistic
RESEMAVAL	Welzel's emancipative values index	Composite index measuring the degree to which individuals emphasize freedom of choice, autonomy, equality, and voice. Higher scores indicate stronger emancipative (freedom-oriented) values	0–1, depending on the construction; higher values = more emancipative	0.324	0.336	−4.632***
AUTONOMY	Welzel autonomy sub-index	Sub-index capturing the value placed on personal independence, self-determination, and free choice in life	0–1; higher values = greater emphasis on autonomy	0.418	0.438	–3.825***
WOMJOB	Gender equality: job	Higher values indicate more supportive or egalitarian views, meaning respondents are more likely to agree that women should be able to work outside the home	0 = Men have more right; 0.5 = Both equal; 1 = Women have more right	0.267	0.312	–8.029***
WOMPOL	Gender equality: politics	A higher value means greater support for female participation in politics	0 = Disagree strongly; 0.33 = Disagree; 0.66 = Agree; 1 = Agree strongly	0.344	0.395	–8.792***

(continued)

Table 1.1 (continued)

Variable	Name	Description	Range	Mean male	Mean female	T-statistic
WOMEDU	Gender equality: education	Higher scores reflect greater endorsement of equal opportunities for females in education	0 = Disagree strongly; 0.33 = Disagree; 0.66 = Agree; 1 = Agree strongly	0.451	0.515	–10.282***
EQUALITY	Equality sub-index	The level of support for social and gender equality	0 to 1; higher values indicate stronger endorsement of egalitarian principles	0.355	0.408	–12.179***
RELATIVISM	Welzel relativism sub-index	It reflects openness to the idea that what is morally right or wrong may depend on cultural, social, or personal contexts rather than fixed universal rules	0–1; higher = greater moral flexibility and tolerance for diverse lifestyles and behaviors	0.439	0.435	0.567
SCEPTICISM	Welzel scepticism index	Higher scepticism indicates a more critical attitude toward established beliefs and institutions, often leading to independent thinking and less acceptance of absolute or dogmatic claims	0–1; higher = greater emphasis on sceptical thinking	0.324	0.333	–2.002***

* $p < 0.10$, ** $p < 0.05$, *** $p < 0.010$; *Source* Author's calculations

Note RESEMAVAL, AUTONOMY, EQUALITY, RELATIVISM and SCEPTICISM are continuous composite indices normalised to range from 0 to 1. WOMJOB, WOMPOL and WOMEDU are single-item gender-attitude variables based on ordered response categories that are rescaled to equally spaced points between 0 and 1 (e.g. 0, 0.5, 1 or 0, 0.33, 0.66, 1), so that higher scores consistently indicate more gender-egalitarian attitudes

The most substantial gender gaps emerge in gender equality measures, with women scoring significantly higher than men on WOMEDU (t = −10.282, $p < 0.001$), EQUALITY (t = −12.179, $p < 0.001$), and WOMPOL (t = −8.792, $p < 0.001$), indicating that rural women express stronger support for gender equality in education, politics, and employment opportunities. Paradoxically, women also show higher scores on RESEMAVAL (t = −4.632, $p < 0.001$) and AUTONOMY (t = −3.825, $p < 0.001$), suggesting greater endorsement of emancipatory values and personal autonomy despite structural constraints. SCEPTICISM shows a modest but significant difference (t = −2.002, $p < 0.05$). These findings provide compelling evidence of systematic gender disparities in socio-political empowerment attitudes among rural populations in developing Asian countries, thereby establishing the relevance of our research questions and analytical approach, which is consistent with recent studies documenting gender differences in empowerment attitudes (Huis et al. 2017). This divergence is further reflected in underlying socio-economic perceptions and civic opinions, revealing significant gender-based disparities in rural individuals' engagement with and evaluation of key institutions, rights, and economic realities (Fig. B.1 in the Appendix).

To address heterogeneity and identify structural determinants, our analysis incorporates comprehensive socio-economic control variables including employment status, age, immigration status, education level, marital status, religious inclination, and income level (Solotaroff and Pande 2014; Graafland and Schilpzand 2025). Income is measured using the WVS ten-step household income ladder, which we collapse into low, medium, and high income based on the WVS three-category country-specific recode. These categories therefore reflect respondents' relative position in their own country's income distribution, rather than a common absolute threshold across countries. In all regressions, they are entered as dummy variables (with low income as the reference group) alongside country fixed effects, so the coefficients capture within-country differences in relative socio-economic status. These variables capture key dimensions of social stratification that previous research has identified as crucial for understanding variations in women's empowerment in developing country contexts (Kabeer 2012; Mahmud et al. 2012). The inclusion of these controls enables examination of structural constructs underlying empowerment patterns while accounting for observable heterogeneity in our sample, following established practices in gender economics research that emphasize the importance of controlling for socio-economic characteristics in empowerment studies (Duflo 2012; Field et al. 2010).

Beyond examining individual SWB questions, we construct a composite Subjective Well-Being Index using min–max and z-score normalization techniques (Greco et al. 2019). The min–max normalization rescales each of the five questions to a 0–1 range, while z-score normalization standardizes responses around sample means with unit variance.[4] Both normalized versions are aggregated using simple arithmetic means, with equal weights assigned to each component, following established practices in composite index construction (Alqararah 2023). This dual normalization approach serves as both a primary analysis tool and a robustness check, ensuring that our findings are not sensitive to specific scaling methodologies. This approach is consistent with recent developments in the empowerment measurement literature, which emphasize methodological robustness (Ewerling et al. 2017; Pratley 2016). The use of simple equal weights reflects a deliberate normative stance that each SWB dimension (life satisfaction, happiness, perceived control and overall well-being) is equally relevant to rural women's lived experiences, consistent with widely used well-being and development indices that prioritise transparency and parsimony in weighting (Greco et al. 2019). Moreover, the five SWB items are highly correlated and, in psychometric work, have been shown to load on a common latent well-being factor across diverse cultural settings (Helliwell et al. 2021), which supports their aggregation into a single index. In our empirical analysis, we primarily rely on the individual SWB items, using the composite index as a complementary robustness measure.

Table 1.2 presents a country-wise heatmap displaying all dependent variables (SPEVI indicators) and composite SWB indices, revealing substantial cross-national heterogeneity in both empowerment outcomes and well-being measures. The variation across countries is particularly striking, with Thailand demonstrating the highest RESEMAVAL score (0.414) and Pakistan the lowest (0.262), a 58% difference between the extremes. Similarly, AUTONOMY scores range from 0.25 in Pakistan to 0.529 in Uzbekistan, highlighting significant cross-country variation in personal autonomy values. Gender equality indicators show even more pronounced disparities, with WOMJOB varying from 0.159 in Pakistan to 0.497 in Thailand, and WOMPOL ranging from 0.293 in Myanmar to 0.539 in India. The composite SWB indices (both SWB Comp and SWB Comp2) show considerable variation, with Kyrgyzstan recording notably high values (3.647 and 0.814, respectively), while Kazakhstan shows relatively low scores (3.093 and 0.156). This substantial cross-country heterogeneity provides essential variation for our empirical strategy, enabling identification of structural determinants while controlling for country-specific factors through fixed effects specifications, and strengthening the external validity of our findings across diverse developing Asian contexts (Welzel 2013).

[4] The composite SWB index was constructed in two stages. First, the raw scores for Q46 (feeling of happiness) and Q47 (state of health), originally coded so that lower values indicated better outcomes, were reversed by computing `$${x}^{\mathrm{\text{'}}}=\text{max}(x)+\text{min}(x)-x$$`,, ensuring that higher values uniformly reflect greater well-being (Pavot and Diener 2008). Each of the five items (Q46–Q50) was then normalized using both min–max and z-score methods. The min–max transformation was applied as $\tilde{x}_i = \frac{x'_i - \min(x')}{\max(x') - \min(x')}$, and z-score standardization as $z_i = \frac{x'_i - \overline{x'}}{\sigma(x')}$. Finally, the normalized scores for Q46–Q50 were aggregated by simple arithmetic mean with equal weights to form the composite SWB index.

Table 1.2 Cross-country heat map of SPEVI indicators and composite SWB scores

Country	RESEMAVAL	AUTONOMY	WOMJOB	WOMPOL	WOMEDU	EQUALITY	RELATIVISM	SCEPTICISM	SWB comp	SWB comp2
Bangladesh	0.312	0.433	0.27	0.43	0.545	0.415	0.361	0.348	3.25	0.342
Indonesia	0.339	0.432	0.3	0.373	0.491	0.388	0.389	0.31	3.362	0.475
India	0.371	0.499	0.448	0.539	0.657	0.546	0.34	0.256	3.196	0.279
Kazakhstan	0.376	0.46	0.373	0.442	0.594	0.47	0.579	0.305	3.093	0.156
Kyrgyzstan	0.273	0.4	0.241	0.322	0.457	0.341	0.223	0.473	3.647	0.814
Myanmar	0.274	0.406	0.193	0.293	0.444	0.31	0.358	0.509	3.192	0.273
Pakistan	0.262	0.25	0.159	0.313	0.477	0.317	0.272	0.35	3.334	0.442
Philippines	0.39	0.426	0.295	0.428	0.504	0.409	0.746	0.282	3.051	0.106
Thailand	0.414	0.492	0.497	0.516	0.588	0.536	0.39	0.387	3.072	0.131
Tajikistan	0.305	0.421	0.362	0.317	0.488	0.389	0.799	0.277	3.422	0.547
Uzbekistan	0.377	0.529	0.223	0.375	0.401	0.332	0.462	0.198	3.154	0.228
Vietnam	0.401	0.335	0.449	0.494	0.595	0.512	0.667	0.271	3.476	0.611

Source Author's calculations

1.4 Empirical Strategy

This empirical strategy deploys a comprehensive multi-methodological framework to examine the complex relationships between subjective well-being and socio-political empowerment among rural women in twelve developing Asian economies. The analytical approach combines baseline linear regression models to establish average effects, quantile regression techniques to capture distributional heterogeneity, and socio-demographic interaction specifications to explore moderation by education, employment, income, and marital status. Additionally, robustness checks are conducted using alternative variable constructions and inference methods. This strategy systematically addresses the research questions concerning structural determinants of empowerment, the influence of well-being, and heterogeneity across key subgroups (Koenker and Bassett 1978; White 1980).

1.4.1 Baseline Linear Regression Framework

The primary model assesses the average association between subjective well-being and each of the eight SPEVI indicators. For individual i in country c and empowerment dimension k The specification is:

$$\text{SPEVI}_{k,i,c} = \alpha_k + \beta_k \text{SWB}_{i,c} + \gamma_k X_{i,c} + \delta_c + \varepsilon_{k,i,c}, \tag{1.1}$$

where $\text{SPEVI}_{k,i,c}$ is the k The empowerment score, $\text{SWB}_{i,c}$ is the subjective well-being measure (component or composite), $X_{i,c}$ is a vector of controls (age, education, employment status, marital status, religion, and income), δ_c are country fixed effects, and $\varepsilon_{k,i,c}$ is the error term (Cameron and Trivedi 2005; Wooldridge 2010). The coefficient β_k captures the mean marginal effect of well-being on empowerment. Standard errors are clustered at the country level and adjusted using White's heteroscedasticity-consistent estimator to guard against within-country correlation and heteroskedasticity (MacKinnon and White 1985; White 1980).

1.4.2 Quantile Regression Specification

To uncover distributional heterogeneity, the τ th conditional quantile of each SPEVI indicator is modeled as:

$$Q_\tau(\text{SPEVI}_{k,i,c} \mid \text{SWB}_{i,c}, X_{i,c}) = \alpha_{k,\tau} + \beta_{k,\tau} \text{SWB}_{i,c} + \gamma_{k,\tau} X_{i,c}, \tag{1.2}$$

where $\beta_{k,\tau}$ reflects the effect of well-being at the τ th quantile ($\tau = 0.1, 0.2, \ldots, 0.9$) of the empowerment distribution. This approach examines whether well-being affects individuals at low, moderate, or high levels of empowerment differently (Buchinsky 1998; Koenker and Bassett 1978; Koenker and Hallock 2001).

1.4.3 Socio-Demographic Heterogeneity Analysis

To test moderation by key socio-demographic factors, interaction terms are added for education, employment, income quintile, and marital status. The quantile model becomes:

$$\begin{aligned} &Q_\tau(SPEVI_{(k,i,c)}|SWB_{(i,c)}, Z_{(i,c)}, X_(i,c)) \\ &= \alpha_{(k,\tau)} + \beta_{(k,\tau)} SWB_{(i,c)} \\ &+ \sum_{f \in (Edu,Inc,Emp,Mar)}^{J_f} \sum_{j=1}^{J_f} \theta_{k,f,j,\tau} \left(\mathrm{SWB}_{i,c} \times Z_{f,j,i,c}\right) + \gamma_{k,\tau} X_{i,c}, \end{aligned} \quad (1.3)$$

where $Z_{f,j,i,c}$ are dummies for: education levels (no formal, primary, secondary, post-secondary, university), employment status (unemployed, student, housewife, self-employed, full-time employed), income (low, medium, high), marital status (single, married, widowed/divorced). Each $\theta_{k,f,j,\tau}$ measures how the well-being effect differs for the subgroup j of factor f. This tests "capability thresholds," in which socio-demographic characteristics buffer or amplify the influence of well-being on empowerment (Sen 1999; Inglehart and Welzel 2005).

1.4.4 Robustness Checks and Alternative Specifications

Multiple robustness checks ensure the reliability of findings (Wooldridge 2010). First, alternative constructions of the composite subjective well-being index—min–max normalization and z-score standardization—are compared:

$$\mathrm{SWB}_{i,c}^{\mathrm{minmax}} = \frac{1}{5} \sum_{l=1}^{5} \frac{\mathrm{SWB}_{i,c}^{l} - \min(\mathrm{SWB}^{l})}{\max(\mathrm{SWB}^{l}) - \min(\mathrm{SWB}^{l})}, \quad (1.4)$$

$$\mathrm{SWB}_{i,c}^{\mathrm{zscore}} = \frac{1}{5} \sum_{l=1}^{5} \frac{\mathrm{SWB}_{i,c}^{l} - \overline{\mathrm{SWB}^{l}}}{\sigma_{\mathrm{SWB}^{l}}}, \quad (1.5)$$

where $\mathrm{SWB}_{i,c}^{l}$ is the l th well-being component (Greco et al. 2019). Second, specifications exclude subsets of control variables to assess coefficient stability. Third, alternative clustering strategies (individual vs. regional) and weighted regressions with sampling weights address potential selection bias. Finally, bootstrap-based inference procedures accommodate non-normal error distributions. These checks confirm that results are not artifacts of methodological choices (MacKinnon and White 1985).

1.5 Results and Discussion

This section presents the empirical findings examining the relationships between subjective well-being dimensions and socio-political empowerment indicators among rural women in developing Asian countries. We analyse the association between happiness and well-being factors and SPEVI, examine how composite SWB indices co-vary with empowerment dimensions, and investigate distributive heterogeneity across socio-economic factors using quantile regression.

1.5.1 The Impact of Happiness and Well-Being Factors on SPEVI

Table 1.3 presents regression results examining the relationship between five subjective well-being dimensions and eight SPEVI indicators, revealing complex patterns that illuminate the psychological foundations of women's empowerment in rural Asian contexts. Across specifications, higher reported happiness is positively associated with most empowerment indicators, whereas greater life satisfaction, perceived freedom and satisfaction with household finances are systematically associated with lower emancipative values, weaker egalitarian attitudes, and reduced scepticism about institutions. Taken together, these patterns indicate a 'satisfaction-empowerment paradox': subjective contentment with life can coexist with, and in some domains accompany, lower motivation to question existing gender hierarchies. This configuration is consistent with theories of adaptation and socially shaped aspirations, whereby individuals adjust expectations to constrained opportunities and report high satisfaction even when agency remains limited (Clark et al. 2008; Graham 2009; Genicot and Ray 2017; Appadurai 2004).

The findings demonstrate a paradoxical relationship between subjective well-being and empowerment attitudes, challenging conventional assumptions about the linear relationship between personal happiness and empowerment aspirations. The most striking finding concerns the consistent positive relationship between feelings of happiness (measured inversely, where lower scores indicate greater happiness) and empowerment indicators. Rural women reporting greater happiness demonstrate significantly higher scores on emancipative values ($\beta = 0.0084, p < 0.05$), autonomy preferences ($\beta = 0.009, p < 0.01$), and gender equality attitudes across employment ($\beta = 0.0237, p < 0.01$), politics ($\beta = 0.0339, p < 0.01$), and overall equality measures ($\beta = 0.0212, p < 0.01$). This counterintuitive relationship suggests that contentment may paradoxically fuel aspirations for greater empowerment, reflecting what Sen

Table 1.3 Impact of individual subjective well-being dimensions on SPEVI - pooled OLS regression results

	Welzel emancipative values index	Welzel autonomy sub-index	Gender equality: job	Gender equality: politics	Gender equality: education	Equality sub-index	Welzel relativism sub-index	Welzel scepticism index
Happiness and Well-being								
Feeling of happiness (lower better)	0.0084** (0.003)	0.009*** (0.002)	0.0237*** (0.008)	0.0339*** (0.008)	0.0077 (0.009)	0.0212*** (0.006)	0.0223** (0.010)	0.0244*** (0.006)
State of health (lower better)	0.0019 (0.002)	0.0041 (0.005)	−0.0003 (0.006)	−0.0025 (0.006)	−0.0034 (0.007)	−0.0021 (0.005)	−0.0095 (0.007)	0.0022 (0.004)
Freedom of choice and control (higher better)	−0.0019** (0.001)	−0.0042** (0.002)	−0.0059*** (0.002)	−0.0052** (0.002)	−0.0068*** (0.002)	0.0060*** (0.002)	−0.0079*** (0.003)	0.0017 (0.002)
Satisfaction with life (higher better)	−0.0019* (0.001)	−0.0044** (0.002)	−0.0059** (0.002)	−0.0080** (0.003)	−0.0071** (0.003)	−0.0002 (0.002)	−0.0117*** (0.003)	−0.0048** (0.002)
Satisfaction with financial situation of household (higher better)	−0.0030*** (0.001)	−0.0036* (0.002)	0.0016 (0.002)	0.0004 (0.003)	0.0080*** (0.003)	−0.0017 (0.002)	0.0040 (0.003)	−0.0087*** (0.002)
Age	−0.0006*** (0.000)	−0.0001 (0.000)	−0.0012*** (0.000)	−0.0007 (0.000)	−0.0012** (0.000)	−0.0011*** (0.000)	0.0008 (0.001)	0.0007** (0.000)
Immigrant to the country	0.0235 (0.019)	−0.0401 (0.043)	0.0643 (0.047)	0.0829* (0.049)	0.0985* (0.053)	0.0815** (0.037)	0.0380 (0.059)	0.0134 (0.034)
Illiterate	−0.0039 (0.006)	−0.0087 (0.013)	−0.0047 (0.014)	0.0070 (0.015)	−0.0406** (0.016)	−0.0132 (0.011)	0.0231 (0.017)	0.0196** (0.010)

(continued)

Table 1.3 (continued)

	Welzel emancipative values index	Welzel autonomy sub-index	Gender equality: job	Gender equality: politics	Gender equality: education	Equality sub-index	Welzel relativism sub-index	Welzel scepticism index
Marital status- married as base								
Marital status: Living together as married	0.0035 (0.014)	−0.0299 (0.031)	0.0404 (0.033)	0.0330 (0.036)	0.0670* (0.038)	0.0475* (0.026)	−0.0503 (0.042)	0.0129 (0.024)
Marital status: Divorced	0.0133 (0.012)	−0.0101 (0.027)	0.0376 (0.029)	−0.0062 (0.030)	−0.0016 (0.033)	0.0075 (0.023)	−0.0036 (0.036)	0.0244 (0.021)
Marital status: Separated	−0.0305 (0.028)	−0.0956 (0.062)	−0.0788 (0.067)	−0.0349 (0.070)	0.0837 (0.076)	−0.0099 (0.052)	−0.0648 (0.086)	−0.0197 (0.048)
Marital status: Widowed	0.0034 (0.009)	0.0049 (0.019)	0.0133 (0.021)	0.0235 (0.022)	0.0108 (0.024)	0.0188 (0.017)	−0.0131 (0.026)	−0.0520*** (0.015)
Marital status: Single	0.0352*** (0.006)	0.0470*** (0.014)	0.0799*** (0.016)	0.0421*** (0.016)	0.0548*** (0.018)	0.0579*** (0.012)	0.0064 (0.019)	0.0022 (0.011)
Religious person: religious person as a base								
Not a religious person	0.0041 (0.006)	−0.0124 (0.013)	0.0159 (0.014)	0.0286* (0.015)	0.0115 (0.016)	0.0178 (0.011)	0.0724*** (0.018)	0.0245** (0.010)
Atheist	0.0320* (0.018)	0.0103 (0.040)	0.0520 (0.043)	0.0193 (0.045)	−0.0050 (0.049)	0.0220 (0.034)	0.0823 (0.054)	0.0689** (0.031)
Income level: low income as base								
Income Level: Medium	0.0241*** (0.005)	0.0044 (0.011)	0.0329*** (0.012)	0.0468*** (0.013)	0.0216 (0.014)	0.0325*** (0.010)	0.0567*** (0.016)	0.0194** (0.016)
Income Level: High	0.0202*** (0.007)	0.0067 (0.017)	0.0055 (0.018)	0.0381** (0.019)	−0.0240 (0.021)	0.0043 (0.014)	0.0772*** (0.023)	−0.0030 (0.013)
Country: Tajikistan as a base								

(continued)

Table 1.3 (continued)

	Welzel emancipative values index	Welzel autonomy sub-index	Gender equality: job	Gender equality: politics	Gender equality: education	Equality sub-index	Welzel relativism sub-index	Welzel scepticism index
Kyrgyzstan	−0.0254*** (0.009)	−0.0246 (0.020)	−0.1044*** (0.022)	0.0274 (0.022)	−0.0310 (0.024)	−0.0361** (0.017)	−0.5244*** (0.027)	0.2304*** (0.015)
Uzbekistan	0.0716*** (0.010)	0.1126*** (0.022)	−0.1346*** (0.024)	0.0587** (0.025)	−0.0963*** (0.027)	−0.0580*** (0.019)	−0.3335*** (0.030)	−0.0753*** (0.017)
Kazakhstan	0.0680*** (0.011)	0.0215 (0.024)	0.0077 (0.026)	0.1291*** (0.027)	0.1000*** (0.029)	0.0797*** (0.020)	−0.1844*** (0.032)	0.0116 (0.018)
India	0.0642*** (0.009)	0.0725*** (0.020)	0.0775*** (0.022)	0.2246*** (0.023)	0.1648*** (0.025)	0.1538*** (0.017)	−0.4343*** (0.028)	−0.0147 (0.016)
Pakistan	−0.0422*** (0.009)	−0.1818*** (0.020)	−0.2016*** (0.021)	0.0004 (0.022)	−0.0051 (0.024)	−0.0697*** (0.017)	−0.4695*** (0.027)	0.0815*** (0.015)
Bangladesh	0.0045 (0.009)	0.0040 (0.021)	−0.0917*** (0.022)	0.1242*** (0.023)	0.0601** (0.025)	0.0295* (0.018)	−0.4073*** (0.028)	0.0780*** (0.016)
Myanmar	−0.0336*** (0.009)	−0.0282 (0.021)	−0.1734*** (0.022)	−0.0134 (0.023)	−0.0514** (0.025)	−0.0800*** (0.018)	−0.3946*** (0.028)	0.2406*** (0.016)
Vietnam	0.0903*** (0.009)	−0.0935*** (0.019)	0.0719*** (0.021)	0.1703*** (0.022)	0.0849*** (0.024)	0.1088*** (0.016)	−0.1167*** (0.026)	−0.0044 (0.015)
Philippines	0.0984*** (0.011)	0.0090 (0.024)	−0.0386 (0.026)	0.1453*** (0.027)	0.0240 (0.029)	0.0427** (0.020)	0.0059 (0.032)	0.0114 (0.018)
Constant	0.2909*** (0.016)	0.4015*** (0.036)	0.3150*** (0.039)	0.2061*** (0.041)	0.4652*** (0.044)	0.3330*** (0.030)	0.7713*** (0.049)	0.2835*** (0.028)
Obs	5958	5880	5958	5858	5951	5881	5901	5799

Source Author's calculations

* $p < 0.10$, ** $p < 0.05$, *** $p < 0.010$

(1999) described as "adaptive preferences" in reverse—where happiness enables women to envision and demand more egalitarian arrangements rather than accepting subordinate positions. This finding aligns with recent theoretical developments in empowerment psychology, where positive emotional states create cognitive space for challenging existing hierarchies and envisioning alternative social arrangements.

Conversely, measures of perceived freedom and control reveal negative associations with most empowerment indicators. Women reporting greater freedom of choice and control demonstrate lower scores on emancipative values ($\beta = -0.0019, p < 0.05$), autonomy preferences ($\beta = -0.0042, p < 0.05$), and gender equality attitudes, with one notable exception: a positive relationship with the equality sub-index ($\beta = 0.0060$, $p < 0.01$). This apparent contradiction suggests that perceived control may reflect adaptation to existing constraints rather than genuine empowerment, consistent with research on "illusory freedom" in constrained environments (Ryan and Deci 2000). The differential effects across SPEVI dimensions indicate that freedom of choice may enable women to support abstract equality principles while simultaneously reducing their inclination to challenge specific institutional arrangements, reflecting the distinction between "preferences within constraints" and "preferences over constraints" identified in development economics literature (Nussbaum 2000; Duflo 2012).

Life satisfaction exhibits predominantly negative relationships with empowerment indicators, with significant negative coefficients for emancipative values ($\beta = -0.0019$, $p < 0.10$), autonomy ($\beta = -0.0044$, $p < 0.05$), and all three gender equality measures. This pattern supports the "satisfaction paradox" identified in the empowerment literature, in which current life satisfaction may reduce motivation for social change (Clark et al. 2008; Easterlin 2013). Our results resonate with recent evidence on gendered well-being paradoxes, where women report equal or higher life satisfaction despite worse mental health or more precarious structural positions (Becchetti and Conzo 2022; Blanchflower and Bryson 2024). They also connect to Graham's (2009) discussion of "happy peasants and miserable millionaires", in which high reported happiness reflects adaptive preferences and bounded aspirations rather than expanded capabilities, suggesting that subjective contentment can coexist with limited socio-political agency. Theoretically, this relationship reflects the tension between hedonic adaptation and aspirational goals- satisfied individuals may lack the "constructive dissatisfaction" necessary for empowerment-seeking behavior (Chen 2024).

Financial satisfaction demonstrates nuanced relationships across SPEVI dimensions, with negative effects on emancipative values ($\beta = -0.0030$, $p < 0.01$) and autonomy ($\beta = -0.0036$, $p < 0.10$), but positive effects on education equality attitudes ($\beta = 0.0080, p < 0.01$). This pattern suggests that economic security may reduce motivation for challenging broader social arrangements while increasing support for specific empowerment domains, particularly education. The differential effects align with theories suggesting that financial security enables a focus on self-actualization goals, such as education, while reducing motivation to challenge existing social arrangements that provide economic stability.

The demographic control variables reveal theoretically consistent patterns that illuminate the structural determinants of empowerment attitudes. Single women demonstrate significantly higher scores across most SPEVI indicators compared to married women, with particularly strong effects for gender equality measures. This finding supports theories of identity conflict in patriarchal societies, where marriage often requires women to adopt more traditional gender role attitudes to maintain family harmony (Kandiyoti 1988). Income effects follow expected patterns, with medium and high-income women showing greater empowerment orientation, particularly for political equality and relativism measures, supporting the "empowerment gradient" hypothesis that economic resources enable women to challenge traditional arrangements (Kabeer 2012). This interpretation aligns with recent philosophical debates on adaptive preferences and constrained agency, which emphasise that women's apparent satisfaction or consent under restrictive gender norms may reflect complex forms of coping and accommodation rather than unconstrained choice (Knowles 2021; Pennings and Symons 2024). Our findings should therefore be read as evidence that high SWB among structurally disadvantaged rural women may signal adaptation to, rather than transformation of, prevailing power relations. The country fixed effects reveal substantial variation in empowerment patterns across developing Asian countries, with India, Vietnam, and the Philippines generally showing higher empowerment scores. In contrast, Pakistan, Myanmar, and Central Asian countries demonstrate more conservative patterns, reflecting complex interactions between cultural values, economic development, and institutional arrangements (Inglehart and Welzel 2005; Welzel 2013).

1.5.2 Composite Subjective Well-Being Index and Empowerment Orientations

The composite Subjective Well-Being (SWB) index was constructed by aggregating five normalized WVS items- feeling of happiness, state of health, freedom of choice and control, life satisfaction, and financial life satisfaction, using min–max normalization to a 0–1 scale, with equal weights assigned to each component (Greco et al. 2019). Table A.2 (Appendix) presents mean comparisons of the eight SPEVI indicators for respondents above versus below the SWB mean, revealing significant differentiation in emancipative values, autonomy, gender equality attitudes, relativism, and scepticism ($p < 0.01$ for most), thereby justifying the examination of SWB as a determinant of empowerment orientations (Ewerling et al. 2017; Pratley 2016).

Table 1.4 reports pooled OLS estimates of SPEVI indicators on the SWB composite index. For the Welzel emancipative values index, higher SWB is associated with a significant negative coefficient ($\beta = -0.0068$), indicating that women with above-average well-being score lower on emancipative values. This result aligns with findings from the "happiness paradox" literature, where contentment reduces the impetus for social change (Clark et al. 2008; Easterlin 2013). The autonomy sub-index shows a non-significant positive association, suggesting that overall well-being does not uniformly translate into greater desire for personal autonomy. Gender equality attitudes in employment ($\beta = -0.0062$), politics ($\beta = -0.0078$), and the equality sub-index ($\beta = -0.0090$) also exhibit negative relationships with SWB, indicating that higher well-being correlates with less support for systemic gender egalitarianism. In contrast, the education equality dimension shows a marginal adverse effect ($\beta = -0.0097$), aligning with theories that economic security may focus women's aspirations on instrumental domains while dampening broader emancipative goals. Notably, the most substantial negative effect is observed for the Welzel scepticism index ($\beta = -0.0520$), suggesting that higher well-being is associated with reduced critical attitudes toward existing social institutions. Similarly, the relativism sub-index exhibits a highly significant negative coefficient ($\beta = -0.0408$), suggesting that well-being may promote moral conservatism rather than openness to diverse lifestyles (Minkov and Bond 2017).

Robustness checks using the z-score–normalized SWB composite (Table A.3) yield qualitatively similar patterns: significant negative effects on emancipative values ($\beta = -0.0057$), gender equality in employment ($\beta = -0.0052$), politics ($\beta = -0.0066$), and scepticism ($\beta = -0.0438$), confirming that the observed relationships are not sensitive to normalization methodology (Alqararah 2023). Thus, the composite SWB index shows a complex pattern of associations with women's empowerment attitudes: higher well-being paradoxically correlates with lower support for structural gender egalitarianism and critical social perspectives.

1.5.3 Distributive Heterogeneity Across Socio-Economic Factors

The quantile regression analysis depicted in Fig. 1.1 through 1.5 reveals pronounced heterogeneity in the influence of Subjective Well-Being (SWB) on women's socio-political empowerment orientations (SPEVI) across different socio-economic and regional strata. These findings underscore that the association between SWB and SPEVI is not uniform but varies systematically across empowerment quantiles and across demographic characteristics, including education, employment status, income level, marital status, and regional groupings.

Figure 1.1 illustrates education-based heterogeneity: women with no formal schooling experience consistently exhibit negative effects on emancipative values in the lower quantiles, whereas post-secondary educated women experience negative effects only in the middle quantiles, and degree holders in the upper quantiles. For autonomy, primary- and secondary-educated women display large negative coefficients at the second and sixth deciles, suggesting episodic disillusionment, while degree-holders remain unaffected. Gender-equality attitudes in employment and politics exhibit large negative SWB coefficients for low-educated women in mid-quantiles, but attenuated or positive effects for educated women at high empowerment

Table 1.4 Regression results of composite SWB Index on SPEVI indicators

	Welzel's emancipative values index	Welzel autonomy sub-index	Gender equality: job	Gender equality: politics	Gender equality: education	Equality sub-index	Welzel relativism sub-index	Welzel scepticism index
Subjective well-being composite (min–max)	−0.0068** (0.003)	0.0055 (0.006)	−0.0062** (0.003)	−0.0078*** (0.003)	−0.0097* (0.005)	−0.009** (0.003)	−0.0408*** (0.009)	−0.0520*** (0.005)
Immigrant to the country	0.0094 (0.018)	−0.0166 (0.040)	0.0108 (0.044)	0.0563 (0.047)	0.0438 (0.050)	0.0337 (0.035)	0.0293 (0.055)	0.0207 (0.031)
Income level: medium	0.0241*** (0.005)	−0.0002 (0.011)	0.0379*** (0.012)	0.0497*** (0.013)	0.0238* (0.014)	0.0362*** (0.010)	0.0644*** (0.015)	0.0206** (0.009)
Income level: high	0.0169** (0.007)	0.0029 (0.016)	0.0082 (0.018)	0.0370** (0.019)	−0.0272 (0.020)	0.0045 (0.014)	0.0863*** (0.022)	−0.0059 (0.012)
Illiterate	−0.0089 (0.005)	−0.0088 (0.012)	−0.0157 (0.013)	0.0021 (0.014)	−0.0530*** (0.015)	−0.0229** (0.010)	0.0257 (0.017)	0.0260*** (0.009)
Kyrgyzstan	−0.0286*** (0.009)	−0.0227 (0.019)	−0.1133*** (0.021)	0.0122 (0.022)	−0.0375 (0.023)	−0.0455*** (0.016)	−0.5549*** (0.026)	0.2167*** (0.015)
Uzbekistan	0.0717*** (0.009)	0.1077*** (0.020)	−0.1366*** (0.022)	0.0607*** (0.023)	−0.0837*** (0.025)	−0.0540*** (0.017)	−0.3412*** (0.027)	−0.0859*** (0.015)
Kazakhstan	0.0683*** (0.010)	0.0350 (0.022)	0.0083 (0.024)	0.1216*** (0.025)	0.0974*** (0.027)	0.0762*** (0.019)	−0.2224*** (0.029)	0.0157 (0.017)
India	0.0699*** (0.008)	0.0794*** (0.019)	0.0947*** (0.020)	0.2295*** (0.021)	0.1769*** (0.023)	0.1657*** (0.016)	−0.4529*** (0.025)	−0.0248* (0.015)
Pakistan	−0.0377*** (0.008)	−0.1728*** (0.018)	−0.1953*** (0.019)	0.0046 (0.020)	0.0010 (0.022)	−0.0629*** (0.015)	−0.5087*** (0.024)	0.0714*** (0.014)

(continued)

Table 1.4 (continued)

	Welzel's emancipative values index	Welzel autonomy sub-index	Gender equality: job	Gender equality: politics	Gender equality: education	Equality sub-index	Welzel relativism sub-index	Welzel scepticism index
Bangladesh	0.0082 (0.008)	0.0117 (0.018)	−0.0890*** (0.020)	0.1178*** (0.021)	0.0605*** (0.023)	0.0294* (0.016)	−0.4378*** (0.025)	0.0683*** (0.014)
Myanmar	−0.0297*** (0.009)	−0.0158 (0.019)	−0.1669*** (0.021)	−0.0160 (0.022)	−0.0479** (0.024)	−0.0771*** (0.016)	−0.4328*** (0.026)	0.2294*** (0.015)
Vietnam	0.0956*** (0.009)	−0.0890*** (0.019)	0.0835*** (0.021)	0.1799*** (0.022)	0.0916*** (0.024)	0.1180*** (0.016)	−0.1176*** (0.026)	0.0029 (0.015)
Philippines	0.0903*** (0.010)	0.0087 (0.023)	−0.0574** (0.025)	0.1286*** (0.026)	0.0192 (0.028)	0.0298 (0.019)	−0.0403 (0.031)	0.0002 (0.017)
Constant	0.3087*** (0.012)	0.4051*** (0.026)	0.3551*** (0.029)	0.2980*** (0.030)	0.4510*** (0.033)	0.3673*** (0.023)	0.8687*** (0.036)	0.4315*** (0.021)
Obs	5958	5880	5958	5858	5951	5881	5901	5799

Source Author's calculations

* $p < 0.10$, ** $p < 0.05$, *** $p < 0.010$

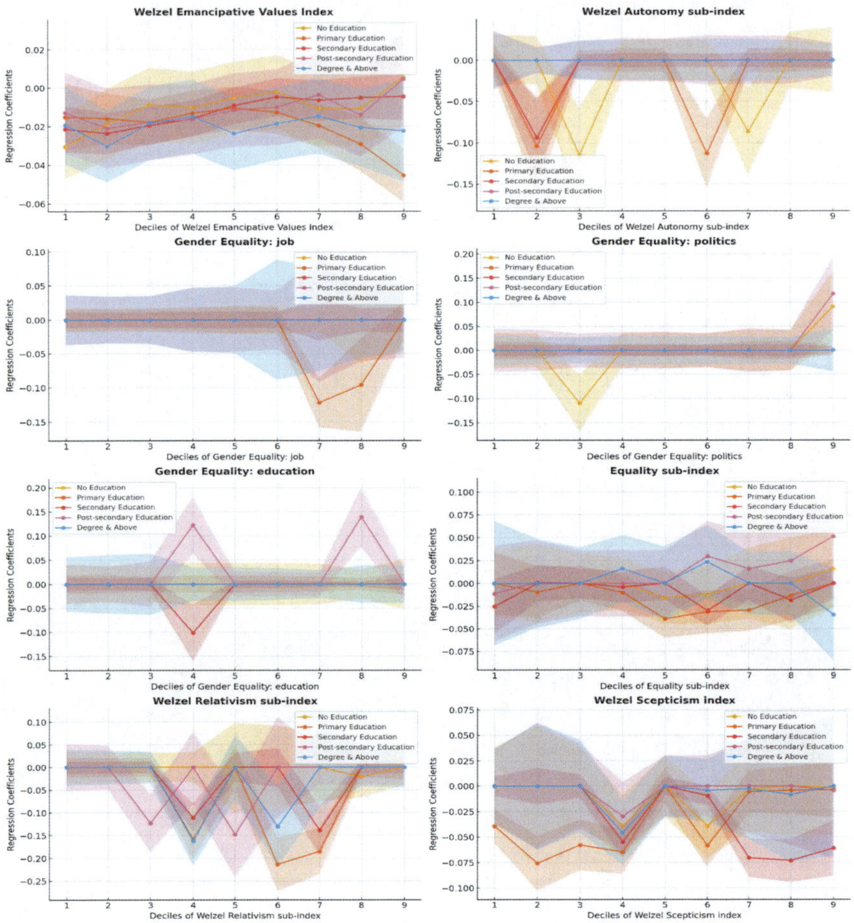

Fig. 1.1 Education-based heterogeneity. *Source* Author's calculations from quantile regression (decile plots)

levels. These patterns align with theories of "capability thresholds," where education enhances resilience against fluctuations in well-being (Jayachandran 2019).

Figure 1.2 compares employment categories. Housewives and self-employed women exhibit steep negative effects on gender-equality job attitudes in the mid to upper deciles, indicating that domestic or precarious work hinders the translation of well-being into empowerment aspirations (Kabeer 2012; Chant and McIlwaine 2016). Full-time employed women show positive effects on SWB autonomy in higher deciles, indicating stable empowerment gains anchored in formal labor participation. Unemployed women exhibit volatile coefficients across indices, highlighting the destabilizing effect of economic marginality on the SWB-empowerment nexus.

Figure 1.3 illustrates income-level heterogeneity. Low-income women exhibit strong negative effects on SWB, including relativism and scepticism, across most

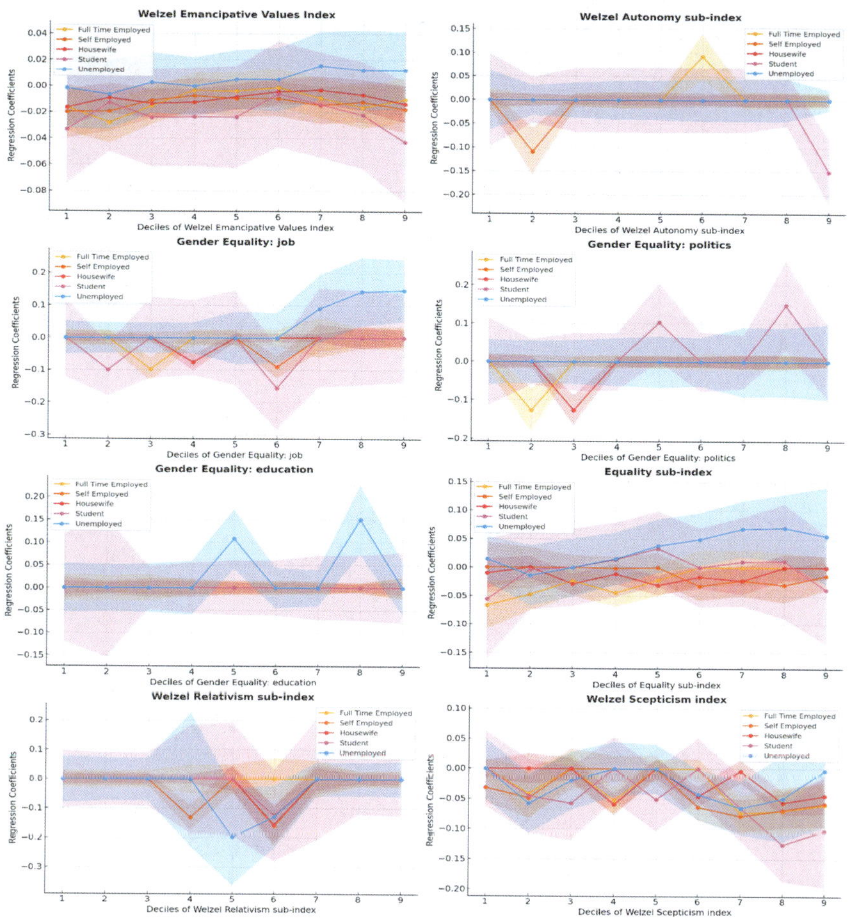

Fig. 1.2 Employment-based heterogeneity. *Source* Author's calculations from quantile regression (decile plots)

quantiles, suggesting that economic insecurity amplifies the constraining influence of well-being on critical social attitudes (Narayan et al. 2000). Middle-income women exhibit moderate negative effects on emancipative values, whereas high-income women in the upper deciles often show positive or null SWB coefficients, supporting the "resource buffer" hypothesis (Duflo 2012).

Figure 1.4 analyzes marital status. Single women consistently show less negative or even positive SWB coefficients across most indices and quantiles, indicating that marital autonomy facilitates the conversion of well-being into empowerment attitudes (Anderson and Eswaran 2009; Doepke et al. 2012). Divorced, separated, and widowed women occupy intermediate positions, reflecting transitional bargaining power dynamics post-marriage dissolution (Kandiyoti 1988).

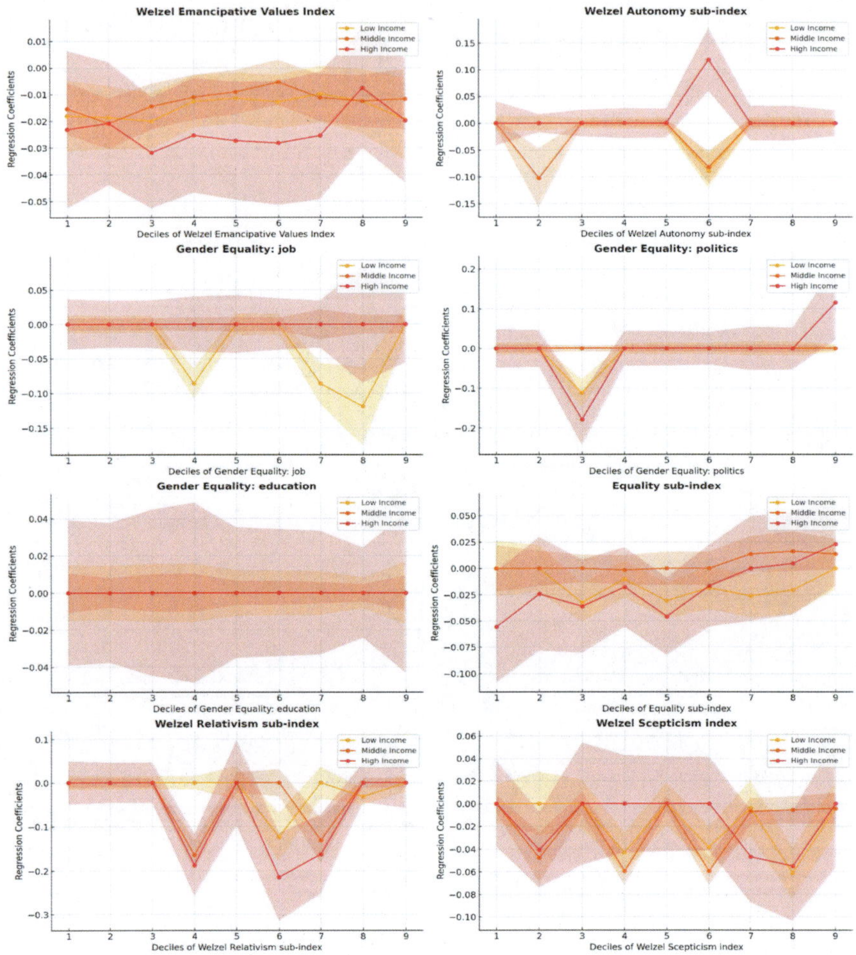

Fig. 1.3 Income-based heterogeneity. *Source* Author's calculations from quantile regression (decile plots)

Finally, Fig. 1.5 groups countries into SAARC, Central Asia, and ASEAN clusters. SAARC women exhibit pronounced negative effects on SWB in gender-equality politics and education in mid-quantiles. In contrast, ASEAN women display more muted and stable coefficients across indices, reflecting regional differences in gender norms and policy contexts (Inglehart and Welzel 2005). Central Asian women show significant negative effects on SWB at specific quantiles, underscoring the interplay between post-Soviet legacies and well-being-empowerment dynamics (Turaeva 2017).

Collectively, these quantile regression results demonstrate that the link between well-being and empowerment is highly context-dependent. Educational attainment, labor force participation, economic resources, marital status, and regional culture

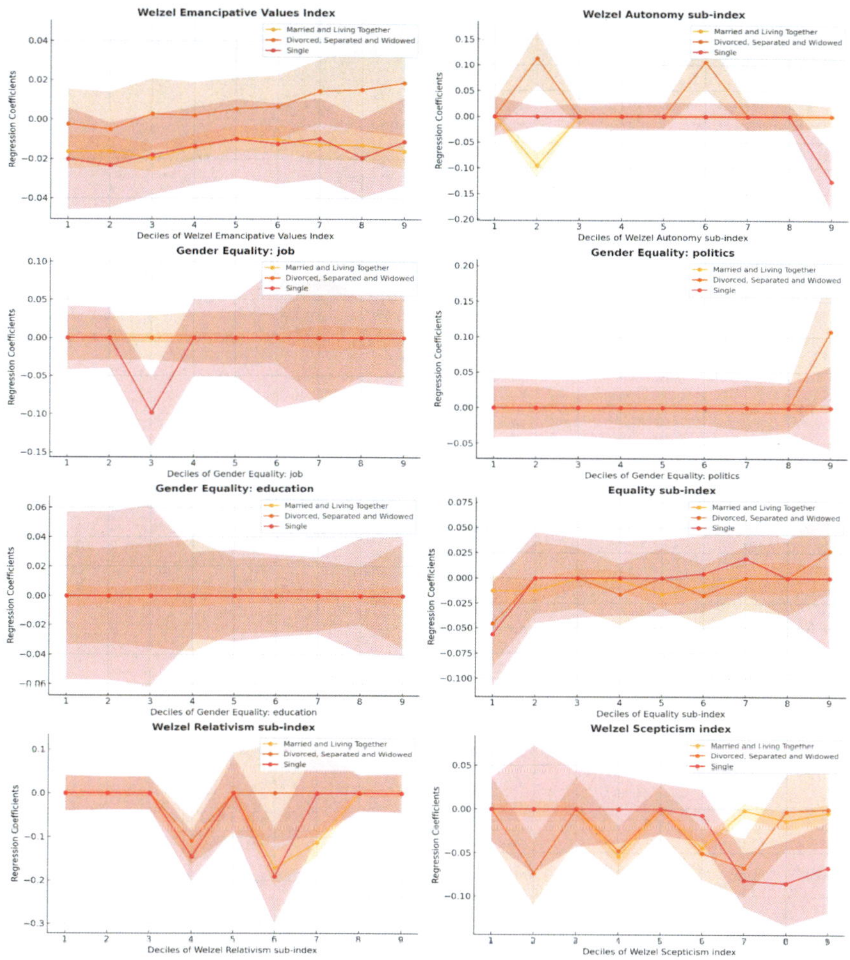

Fig. 1.4 Marriage-based heterogeneity. *Source* Author's calculations from quantile regression (decile plots)

critically shape whether higher SWB enhances or dampens empowerment orientations. Policies aiming to leverage well-being for empowerment must therefore tailor interventions to these socio-economic and cultural subgroups, rather than apply one-size-fits-all approaches (Firpo et al. 2009). Conceptually, the changing signs and magnitudes of coefficients across quantiles (Koenker and Hallock 2001) suggest that the satisfaction-empowerment paradox is experienced differently by women at low, middle, and high levels of empowerment. This is compatible with theories of adaptive preferences and socially determined aspirations, which argue that satisfaction can either mute or amplify emancipative impulses depending on one's position in the

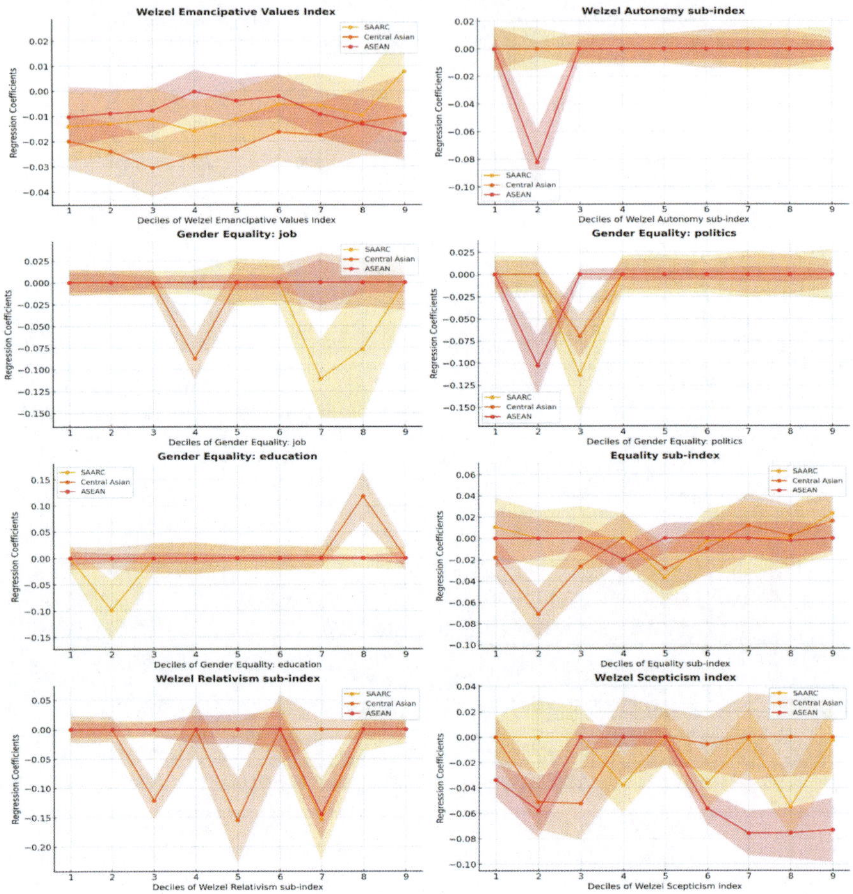

Fig. 1.5 Heterogeneity in country grouping. *Source* Author's calculations from quantile regression (decile plots)

empowerment distribution (Clark et al. 2008; Graham 2009; Genicot and Ray 2017; Appadurai 2004).

1.6 Conclusions, Policy Implications, and Limitations

1.6.1 Conclusions

This paper examines how subjective well-being and socio-political empowerment interact for rural women across 12 developing Asian economies, using individual-level data from the World Values Survey. We constructed a multidimensional Socio-Political Empowerment and Values Indicators framework and considered several dimensions of subjective well-being, including happiness, life satisfaction, perceived freedom and satisfaction with household finances. Methodologically, the analysis combined linear and quantile regressions with checks for socio-demographic heterogeneity to capture both average associations and distributional patterns. Reported happiness exhibits positive associations with empowerment indicators- emancipative values, autonomy, and gender equality in employment, politics, and education. Conversely, life satisfaction, perceived freedom, and financial satisfaction show predominantly negative associations with most empowerment dimensions, with composite SWB displaying negative coefficients for emancipative values, gender equality attitudes, and institutional scepticism.

Quantile analysis reveals pronounced heterogeneity. Women with higher education show weaker negative effects on SWB in higher empowerment quantiles. Full-time employed women show positive associations between SWB and empowerment in higher deciles, whereas housewives exhibit steep negative coefficients. Single women convert SWB gains into empowerment orientations more readily than married women. Regional variation is striking: SAARC countries show the strongest negative SWB-SPEVI associations in the middle quantiles; ASEAN nations display stronger positive associations; Central Asian countries exhibit distinctive post-Soviet patterns. These distributional patterns suggest that satisfaction may reflect constrained adaptation rather than genuine empowerment, particularly among less educated, economically marginalized, and married women facing structural constraints.

1.6.2 Policy Implications

Four interconnected policy strategies flow directly from these findings. First, governments should embed critical consciousness training into rural education systems. The education gradient is pronounced: women with no formal schooling experience persistent negative SWB-empowerment associations, while university-educated women show negative effects only at high empowerment levels. Secondary and tertiary curricula in SAARC countries (Bangladesh, India, Pakistan), where the paradox is most acute, should integrate modules on gender rights, patriarchal norm analysis, and democratic participation. Central Asian governments should supplement technical education with civic leadership and critical media literacy programs. ASEAN nations that demonstrate more integrated welfare-empowerment outcomes should scale their successful gender-responsive pedagogy models across the region.

Second, policymakers should embed empowerment metrics into economic empowerment schemes. The employment heterogeneity is striking: full-time employed women show positive associations between SWB and autonomy (in the upper quantiles), whereas housewives show steep negative coefficients. Microfinance institutions in South Asia should condition loan continuation on measurable empowerment outcomes- participation in women's councils, completion of leadership training, or collective action around local governance. Conditional cash transfer programs should tie disbursements not only to education and health outcomes but also to women's participation in community leadership forums and civic workshops. Myanmar, where gender equality attitudes are particularly low, should couple economic initiatives with explicit norm-change programs including male engagement and community dialogues challenging patriarchal attitudes.

Third, governments must strengthen legal protections for married women's economic independence. The marital status heterogeneity is stark and consistent: married women's SWB coefficients for autonomy are approximately 40% more negative than those of single women. This compressed empowerment space for married women reflects entrenched patriarchal marital arrangements. Bangladesh and Pakistan should accelerate family law reforms that guarantee equal property division upon marital dissolution and establish specialized legal aid clinics in rural areas. All countries should introduce psycho-social support services for divorced and widowed women, rebuilding agency following marital transitions.

Fourth, policymakers should implement region-specific policy frameworks recognizing the distinct SWB-empowerment dynamics. SAARC countries require intensive norm-change interventions- community dialogues, male-engagement programs, and civil society scaling- coupled with economic and educational policies. ASEAN nations should position themselves as regional knowledge hubs, systematizing and disseminating successful policy designs in gender-responsive budgeting and women's civic participation programs to SAARC and Central Asian governments.

Central Asian governments should revitalize local governance participation by implementing quotas for women's representation, leadership training, and linking grassroots women's groups with municipal administrations. Across all regions, policymakers must accept that some degree of constructive dissatisfaction- where women recognize gaps between actual and potential freedoms- is necessary for genuine empowerment.

1.6.3 Limitations

First, the analysis is based on cross-sectional survey data, which restricts the ability to establish temporal ordering and to trace dynamic co-evolution between SWB and empowerment over time. Second, the study relies on self-reported measures and constructed indices; while this enables cross-country comparability, it may not fully capture context-specific constraints operating at household or community levels. The study does not systematically examine the intersectional effects of caste, ethnicity, religion, or disability, nor does it analyze gender-relational dynamics or men's responses to shifts in women's empowerment. Third, although the paper documents robust multi-dimensional patterns and heterogeneity, stronger causal attribution would require designs with additional identification leverage.

Future work can build on these results by leveraging repeated surveys or panel data when available, combining household responses with richer institutional and community indicators, and conducting more granular subnational analyses. These may examine how local governance and normative environments condition the SWB–empowerment relationship for rural women.

Appendix

See Tables A.1, A.2, and A.3 and Fig. B.1.

Table A.1 Country-wise distribution of WVS wave 7 sample

Country	Total WVS respondents	Rural respondents	Rural women respondents	Rural women as % of national sample
Bangladesh	1200	920	467	38.9
India	1692	1058	464	27.4
Indonesia	3196	2367	1279	40.0
Kazakhstan	1276	521	278	21.8
Kyrgyzstan	1200	730	452	37.7
Myanmar	1200	840	420	35.0
Pakistan	1995	1331	642	32.2
Philippines	1200	510	255	21.2
Tajikistan	1200	880	432	36.0
Thailand	1491	915	499	33.5
Uzbekistan	1250	699	351	28.1
Vietnam	1200	784	419	34.9

Source Authors' calculation

Table A.2 Mean comparison of SPEVI indicators by above- and below-average SWB groups

Variable	SWB > SWB (mean)	SWB ≤ SWB (mean)	t-stat
Welzel emancipative values index	0.3304	0.3412	−3.1689***
Welzel Autonomy sub-index	0.4249	0.4105	1.9474*
Gender equality: job	0.3072	0.3264	−2.9504***
Gender equality: politics	0.3736	0.3967	−2.3733***
Gender equality: education	0.5093	0.5207	−1.3237
Equality sub-index	0.4078	0.4679	−5.0573***
Welzel relativism sub-index	0.4035	0.4667	−5.8509***
Welzel scepticism index	0.3151	0.3509	−6.0499***

Source Authors' calculation

Table A.3 Regression results- robustness test

	Welzel emancipative values index	Welzel autonomy sub-index	Gender equality: job	Gender equality: politics	Gender equality: education	Equality sub-index	Welzel relativism sub-index	Welzel scepticism index
Subjective well-being composite (Z-score)	−0.0057** (0.002)	0.0046 (0.005)	−0.0052** (0.002)	−0.0066*** (0.002)	−0.0082 (0.007)	−0.007** (0.003)	−0.0343*** (0.007)	−0.0438*** (0.004)
Immigrant to the country	0.0094 (0.018)	−0.0166 (0.040)	0.0108 (0.044)	0.0563 (0.047)	0.0438 (0.050)	0.0337 (0.035)	0.0293 (0.055)	0.0207 (0.031)
Income level: medium	0.0241*** (0.005)	−0.0002 (0.011)	0.0379*** (0.012)	0.0497*** (0.013)	0.0238* (0.014)	0.0362*** (0.010)	0.0644*** (0.015)	0.0206** (0.009)
Income level: high	0.0169** (0.007)	0.0029 (0.016)	0.0082 (0.018)	0.0370** (0.019)	−0.0272 (0.020)	0.0045 (0.014)	0.0863*** (0.022)	−0.0059 (0.012)
Illiterate	−0.0089 (0.005)	−0.0088 (0.012)	−0.0157 (0.013)	0.0021 (0.014)	−0.0530*** (0.015)	−0.0229** (0.010)	0.0257 (0.017)	0.0260*** (0.009)
Kyrgyzstan	−0.0286*** (0.009)	−0.0227 (0.019)	−0.1133*** (0.021)	0.0122 (0.022)	−0.0375 (0.023)	−0.0455*** (0.016)	−0.5549*** (0.026)	0.2167*** (0.015)
Uzbekistan	0.0717*** (0.009)	0.1077*** (0.020)	−0.1366*** (0.022)	0.0607*** (0.023)	−0.0837*** (0.025)	−0.0540*** (0.017)	−0.3412*** (0.027)	−0.0859*** (0.015)
Kazakhstan	0.0683*** (0.010)	0.0350 (0.022)	0.0083 (0.024)	0.1216*** (0.025)	0.0974*** (0.027)	0.0762*** (0.019)	−0.2224*** (0.029)	0.0157 (0.017)
India	0.0699*** (0.008)	0.0794*** (0.019)	0.0947*** (0.020)	0.2295*** (0.021)	0.1769*** (0.023)	0.1657*** (0.016)	−0.4529*** (0.025)	−0.0248* (0.015)
Pakistan	−0.0377*** (0.008)	−0.1728*** (0.018)	−0.1953*** (0.019)	0.0046 (0.020)	0.0010 (0.022)	−0.0629*** (0.015)	−0.5087*** (0.024)	0.0714*** (0.014)

(continued)

Table A.3 (continued)

	Welzel emancipative values index	Welzel autonomy sub-index	Gender equality: job	Gender equality: politics	Gender equality: education	Equality sub-index	Welzel relativism sub-index	Welzel scepticism index
Bangladesh	0.0082 (0.008)	0.0117 (0.018)	−0.0890*** (0.020)	0.1178*** (0.021)	0.0605*** (0.023)	0.0294* (0.016)	−0.4378*** (0.025)	0.0683*** (0.014)
Myanmar	−0.0297*** (0.009)	−0.0158 (0.019)	−0.1669*** (0.021)	−0.0160 (0.022)	−0.0479** (0.024)	−0.0771*** (0.016)	−0.4328*** (0.026)	0.2294*** (0.015)
Vietnam	0.0956*** (0.009)	−0.0890*** (0.019)	0.0835*** (0.021)	0.1799*** (0.022)	0.0916*** (0.024)	0.1180*** (0.016)	−0.1176*** (0.026)	0.0029 (0.015)
Philippines	0.0903*** (0.010)	0.0087 (0.023)	−0.0574** (0.025)	0.1286*** (0.026)	0.0192 (0.028)	0.0298 (0.019)	−0.0403 (0.031)	0.0002 (0.017)
constant	0.2884*** (0.008)	0.4212*** (0.017)	0.3367*** (0.019)	0.2749*** (0.020)	0.4799*** (0.021)	0.3647*** (0.015)	0.7480*** (0.023)	0.2775*** (0.013)
Obs	5958	5880	5958	5858	5951	5881	5901	5799

Source Authors' calculation

* $p < 0.10$, ** $p < 0.05$, *** $p < 0.010$

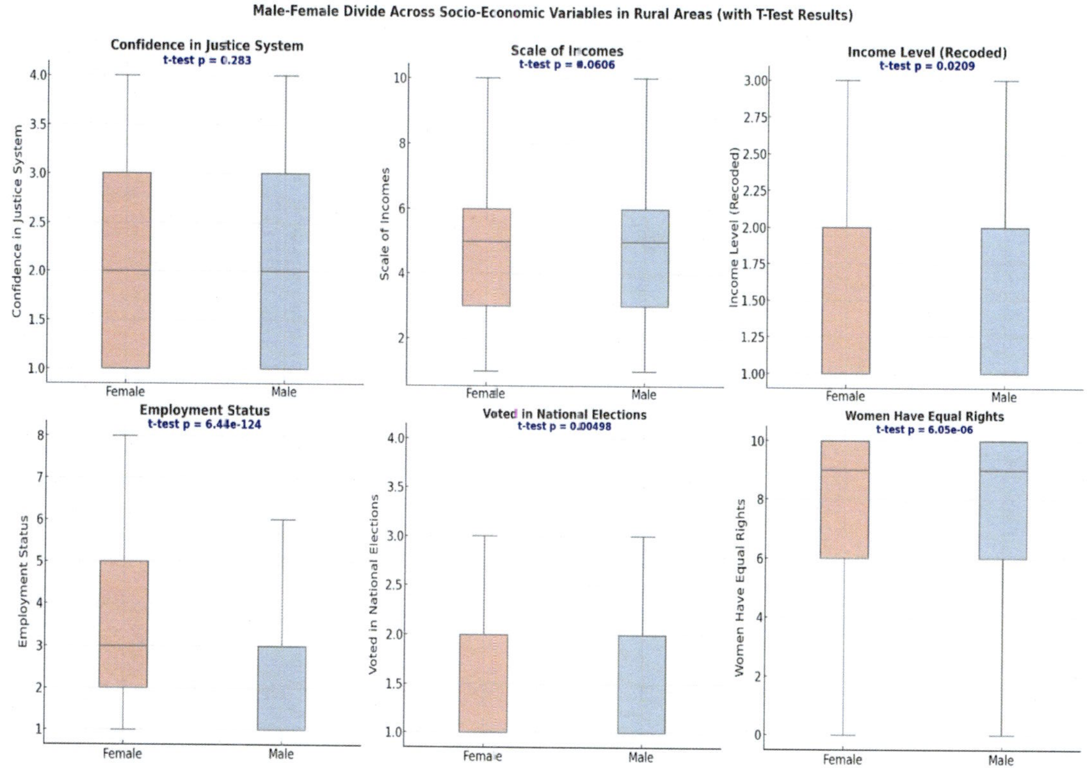

Fig. B.1 Male–female divide across socio-economic variables in rural areas. *Source* Author's illustration. WVS questions Q70: Confidence: Justice system/courts, Q288: scale of incomes, Q288R: Income level (recoded), Q279: Employment status, Q222: Vote in elections: National level, Q249: Democracy: Women have the same rights as men

References

Abrar-ul-Haq, M., Abbas, N., & Ashiq, U. (2025). Happiness and well-being of women working in a modern corporate environment. Asian Social Work and Policy Review, 19(3), e70015. https://doi.org/10.1111/aswp.70015.

Acemoglu, D., Naidu, S., Restrepo, P., & Robinson, J. A. (2019). Democracy does cause growth. Journal of Political Economy, 127(1), 47–100. https://doi.org/10.1086/700936.

Alkire, S., Meinzen-Dick, R., Peterman, A., Quisumbing, A., Seymour, G., & Vaz, A. (2013). The Women's Empowerment in Agriculture Index. World Development, 52. https://doi.org/10.2139/ssrn.2197300.

Allendorf, K. (2007). Do women's land rights promote empowerment? Evidence from Nepal. World Development, 35(11), 1975–1988. https://doi.org/10.1016/j.worlddev.2006.12.005.

Alqararah, K. (2023). Assessing the robustness of composite indicators: The case of the Global Innovation Index. Journal of Innovation and Entrepreneurship, 12(1), 61. https://doi.org/10.1186/s13731-023-00332-w.

Ambler, K., Jones, K. M., & O'Sullivan, M. (2026). Increasing women's empowerment: Evaluating two interventions in Uganda. Journal of Development Economics, 178, 103575. https://doi.org/10.1016/j.jdeveco.2025.103575.

Anderson, S., & Eswaran, M. (2009). What determines female autonomy? Evidence from Bangladesh. Journal of Development Economics, 90(2), 179–191. https://doi.org/10.1016/j.jdeveco.2008.10.004.

Annan, J., Donald, A., Goldstein, M., Gonzalez Martinez, P., & Koolwal, G. (2021). Taking power: Women's empowerment and household well-being in Sub-Saharan Africa. World Development, 140, 105292. https://doi.org/10.1016/j.worlddev.2020.105292.

Appadurai, A. (2004). The capacity to aspire: Culture and the terms of recognition. In V. Rao & M. Walton (Eds.), Culture and public action (pp. 59–84). Stanford, CA: Stanford University Press.

Ara, J. (2025). Beyond economic gains: Asset transfer programs and psychological well-being of ultra-poor women in Bangladesh. Journal of International Development, 38(1), 140–158. https://doi.org/10.1002/jid.70045.

Båge, K., Kågesten, A., Fagbemi, M., Uthman, O., Arunda, M. O., Puranen, B., Ekström, A. M., & Litorp, H. (2025). Is reproductive agency associated with subjective well-being? A population-based cross-sectional study among men and women in four sub-Saharan African countries using the World Values Survey. Critical Public Health. https://doi.org/10.1080/09581596.2025.2604450.

Balasubramanian, P., Ibanez, M., Khan, S., & Sahoo, S. (2024). Does women's economic empowerment promote human development in low- and middle-income countries? A meta-analysis. World Development, 178, 106588. https://doi.org/10.1016/j.worlddev.2024.106588.

Becchetti, L., & Conzo, G. (2022). The gender life satisfaction/depression paradox. Social Indicators Research, 160(1), 35–113. https://doi.org/10.1007/s11205-021-02740-5.

Blanchflower, D. G., & Bryson, A. (2024). The female happiness paradox. Journal of Population Economics, 37(1), 1–27. https://doi.org/10.1007/s00148-024-00981-5.

Bortolotti, A., Di Berardino, C., & Palumbo, R. (2026). Living well or spending more? A 25-year review of income, consumption, and life satisfaction. Journal of Happiness Studies. https://doi.org/10.1007/s10902-026-01006-6.

Buchinsky, M. (1998). Recent advances in quantile regression models: A practical guideline for empirical research. Journal of Human Resources, 33(1), 88–126. https://doi.org/10.2307/146316.

Cameron, A. C., & Trivedi, P. K. (2005). Microeconometrics: Methods and applications. Cambridge University Press. https://doi.org/10.1017/CBO9780511811241.

Chang, M., Chu, Y., & Yao, S. (2011). Asian Barometer Survey: Social development report. Taiwan: Asian Barometer Foundation.

Chant, S., & McIlwaine, C. (2016). Cities, slums and gender in the global South: Towards a feminised urban future. Routledge.

Chattopadhyay, R., & Duflo, E. (2004). Women as policy makers: Evidence from a randomized policy experiment in India. Econometrica, 72(5), 1409–1443. https://doi.org/10.1111/j.1468-0262.2004.00539.x.

Chen, Y. (2024). Early exposure to air pollution and cognitive development later in life: Evidence from China. China Economic Review, 83, 102098. https://doi.org/10.1016/j.chieco.2023.102098.

Clark, A. E., Frijters, P., & Shields, M. A. (2008). Relative income, happiness, and utility: An explanation for the Easterlin paradox and other puzzles. Journal of Economic Literature, 46(1), 95–144. https://doi.org/10.1257/jel.46.1.95.

Cornwall, A., & Rivas, A.M. (2015). From 'gender equality' and 'women's empowerment' to global justice: Reclaiming a transformative agenda for gender and development. Third World Quarterly, 36(2), 396–415. https://doi.org/10.1080/01436597.2015.1013341.

Diener, E., Oishi, S., & Tay, L. (2018). Advances in subjective well-being research. Nature Human Behaviour, 2(4), 253–260. https://doi.org/10.1038/s41562-018-0307-6.

Doepke, M., Tertilt, M., & Voena, A. (2012). The economics and politics of women's rights. Annual Review of Economics, 4, 339–372. https://doi.org/10.1146/annurev-economics-061109-080201.

Duflo, E. (2012). Women's empowerment and economic development. Journal of Economic Literature, 50(4), 1051–1079. https://doi.org/10.1257/jel.50.4.1051.

Easterlin, R. A. (2013). Happiness, growth, and public policy. Economic Inquiry, 51(1), 1–15. https://doi.org/10.1111/j.1465-7295.2012.00505.x.

Ewerling, F., Lynch, J. W., Victora, C. G., van Eerdewijk, A., Tyszler, M., & Barros, A. J. (2017). The SWPER index for women's empowerment in Africa: Development and validation of a measurement framework. The Lancet Global Health, 5(9), e916–e923. https://doi.org/10.1016/S2214-109X(17)30292-9.

Field, E., Jayachandran, S., & Pande, R. (2010). Do traditional institutions constrain female entrepreneurship? A field experiment on business training in India. American Economic Review, 100(2), 125–129. https://doi.org/10.1257/aer.100.2.125.

Fielding, D., & Lepine, A. (2016). Women's empowerment and well-being: Evidence from Africa. The Journal of Development Studies, 53(6), 826–840. https://doi.org/10.1080/00220388.2016.1219345.

Firpo, S., Fortin, N. M., & Lemieux, T. (2009). Unconditional quantile regressions. Econometrica, 77(3), 953–973. https://doi.org/10.3982/ECTA6822.

Freire, P. (1970). Pedagogy of the oppressed. Herder and Herder.

Genicot, G., & Ray, D. (2017). Aspirations and inequality. Econometrica, 85(2), 489–519. https://doi.org/10.3982/ECTA13865.

Graafland, J., & Schilpzand, A. (2025). Gender equality and life satisfaction: A mediation model with individual autonomy, income per capita and trust. Journal of Happiness Studies, 26(3), 1–27. https://doi.org/10.1007/s10902-024-00850-8.

Graham, C. (2009). Happiness around the world: The paradox of happy peasants and miserable millionaires. Oxford University Press. https://doi.org/10.1093/acprof:osobl/9780199549054.001.0001.

Greco, S., Ishizaka, A., Tasiou, M., & Torrisi, G. (2019). On the methodological framework of composite indices: A review of the issues of weighting, aggregation, and robustness. Social Indicators Research, 141(1), 61–94. https://doi.org/10.1007/s11205-017-1832-9.

Haerpfer, C., Inglehart, R., Moreno, A., Welzel, C., Kizilova, K., Diez-Medrano, J., … Puranen, B. (Eds.). (2022). World Values Survey Wave 7 (2017–2022) cross-national data-set. World Values Survey Association. https://doi.org/10.14281/18241.18.

Hasan, Z. (2023). Gender inequality in South Asia: Tracing impediments to SDG 5 of UN Sustainable Development Goals. IntechOpen. https://doi.org/10.5772/intechopen.112617.

Helliwell, J. F., Layard, R., Sachs, J. D., De Neve, J. E., Aknin, L. B., & Wang, S. (2021). World Happiness Report 2021. Sustainable Development Solutions Network. Retrieved from https://worldhappiness.report/ed/2021/.

Hirai, T. (2025). The validity of subjective assessments of deprivation: Can it be true that poor people are happier than those who are well off? Humanities and Social Sciences Communications, 12, Article 1719. https://doi.org/10.1057/s41599-025-05987-2.

Hortas-Rico, M., & Rodríguez-Crespo, E. (2025). How does women's political empowerment relate to subjective well-being? The moderating role of institutional quality. European Journal of Political Economy, 86, 102639. https://doi.org/10.1016/j.ejpoleco.2024.102639.

Huis, M. A., Hansen, N., Otten, S., & Lensink, R. (2017). A three-dimensional model of women's empowerment: Implications in the field of microfinance and future directions. Frontiers in Psychology, 8, 1678. https://doi.org/10.3389/fpsyg.2017.01678.

International Finance Corporation (IFC). (2020). IFC's work on gender in South Asia.

Inglehart, R., & Welzel, C. (2005). Modernization, cultural change, and democracy: The human development sequence. Cambridge University Press. https://doi.org/10.1017/CBO9780511790881.

Jayachandran, S. (2019). Social norms as a barrier to women's employment in developing countries (WIDER Working Paper No. 2019/74). UNU-WIDER. https://doi.org/10.35188/UNU-WIDER/2019/708-8.

Kabeer, N. (2012). Women's economic empowerment and inclusive growth: Labour markets and enterprise development. Discussion Paper No. 29. Centre for Development Policy & Research, SOAS, University of London.

Kandiyoti, D. (1988). Bargaining with patriarchy. Gender & Society, 2(3), 274–290. https://doi.org/10.1177/089124388002003004.

Kar, R. N., & Tiwari, K. (2020). Realms of gender interactions: South Asian perspectives. South Asian Survey, 27(2), 91–97. https://doi.org/10.1177/0971523120951575.

Khader, S. J. (2011). Adaptive preferences and women's empowerment. Oxford University Press.

Knowles, C. (2021). Beyond adaptive preferences: Rethinking women's complicity in their own subordination. European Journal of Philosophy, 30(4), 1317–1334. https://doi.org/10.1111/ejop.12742.

Koenker, R., & Bassett, G. (1978). Regression quantiles. Econometrica, 46(1), 33–50. https://doi.org/10.2307/1913643.

Koenker, R., & Hallock, K. F. (2001). Quantile regression. Journal of Economic Perspectives, 15(4), 143–156. https://doi.org/10.1257/jep.15.4.143.

Kumar, V., Maral, P., Upadhyay, A., & Azam, S. (2024). Women: Autonomous bodies, are they? Understanding autonomy and well-being. The Oriental Anthropologist, 24(2), 246–261. https://doi.org/10.1177/0972558X241277121.

Longwe, S.H. (1991). Gender awareness: the missing element in the Third World development project. Oxfam.

MacKinnon, J. G., & White, H. (1985). Some heteroskedasticity-consistent covariance matrix estimators with improved finite sample properties. Journal of Econometrics, 29(3), 305–325. https://doi.org/10.1016/0304-4076(85)90158-7.

Mahmud, S., Shah, N. M., & Becker, S. (2012). Measurement of women's empowerment in rural Bangladesh. World Development, 40(3), 610–619. https://doi.org/10.1016/j.worlddev.2011.08.003.

Malah, Y. F. K. (2021). Is happiness in the hands of women? Women's political empowerment and subjective well-being. Economics Bulletin, 41(2), 573–587.

Manda, S. (2023). COVID-19, livelihoods and gender: Material, relational and subjective realities in rural Zambia. World Development Perspectives, 32, 100547. https://doi.org/10.1016/j.wdp.2023.100547.

Mantsi, L., Lesaoana, R., & Motlamelle, T. (2025). Does being male or female affect life satisfaction? Empirical evidence from Lesotho. Development Southern Africa, 42(3), 477–495. https://doi.org/10.1080/0376835X.2025.2485936.

Miedema, S. S., Haardörfer, R., Girard, A. W., & Yount, K. M. (2018). Women's empowerment in East Africa: Development of a cross-country comparable measure. World Development, 110, 453–464. https://doi.org/10.1016/j.worlddev.2018.05.031.

Minkov, M., & Bond, M. H. (2017). A genetic component to national differences in happiness. Journal of Happiness Studies, 18(1), 233–254. https://doi.org/10.1007/s10902-015-9712-y.
Narayan, D., Chambers, R., Shah, M. K., & Petesch, P. (2000). Voices of the poor: Crying out for change. World Bank. https://hdl.handle.net/10986/13848.
Turaeva, R. (2017). Women as change agents: Gender in post-Soviet Central Asia. Routledge.
Njiru, N., Omia, D., Galiè, A., Loriba, A., & Cislaghi, B. (2026). Gender norms and implications on women's empowerment within the livestock and vaccines delivery systems: A multisite qualitative study in the Upper East Region of Northern Ghana. Heliyon, 12(1), Article e44514. https://doi.org/10.1016/j.heliyon.2026.e44514.
Nussbaum, M. C. (2000). Women and human development: The capabilities approach. Cambridge University Press.
Olivos, F., Sun, Y., & Ho, L.-S. (2026). The structural fit of personal gender beliefs: A cross-national analysis of its implications for life satisfaction. Social Science Research, 135, 103308. https://doi.org/10.1016/j.ssresearch.2026.103308.
Pennings, S., & Symons, X. (2024). First among equals? Adaptive preferences and the limits of autonomy in medical ethics. Journal of Medical Ethics, 50(3), 212–218. https://doi.org/10.1136/medethics-2021-107942.
Pratley, P. (2016). Associations between quantitative measures of women's empowerment and access to care and health status for mothers and their children: A systematic review of evidence from the developing world. Social Science & Medicine, 169, 119–131. https://doi.org/10.1016/j.socscimed.2016.08.001.
Rowlands, J. (1997). Questioning empowerment: Working with women in Honduras, Oxfam.
Ryan, R. M., & Deci, E. L. (2000). Self-determination theory and the facilitation of intrinsic motivation, social development, and well-being. American Psychologist, 55(1), 68–78. https://doi.org/10.1037/0003-066X.55.1.68.
Samartzidis, L., Quatrosi, M., & von Dulong, A. (2025). Gender and age matter! Identifying important predictors for subjective well-being using machine learning methods. Social Indicators Research, 179(2), 955–978. https://doi.org/10.1007/s11205-025-03643-5.
Samman, E., Presler-Marshall, E., & Jones, N., with Bhatkal, T., Melamed, C., Stavropoulou, M., & Wallace, J. (2016). Women's work: Mothers, children and the global childcare crisis. Overseas Development Institute. https://media.odi.org/documents/10331.pdf.
Sen, A. (1999). Development as freedom. Oxford University Press.
Solotaroff, J. L., & Pande, R. P. (2014). Violence against women and girls: Lessons from South Asia. World Bank. https://doi.org/10.1596/978-1-4648-0171-6.
Stiglitz, J. E., Sen, A., & Fitoussi, J.-P. (2009). Report by the Commission on the Measurement of Economic Performance and Social Progress. Paris: Commission on the Measurement of Economic Performance and Social Progress.
Terefe, B., Workneh, B. S., Zeleke, G. A., Mekonen, E. G., Zegeye, A. F., Aemro, A., Tekeba, B., Tamir, T. T., Wassie, M., & Ali, M. S. (2025). Uncovering women's healthcare access challenges in low- and middle-income countries using mixed effects modelling approach: Insights for achieving the Sustainable Development Goals. PLoS One, 20(1), e0314309. https://doi.org/10.1371/journal.pone.0314309.
Welzel, C. (2013). Freedom rising: Human empowerment and the quest for emancipation. Cambridge University Press. https://doi.org/10.1017/CBO9781139540919.
White, H. (1980). A heteroskedasticity-consistent covariance matrix estimator and a direct test for heteroskedasticity. Econometrica, 48(4), 817–838. https://doi.org/10.2307/1912934.

Wooldridge, J. M. (2010). Econometric analysis of cross section and panel data (2nd ed.). MIT Press.
World Bank. (2024). Clearing the path for women to work: Gender gaps in labor force participation in South Asia. Washington, DC: World Bank.
World Economic Forum (WEF). (2024). Why we must close South Asia's digital gender divide.
Yuniati, F., Shobur, S., Kumalasari, I., Lukman, Mediarti, D., & Haryanti, R. S. (2022). The importance of physical activity and community participation amongst women for a better quality of life: A cross-sectional study of Indonesia Family Life Survey. International Journal of Health Engineering and Technology, 1(2). https://doi.org/10.55227/ijhet.v1i2.25.

Chapter 2
Happy Farmers, Efficient Farms: Insights from Potato Production in India

Lixue Qu, Wanglin Ma, and Nozomi Kawarazuka

2.1 Introduction

Enhancing agricultural productivity is vital for ensuring food security and sustainable rural development, particularly in developing nations where agriculture remains the backbone of the economy. Productivity can be improved by either increasing production inputs, such as labor, land, water, fertiliser, and machinery, or by enhancing technical efficiency, which refers to achieving higher output under given input conditions (Njuki et al. 2025; Xin et al. 2025). Increasing productivity by increasing production inputs often leads to rising production costs, inefficient resource allocation, and increasing environmental pressure. In comparison, increasing agricultural productivity through improved technical efficiency requires better utilization of existing resources, without increasing production costs, which has become a priority in enhancing farm performance and food security (Chen 2025; Mohamed et al. 2026).

A growing number of studies have explored the factors that determine the technical efficiency of crop production. There exist three strands of literature. The first strand of literature examines how the characteristics of farmers and households influence the technical efficiency of crop production (Hossain et al. 2008; Shavgulidze et al. 2017; Andaregie and Astatkie 2020; Fikadu and Mulatu 2023). For example, Hossain et al. (2008) demonstrated that higher levels of education among farmers significantly improved rice production efficiency in Bangladesh. Andaregie and Astatkie

L. Qu · W. Ma (✉)
Department of Global Value Chains and Trade, Faculty of Agribusiness and Commerce, Lincoln University, Christchurch, New Zealand
e-mail: Wanglin.Ma@lincoln.ac.nz

L. Qu
e-mail: Lixue.Qu@lincolnuni.ac.nz

N. Kawarazuka
Department of Regenerative Agriculture, International Potato Center, Hanoi, Vietnam
e-mail: N.Kawarazuka@cgiar.org

W. Ma et al. (eds.), *Beyond Income*, Contributions to Economics,
https://doi.org/10.1007/978-981-92-4957-2_2

(2020) reported that education, farming experience, off-farm income, household size, membership in farmers' association, access to irrigation, extension contact, and adoption of improved seed all contributed positively to the technical efficiency of potato production in Ethiopia. Similarly, Fikadu and Mulatu (2023) found that the frequency of extension contact, agronomic practice training, and cooperative membership significantly improved the technical efficiency of potato production in Ethiopia.

The second strand of literature focuses on how variations in resource endowments and environmental conditions influence the technical efficiency of crop production (DeLay et al. 2022; Geffersa et al. 2019; Liu et al. 2019; Mayen et al. 2010; Yin et al. 2024; Zhang et al. 2011). For example, analyzing panel data from rural households in Zhejiang, Hubei, and Yunnan provinces of China, Zhang et al. (2011) demonstrated that land reallocation (i.e., the redistribution of contracted farmland among farmers) significantly affected the technical efficiency of aggregate crop production. Specifically, land reallocation increased technical efficiency in Zhejiang but decreased it in Hubei and Yunnan. Further, Liu et al. (2019) demonstrated that land fragmentation imposed a strong negative effect on the technical efficiency of wheat production. Yin et al. (2024) found that land consolidation, the merging of small, scattered plots into larger, more contiguous farmland, significantly improves land-use efficiency in China's developed agricultural regions by promoting economies of scale and mechanization. Beyond land, technological adoption and access to information also play a role. Using U.S. Agricultural Resource Management Survey (ARMS) data, Mayen et al. (2010) compared the technical efficiency between organic and conventional dairy farms. They found no significant difference in technical efficiency when efficiency was measured relative to the appropriate production technology. However, the organic dairy technology was about 13% less productive than the conventional one. Geffersa et al. (2019) demonstrated that easier access to technical information improves the technical efficiency of maize production among farmers.

The third strand emphasizes the impact of institutional support and social mechanisms on technical efficiency (Solís et al. 2009; Djoumessi et al. 2018; Biswas et al. 2021; Missiame et al. 2021; Rajkhowa and Qaim 2021). For example, Solís et al. (2009) found that farmers who adopted soil conservation practices, such as crop residue mulching, contour tillage, green manure, and crop rotation, under these projects achieved significantly higher technical efficiency than those who did not. Djoumessi et al. (2018) reported that access to agricultural technology extension significantly improved technical efficiency among smallholder vegetable farmers in Cameroon, as those who received extension support achieved higher output with the same level of inputs. Missiame et al. (2021) examined the impact of access to credit from rural and community banks (RCBs) on the technical efficiency of smallholder cassava farmers in Ghana. They found that farmers who obtained credit from RCBs achieved significantly higher technical efficiency, suggesting that rural credit access enables farmers to utilize inputs more effectively and improve the efficiency of cassava production.

In addition to household, resources, and institutional factors, farmers' psychological well-being may also affect their technical efficiency in crop production. In theory, farmers who are psychologically performing better would have a higher technical efficiency than their counterparts who are performing less well, because the former are generally more motivated, energetic, and goal-oriented in agricultural production. Additionally, farmers with higher psychological well-being tend to be more open-minded and confident in adopting new agricultural technologies and management practices, and they experience better physical health and greater work capacity, which enhances their overall productivity. Happier farmers are more socially connected and collaborative within their communities, fostering communication and knowledge exchange on farm management practices that improve technical efficiency.

To date, only a small number of recent works have begun to consider farmers' subjective well-being in explaining farm performance (Bukchin-peles 2022; Ma et al. 2022; Khaled and Ben 2024). Bukchin-peles (2022) utilized field survey data from smallholder farmers in Nepal to investigate the relationship between farmers' positivity and agricultural productivity. They found that a higher positivity ratio is associated with higher agricultural income and output. Ma et al. (2022) reported that Chinese farmers with higher levels of happiness achieved higher maize productivity. Khaled and Ben (2024) conducted a panel data analysis of 34 African countries from 2006 to 2020 to examine the bidirectional relationship between agricultural productivity and happiness. Their findings indicate a positive but very weak two-way relationship: agricultural productivity slightly improves happiness, while higher happiness levels marginally enhance agricultural productivity. Nevertheless, no previous studies have explored the relationship between farmers' subjective well-being and the technical efficiency of crop production. This study addresses the research gap.

This study empirically examines how farmers' subjective well-being, with a focus on happiness, influences the technical efficiency of potato production, using micro-survey data from 793 potato growers in Uttar Pradesh, India. We focus on happiness because it directly influences farmers' motivation and decision-making in farm production, shaping how efficiently they utilize available resources to optimize farm output. By examining how farmers' happiness influences their technical efficiency of potato production, this study provides new insights for formulating policies that would enhance farmers' subjective well-being while promoting the sustainable development of the agricultural sector.

This study makes two contributions to the literature. First, this study contributes to the literature by explicitly considering farmers' subjective well-being as a determinant of technical efficiency, thereby introducing a behavioural perspective into agricultural efficiency analysis. Second, methodologically, this paper integrates stochastic frontier analysis with a conditional mixed process framework to estimate the impact of farmers' happiness on the technical efficiency of potato production, while addressing potential endogeneity in happiness. This unified econometric approach enables the simultaneous estimation of happiness and technical efficiency equations, thereby capturing possible correlated error structures more accurately.

The rest of the paper is organised as follows. Section 2.2 provides a brief overview of the background of potato production in India. Section 2.3 discusses the estimation strategies. Section 2.4 presents the data and descriptive statistics. Section 2.5 presents and discusses empirical results. The final section contains the conclusions and policy implications.

2.2 Potato Production in India

Potatoes are one of the most important food and cash crops in India. They are not only an essential part of residents' daily diet, but also of great significance to the livelihood stability of smallholder farmers (FAOSTAT 2025). Figure 2.1 illustrates the trend in potato production in India from 2014 to 2023, indicating an upward trend. In 2014, India's potato production was 46.60 million tons. By 2023, India's potato production had increased to 60.14 million tons, up 13.54 million tons, a growth rate of 29.06%. In general, Fig. 2.1 highlights that potatoes play a vital role in India's food security and rural livelihoods.

Moreover, India is a significant global producer of potatoes. Figure 2.2 presents total potato output across the world's top ten producers, showing that India ranks second after China, which produced 93.43 million tons of potatoes in 2023. However, despite this substantial contribution to global output, India's potato yield remains relatively low at 25.79 tons per hectare, placing it 53rd worldwide (FAOSTAT 2025). This yield is considerably lower than that of high-yielding developed countries such as the United States (51.45 tons/ha), New Zealand (50.88 tons/ha), and Denmark (45.13 tons/ha), and below several Asian developing countries, including Türkiye (37.77 tons/ha), Palestine (36.25 tons/ha), and Uzbekistan (31.88 tons/ha). Because potato yield directly affects food and nutrition security, and improving technical efficiency can enhance yields, it is crucial to explore ways to further increase potato production's technical efficiency. From the perspective of sustainable agriculture and farmers' psychological well-being, this study contributes to the literature by

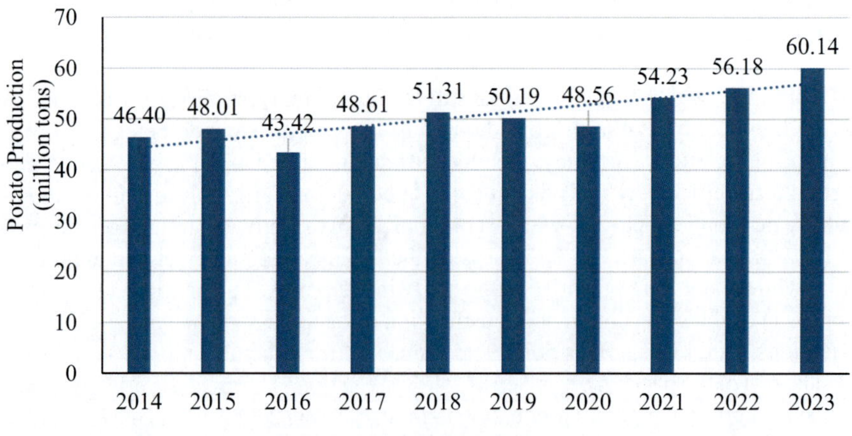

Fig. 2.1 Potato production in India 2014–2023. *Source* FAOSTAT

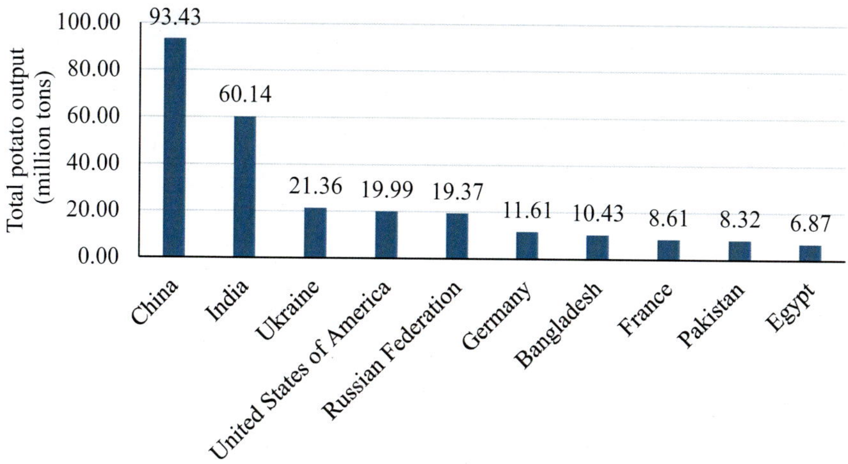

Fig. 2.2 Top 10 potato producing countries in 2023. *Source* FAOSTAT

examining how farmers' happiness influences the technical efficiency in their potato production.

2.3 Estimation Strategies

2.3.1 Stochastic Production Frontier Model

In the efficiency measurement literature, two broad approaches are commonly adopted: non-parametric methods, such as data envelopment analysis (DEA) (Wang et al. 2013), and parametric methods, such as stochastic frontier analysis (SFA) (González-Flores et al. 2014). DEA constructs an efficiency frontier using linear programming without imposing a specific functional form, making it flexible and easy to implement. However, DEA is deterministic in nature and attributes all deviations from the frontier to inefficiency, without explicitly accounting for statistical noise. This limitation is particularly relevant in agricultural production, where output and input use are frequently affected by random shocks, including weather variability, pest and disease outbreaks, and other unforeseen disturbances (Ma et al. 2018). In contrast, the SFA framework decomposes the composite error term into a random noise component and an inefficiency component, allowing for the estimation of technical inefficiency while controlling for stochastic shocks. Therefore, this study uses a parametric SFA model to estimate technical efficiency in potato production by estimating a stochastic production frontier (SPF). The SPF model has been widely used in the production economics literature to estimate farm technical efficiency (e.g., Abdul-Rahaman et al. 2023; Feng et al. 2022; Ma, Zheng, et al. 2023).

The econometric specification of the SPF model can be expressed as follows:

$$Y_i = f(X_i; \beta_i) \cdot \exp(\upsilon_i - \nu_i) \tag{2.1}$$

where Y_i refers to the output of farm household i, measured as the total value of potato production per acre. X_i is a vector of inputs, including expenditures on pesticides, fertilizers, machinery, labor, and land area. β_i is a vector of parameters to be estimated. υ_i a stochastic term that represents random noise (e.g., weather, pests, and market volatility) that can increase or decrease farm output. υ_i is assumed to be independent and identically distributed, i.e., $\upsilon_i \sim N(0, \sigma_\upsilon^2)$. ν_i is a non-negative stochastic term representing inefficiency.

2.3.2 *Technical Efficiency Score Calculation*

Equation (2.1) can be estimated by either a Cobb–Douglas functional form (e.g., Fikadu and Mulatu 2023; Muteti et al. 2024; Obalola et al. 2025) or a translog functional form (e.g., Lin et al. 2023; Obalola et al. 2025; Selorm et al. 2023). We use the likelihood ratio test to check whether the Cobb–Douglas or the translog functional form is more appropriate. The test results report a likelihood-ratio test statistic of 21.27 (Prob = 0.443), suggesting that the translog function is nested within the Cobb–Douglas function. In other words, we should use the Cobb–Douglas function to estimate our data. The Cobb–Douglas SPF model is expressed as follows:

$$\ln Y_i = A + \sum_{k=1}^{6} \beta_k \mathrm{Ln} X_{ki} + \upsilon_i - \nu_i \tag{2.2}$$

where $\ln(Y_i)$ refers to the logarithm of the total value of potato production in farmer i. $\ln(X_{ki})$ is the logarithm of input k for farm household i. A is a constant term capturing the overall technology level. β_k measures the output elasticity with respect to the input X_k. $\upsilon_i - \nu_i$ are defined earlier.

After estimating Eq. (2.2), the output-oriented technical efficiency (TE) of potato production for the i-th farm household can be calculated as follows:

$$\mathrm{TE}_i = \frac{\mathrm{In} Yi}{\mathrm{In} Y_i^*} = \exp(-\nu_i) \tag{2.3}$$

where TE_i captures the ratio of the observed potato output, $\ln(Y_i)$, to the predicted optimal output, $\ln(Y_i^*)$, on the condition that all inputs have been efficiently used. Because $\ln(Y_i) \leq \ln(Y_i^*)$, the facts result in $0 < \mathrm{TE}_i \leq 1$, with one indicating that farmer i is technically efficient in potato production.

2.3.3 *Modelling the Impact of Happiness on Technical Efficiency: Conditional Mixed Process Model*

To analyse the impact of farmers' happiness on the technical efficiency (TE) of potato production, we employ the conditional mixed process (CMP) estimator (Ma et al. 2022; Li et al. 2024; Li and Ma 2025). The rationale for this choice is twofold. First, happiness is potentially endogenous: more efficient farmers may also feel happier because of higher yields or incomes (reverse causality). Second, unobserved factors, such as farmers' innate abilities, risk preferences, or social capital status, may simultaneously affect farmers' happiness and their TE in potato production, thereby biasing results in conventional regression frameworks. The CMP framework is particularly suitable because it can estimate a system of equations with different outcome types and correlated disturbances.

The CMP model jointly estimates two equations. The first equation estimates the impact of control variables on happiness, incorporating at least one instrumental variable as a regressor. The second equation captures the impact of happiness and control variables on the technical efficiency of potato production. The two equations are specified as follows:

$$H_i^* = \gamma_0 + \pi IV_i + Z_i\prime\gamma + \xi_i, H_i = m if \tau_{m-1} < H_i^* \leq \tau_m, m = 1,2, \ldots, 10 \quad (2.4)$$

$$\mathrm{TE}_i = \alpha + \beta H_i + Z_i\prime\delta + \varepsilon_i \quad (2.5)$$

where H_i^* is a latent continuous variable representing the farmer's happiness levels, H_i is the observed ordinal happiness score ranging from 0 to 10, $Z_i\prime$ is a vector of household and demographic characteristics. IV_i refers to an instrumental variable. τ_{m-1} and τ_m are estimated threshold parameters. TE_i is the technical efficiency score estimated from Eq. (2.2), and ε_i is an error term, which is comprised of two parts, including the random noise υ_i with $\upsilon_i \sim N(0, \sigma_\upsilon^2)$ and a half-normal non-negative technical inefficiency term ν_i with $\nu_i \sim N^+(0, \sigma_\nu^2)$.

In Eq. (2.4), we use a variable representing the distance from the respondent's residential house to the nearest agricultural government office as an instrumental variable (IV). The distance variable can reflect the ease with which farmers can access formal agricultural services, including information, technical extension guidance, administrative procedures, and policy support. Therefore, we expect the distance variable to be closely related to farmers' happiness: the shorter the distance, the happier a farmer is. However, we do not expect the distance variable to have a significant impact on the technical efficiency.

We further employ the falsification test to check the statistical validity of the IV (Adhvaryu and Nyshadham 2017; Li et al. 2024). As reported in Table 2.8 in the Appendix, the IV significantly predicts farmers' happiness, but its correlation with technical efficiency is statistically insignificant. These results support the exclusion restriction and confirm the effectiveness and validity of the IV employed in the present study.

2.4 Data and Descriptive Statistics

2.4.1 Data

The data for this study comes from a farmer-level questionnaire survey conducted in Uttar Pradesh, India, between December 2024 and January 2025, targeting potato farmers. This survey was funded by the Asian Development Bank Institute (ADBI) in Tokyo, Japan, with technical support and execution provided by a local Indian research institution. India was chosen as the research subject primarily because it is the world's second-largest agricultural producer and one of the world's most important potato producers. Its agricultural system is dominated by smallholder farmers, with highly fragmented land management and significant heterogeneity among farmers in terms of production resources and technology adoption. Therefore, it provides an ideal research context for exploring the impact of behavioral factors such as happiness on agricultural technology efficiency.

A multistage sampling procedure was used to select survey respondents. First, India was purposively selected as the study country due to its importance in global potato production and the dominance of smallholder farming systems. Within India, Uttar Pradesh was identified as the primary study region because it accounts for approximately 30% of total potato production. Second, three major potato-producing regions in Uttar Pradesh—Agra, Firozabad, and Hathras—were purposively selected as the survey sample areas. Third, within each selected region, cities were randomly selected, followed by the random selection of villages within those cities. Last, potato-growing households within the selected villages were randomly selected and interviewed. Ultimately, 793 valid samples were collected, including 334 from Agra, 237 from Firozabad, and 222 from Hathras.

A face-to-face interview was conducted by well-trained enumerators using a structured and pre-tested questionnaire. The survey questionnaire collected information on the personal characteristics of household heads (e.g., age, gender, education, and health status), household- and farm-level characteristics (e.g., number of household members, farm size, and ownership of machines), inputs and outputs of potato production, resource allocation, socioeconomic characteristics, and subjective well-being such as farmers' happiness. In particular, the happiness variable is measured on an integer scale from 0 to 10. In the questionnaire, we included the question "*To what extent do you feel happy?*" to collect information. The respondents were asked to select an answer from an 11-point scale ranging from 0 (completely unhappy) to 10 (completely happy). We also collected detailed information on input use (e.g., seeds, fertilizers, pesticides, and labor), output, and the sale price of potato production in the 2023/2024 potato production season.

2.4.2 Descriptive Statistics

Table 2.1 presents the definitions and descriptive statistics of the variables used in the empirical analyses. The average value of potato output was 209,600 INR/acre (1 USD = 83.423 INR). Potato farmers spent an average of 400 INR/acre on pesticides, 12,300 INR/acre on fertilizers, 9,600 INR/acre on machinery, and 700 INR/acre on hired labor. Each household can provide 2.6 laborers, and 6.0 acres of land are used for potato cultivation. In the sample, the mean happiness score is 8.371, with a standard deviation of 1.640, indicating that most household heads report a high level of happiness. Technical efficiency is estimated using the stochastic frontier production function (SPF) and Eq. (2.3), which range from 0 to 1, with higher values indicating greater production efficiency. The average technical efficiency in the sample is 0.851, suggesting that most farmers produce at an efficiency level close to the frontier.

The lower part of Table 2.1 also presents the definitions and descriptive statistics of the control variables.[1] The average age of household heads in the sample is 47.3 years. Most household heads (84.7%) are married, and the average education level is 10.7 years. Elderly individuals aged 64 and above account for 7%. The mean annual household income is INR 1,712,900 (1 USD = 86.444 INR). On average, each household owns 4.47 farming plots, and 77.4% of households possess at least one potato production machine. Furthermore, 17.1% of households incurred gift expenditures during the production season, while 87.4% reported economic losses due to climate-related events. 17.9% of households reported having family members or friends in leadership positions. Moreover, 87.4% of households reported having suffered economic losses due to climate-related events. Spatially, 29.8%, 28.0%, and 42.1% of the sampled farmers are in Firozabad, Hathras, and Agra districts, respectively. The descriptive statistics also show that the average distance from respondents' residences to the nearest agricultural government office is 13.30 km, which is used as the instrumental variable in this study.

2.5 Results and Discussion

2.5.1 Results of the Stochastic Production Frontier

Table 2.2 presents the SPF parameter estimates under the Cobb–Douglas (CD) specification, estimated by Eq. (2.2). The coefficients related to production inputs shed light on their relative importance for potato yields. The coefficient for the pesticide variable (Ln (Pesticides)) is negative and significant at the 5% level, indicating that increased pesticide use would reduce potato yields. Although previous studies have

[1] We do not include the gender variable in our analysis because 99% of household heads in our sample are male.

Table 2.1 Variable definitions and summary statistics

Variables	Definitions	Mean (S.D.)
Output and input variables used in the SPF model		
Potato output	Total value of potato production (100,000 INR/acre)	2.096 (0.764)
Pesticides	Expenditures on chemical pesticides (100,000 INR/acre)	0.004 (0.009)
Fertilizers	Expenditures on chemical and organic fertilizers (100,000 INR/acre)	0.123 (0.058)
Machinery	Expenditure on machinery rent (100,000 INR/acre)	0.096 (0.053)
Family Labor	Total household labor number (person)	2.613 (1.674)
Hired Labor	Total cost of hiring labor (100,000 INR/acre)	0.007 (0.007)
Land	Total size of land for potato production (acres)	6.047 (8.826)
Variables used in the CMP Model		
Treatment variables		
Happiness	Household head's self-reported happiness level from 0 = completely unhappy to 10 = completely happy	8.371 (1.640)
Outcome variables		
TE	Technical efficiency calculated by the SPF model	0.851 (0.059)
Control variables		
Age	Age of household head (years)	47.349 (14.186)
Education	Household head's years of education (years)	10.632 (4.069)
Marital status	1 if the household head was married,0 otherwise	0.847 (0.360)
Elderly ratio	Ratio of the number of residents aged over 64 years to household size	0.073 (0.121)
Household income	Total household income from all sources during the 2023/2024 production season (100,000 INR)	17.129 (23.909)
Total plots	The total number of farming land plots owned by the household in the 2023/2024 production season	4.469 (11.272)
Machine ownership	1 if the household head owns any machine for potato production; 0 otherwise	0.774 (0.418)
Gift expenditure	Total household expenditure on gifts given to relatives, friends, or others during the 2023/2024 production season (100,000 INR)	0.172 (0.171)
Climate-related events	1 if the household experienced any economic losses due to a climate-related event; 0 otherwise	0.874 (0.332)

(continued)

Table 2.1 (continued)

Variables	Definitions	Mean (S.D.)
Leadership	1 if family members or friends who work in leadership positions; 0 otherwise	0.179 (0.384)
Firozabad	Equal 1 if the household is in Firozabad, 0 otherwise	0.298 (0.458)
Hathras	Equal 1 if the household is in Hathras, 0 otherwise	0.280 (0.449)
Agra	Equal 1 if the household is in Agra, 0 otherwise	0.421 (0.494)
Instrument variable		
IV	Distance from the respondent's residential house to the nearest agricultural government office (km)	13.299 (7.312)
Sample size		793

Note S.D. refers to the standard deviation. 1 USD = 86.444 INR in January 2025
Source Authors

shown a positive impact of pesticides on output (Yekti et al. 2015; Sultana et al. 2023), our findings of negative elasticity suggest that the overuse of pesticides, which can lead to soil pollution, may decrease potato yields. Family labor (*Ln(Family Labor)*) exhibits a negative and significant impact on potato yields, while the hired labor variable (*Ln(Hired Labor)*) has a positive and statistically significant impact. In rural areas, family laborers may choose to migrate in search of better job opportunities, resulting in crop yield losses due to the labor lost effect of off-farm work. However, hiring professional laborers can offset the labor shortage, thereby increasing potato yields. The land size (*Ln(Land)*) shows a small but significant and positive coefficient, indicating that households cultivating on large farms are associated with increased potato production. The positive elasticity of land is consistent with expectations that land availability remains a primary driver of production. Đokić et al. (2022) and Sultana et al. (2023) found a significant positive relationship between land size and farm output.

The model's log-likelihood value is 37.031, and the *LR* test of model significance yields a result of $Chi-squared\,(\chi^2)$=11, and is statistically significant, confirming the overall statistical validity of the Cobb–Douglas specification. The variance components, σ_ν and σ_υ, are both highly significant, indicating that deviations from the production frontier are not purely random but are partly explained by technical inefficiency. The estimated constant term (-3.296, $p < 0.01$) suggests that inefficiency plays a substantial role in output variation among farmers.

Table 2.2 Results of the SPF model estimation: CD specification

Variables	Coefficients
Ln (Pesticides)	−2.106 (0.945)**
Ln (Fertilizers)	−0.146 (0.164)
Ln (Machinery)	−0.111 (0.216)
Ln(Family Labor)	−0.041 (0.024)*
Ln (Hired Labor)	2.359 (1.312)*
Ln (Land)	0.051 (0.015)***
Constant	1.260 (0.022)***
$\sigma_{(v)}$	−3.296 (0.105)***
$\sigma_{(u)}$	−3.088 (230)***
Log-likelihood	37.031
Likelihood-ratio test	LR chi^2=11.00, ***Prob > chi = 0.000
Sample size	793

*Note** $p < 0.10$, ** $p < 0.05$, and *** $p < 0.01$. Standard errors are presented in parentheses
Source Authors

2.5.2 *Technical Efficiency Scores*

Table 2.3 summarizes the technical efficiency (TE) scores of potato farmers. On average, TE is estimated at 0.851, with a range of 0.492 to 0.970. The finding suggests that technical efficiency can be improved by 14.9% if all resources in potato production are used efficiently. The existing literature reveals significant differences in the technical efficiency of potato production across various countries and regions. Taking East Africa as an example, Fikadu & Mulatu (2023) estimated an average technical efficiency of 0.737 in potato production based on a farmer survey in the Welmera region of Ethiopia during the 2019/2020 production season. Sultana et al. (2023) surveyed major potato-producing areas in Bangladesh in 2022/2023 and found that farmers' average technical efficiency was 0.88, indicating a medium-to-high level of efficiency. Hanani et al. (2024) found an average technical efficiency of approximately 0.791 for potato production in East Java, Indonesia, which falls between the two countries mentioned above. Compared with these findings, the TE level observed in the present study positions Indian potato farmers between those of Bangladesh and Ethiopia, and slightly above those of Indonesia. This suggests that while Indian potato farmers are performing relatively well, there remains considerable room for improvement in their technical efficiency, which, in turn, contributes to higher potato yields and enhanced food security.

Table 2.4 shows the distributions of TE scores among sample households. The results show that TE is primarily concentrated in the higher range, with 69.36% of households falling within the 0.80–0.90 range and another 16.39% reaching the near-frontier level of 0.90–1.00. Meanwhile, less than 2% of households have a TE below 0.70. Overall, while most households demonstrate high production efficiency,

Table 2.3 Summary statistics of the technical efficiency scores

Mean	Standard deviation	Min	Max
0.851	0.059	0.492	0.970

Source Authors

Table 2.4 Distributions of technical efficiency scores

Range of TE	Frequency	% of farms in TE interval
0.40 < TE < = 0.50	1	0.13
0.50 < TE < = 0.60	6	0.76
0.60 < TE < = 0.70	8	1.01
0.70 < TE < = 0.80	98	12.36
0.80 < TE < = 0.90	550	69.36
0.90 < TE < = 1.00	130	16.39
Total	793	100

Source Authors

a significant proportion remain underachieving their full technological potential. This provides a realistic basis for further exploring the factors influencing efficiency disparities.

Figure 2.3 shows the kernel density distribution of technical inefficiency for the sample households. It can be observed that inefficiency values are primarily concentrated below 0.20, with a distinct peak near 0. This suggests that most households exhibit low levels of technical inefficiency, indicating relatively high production efficiency. Overall, extreme inefficiency is relatively rare, indicating that the sample households generally operate relatively close to the production frontier. However, a significant proportion of households still fall within the moderate inefficiency range, suggesting room for further efficiency improvement and providing a foundation for further analysis of the factors influencing efficiency differences.

2.5.3 *Impact of Happiness on Technical Efficiency*

Table 2.5 shows the results of household heads' happiness impacts on TE of potato production. The CMP approach was used to jointly estimate Eqs. (2.4) and (2.5), accounting for the happiness variable's endogeneity. Below, we will first explain the factors influencing farmers' happiness. Then, we will investigate factors that determine TE of potation production.

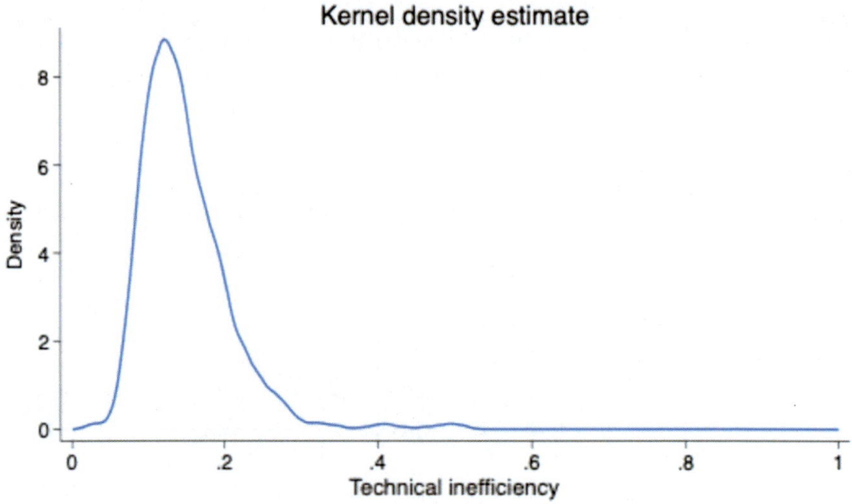

Fig. 2.3 Distributions of technical inefficiency. *Source* Authors

Table 2.5 Association between happiness and technical efficiency: CMP model estimates

Variables	Happiness (oprobit model)	TE (fractional probit model)
Happiness		0.045 (0.026)*
Age	−0.008 (0.003)**	−0.001 (0.001)
Education	0.040 (0.010)***	−0.003 (0.003)
Marital status	0.461 (0.113)***	−0.042 (0.033)
Elderly ratio	−0.468 (0.309)	0.118 (0.076)
Household income	0.005 (0.002)**	0.000 (0.000)
Total plots	−0.003 (0.001)**	0.000 (0.000)
Machine ownership	0.228 (0.093)**	−0.037 (0.027)
Gift expenditure	0.577 (0.312)*	0.128 (0.079)
Climate-related events	0.066 (0.116)	−0.046 (0.031)
Leadership	0.230 (0.120)*	0.019 (0.020)
Hathras	0.172 (0.103)*	0.095 (0.027)***
Agra	0.451 (0.100)***	0.102 (0.026)***
IV	−0.011 (0.006)*	
Observations	793	
ρ_{12}	−0.070 (0.041)*	

Note * $p < 0.10$, ** $p < 0.05$, and *** $p < 0.01$. Standard errors are presented in parentheses. The reference region is Firozabad
Source Authors

2.5.3.1 Determinants of Farmers' Happiness

Column 2 of Table 2.5 presents the first-stage results of the CMP model, specifically the factors influencing household heads' happiness. The results indicate that age is negatively and significantly associated with happiness. The negative association between age and happiness may be linked to deteriorating physical health, heavier workloads, and uncertainty about the future. Besides, older farmers are often disadvantaged in adopting new technologies or accessing market information and social resources, which further exacerbates their financial difficulties and reduces their overall happiness. Education, on the other hand, exerts a positive and significant influence on the happiness of potato farmers. Education enhances farmers' cognitive skills, improves their access to information, and facilitates better decision-making in both agricultural and daily life, ultimately contributing to increased happiness. Casinillo & Seriño (2022) found that more years of formal education significantly increase the happiness of rice farmers in the Philippines, as education equips them with greater knowledge and problem-solving abilities. Similarly, Rahman et al. (2023) found that education is a strong positive predictor of subjective well-being among Indonesian farmers, as it enhances their confidence and capacity to cope with risks.

Marital status also emerges as a significant factor in determining farmers' happiness. Married farmers are more likely to be happier, mainly due to the emotional support and psychological comfort provided by their families (Rahman et al. 2023). Marriage facilitates the division of labor and the pooling of resources within households, thereby allowing families to better cope with production risks and uncertainties. Household income is another strong predictor of happiness. Multiple studies have confirmed that income is a core determinant of farmers' subjective well-being. For example, Li et al. (2023) found that higher household income was associated with greater happiness, life satisfaction, and confidence in the future. In addition, Wu et al. (2022) reported that approximately 28.9% of the increase in happiness was attributed to "increased agricultural income", indicating that higher agricultural income plays a crucial role in enhancing farmers' happiness. Their conclusion clearly indicates that income directly improves happiness and, indirectly, enhances it through improved living conditions and increased consumption capacity. This further demonstrates that abundant economic resources enhance farmers' sense of security and life satisfaction.

The number of plots (land fragmentation) a farmer operates has a negative and significant impact on farmers' happiness. Existing research also suggests that land fragmentation negatively affects farmers' happiness. For example, analyzing data from China, Wang et al. (2020) found that land fragmentation increases commuting time and field monitoring costs, reduces crop management efficiency, and exacerbates production risks, thus causing psychological stress for smallholder farmers. Brien (2022) showed that while larger farmland sizes can improve rural household welfare, greater land fragmentation significantly reduces household income and asset levels in Vietnam.

Machinery ownership also has a highly positive and significant impact on happiness. Farmers with access to machinery face less physical strain, save considerable time and energy, and reduce psychological stress. Released from burdensome manual labor, they can devote more time to family life, leisure, and social activities, thereby increasing their subjective well-being (Ma et al. 2022). The findings show that gift expenditure has a positive and significant impact on farmers' happiness. Higher gift expenditure typically reflects more frequent, closer social interactions among farmers and their relatives, friends, and community members (Wang et al. 2025). This reciprocal behavior not only strengthens interpersonal relationships (Herrera Sabillón et al. 2022), but also enhances farmers' sense of social belonging, reciprocity, and social support, thereby significantly improving their subjective well-being.

Our findings show a positive significant association between leadership and farmers' happiness. This is likely because holding a leadership role can reduce uncertainty, provide informal support, and enhance the coordination of community affairs. Duan et al. (2025) indicated that maintaining close relationships with grassroots cadres can reduce farmers' uncertainty in production and life, providing them with timely informal support and effectively alleviating stress. Finally, the results showed that the distance between the respondents' residences and the nearest agricultural government service agency, as an instrumental variable, was significantly negatively correlated with farmers' happiness. The results suggest that farmers living farther from agricultural service agencies tend to be less satisfied, likely because reduced access to services reduces support for farming, income opportunities, and overall life satisfaction. Brew et al. (2016) indicated that farmers living in remote areas were significantly worse off than non-agricultural workers in terms of mental health and well-being.

2.5.3.2 Impacts of Happiness and Control Variables on Technical Efficiency

The last column of Table 2.5 illustrates the main factors influencing the technical efficiency of potato production. The positive and significant coefficient of the happiness variable suggests that farmers with a higher level of happiness obtain a higher level of technical efficiency. Higher levels of happiness are typically accompanied by stronger intrinsic motivation, a more optimistic production outlook (Waterman et al. 2024), and greater psychological resilience. As a result, farmers are more willing to invest time and effort when confronting risks and uncertainties (Xie et al. 2023), enabling them to make more rational production decisions and ultimately enhance both resource allocation efficiency and input–output performance. Finally, the significant coefficients of the location variables indicate that, relative to farmers in Firozabad, those cultivating potatoes in Hathras and Agra exhibit higher levels of technical efficiency. The findings suggest that Hathras and Agra tend to have more favorable soil quality, water availability, or climatic conditions for potato cultivation, enabling farmers to convert production inputs into outputs more efficiently.

2.5.4 Disaggregated Analyses

To improve our understanding, we further investigated the education-differentiated impacts of farmers' happiness on the technical efficiency of potato production. We classified the education level into three groups using the "tertile" commands of Stata, including low (0 ~ 9 years), middle (10 ~ 12 years), and high (13 ~ 17 years). The results are presented in Table 2.6. In general, the results indicate that among households with low and middle levels of education, happiness has no significant impact on the technical efficiency of potato production, even at the 5% significance level. However, the happiness of household heads with a high level of education is positively associated with high technical efficiency, and the coefficient is significant at the 1% level. Ali and Erenstein (2017) found that farmers with higher levels of education were more efficient in adopting technology, allocating resources, and making production decisions. Similarly, Ma and Abdulai (2016) suggested that education enhances farmers' cognitive abilities, risk management capabilities, and learning abilities, making it easier for them to adopt agricultural production practices efficiently. Overall, this finding suggests that education moderates the relationship between happiness and technical efficiency: happiness contributes more strongly to efficiency among farmers with higher levels of human capital, highlighting the complementary roles of education and psychological well-being in boosting agricultural productivity.

The education groups are classified using the "tertile" command in Stata. *Source* Authors.

Table 2.6 Impact of happiness on TE across Education Groups: CMP model estimates

Variables	Low (0 ~ 10 years)		Middle (11 ~ 12 years)		High (13 ~ 17 years)	
	Happiness (oprobit model)	TE (fractional probit model)	Happiness (oprobit model)	TE (fractional probit model)	Happiness (oprobit model)	TE (fractional probit model)
Happiness		0.003 (0.006)		−0.004 (0.015)		0.035 (0.012)***
Control variables	Yes	Yes	Yes	Yes	Yes	Yes
Location variables	Yes	Yes	Yes	Yes	Yes	Yes
IV	−0.006 (0.009)		−0.023 (0.012)*		−0.013 (0.008)*	
Observations	404		195		194	
ρ_{12}	−0.020 (0.148)		0.078 (0.427)		−1.145 (0.329)***	

Note * $p < 0.10$ and *** $p < 0.01$. Standard errors are presented in parentheses. The reference region is Firozabad

2.5.5 *Further Analysis*

A higher level of technical efficiency is a prerequisite for higher crop yields (Murthy et al. 2009). To deepen our understanding, we also estimate the impact of happiness on potato yields. We also use the CMP method to conduct empirical analysis. The results are presented in Table 2.7. For simplicity, we list only the coefficients for variables related to happiness and potato output.

The results show that the happiness variable is positive and statistically significant, indicating that higher levels of farmers' happiness are associated with higher potato yields. The finding is consistent with Ma et al. (2022), who reported a positive relationship between farmers' happiness and maize productivity in China. Farmers with higher levels of happiness tend to exhibit more stable and positive mental states, which, in turn, leads them to be more rational and risk-averse when making production-related decisions. For example, they may be more cautious in controlling the timing and dosage of pesticides and fertilizers, thereby reducing uncertainty and risk of loss during the production process (Jones et al. 2019). Furthermore, a positive mental state has been shown to enhance farmers' labor organization and resource allocation efficiency, resulting in more effective field management, labor scheduling, and coordination of the production process (Riethmuller et al. 2023). This is consistent with previous research showing that higher levels of psychological well-being can enhance farmers' decision-making resilience and their ability to recover in the face of uncertainty (Liu et al. 2024), thereby reducing impulsive or inefficient short-term, emergency-driven behaviors.

Table 2.7 Effects of Happiness on Potato output: CMP model estimates

Variables	Happiness (Oprobit model)	Potato yields (OLS model)
Hppiness		0.128 (0.054)**
Control variables	Yes	Yes
Location variables	Yes	Yes
IV	−0.010 (0.006)*	
Observations	793	793
ρ_{12}	−0.250 (0.120)**	

Note * $p < 0.10$ and ** $p < 0.05$. Standard errors are presented in parentheses
Source Authors

2.6 Conclusion and Policy Implications

2.6.1 Conclusions

This study examines how farmers' happiness influences the technical efficiency of potato production, using the first-hand survey data from 793 farming households across India's three major potato-producing districts (Firozabad, Hathras, and Agra). It uses a conditional mixed-process model to address endogeneity in the happiness variable. We also explore the moderating role of the education variable on the relationship between happiness and technical efficiency. This study provides evidence that farmers' happiness is positively and significantly associated with technical efficiency, suggesting that farmers' psychological well-being plays an important role in improving farm performance. We also find that farmers' happiness is positively and significantly associated with their education, marital status, household income, machine ownership, gift expenditure, and leadership, but is negatively and significantly associated with their age and total plots cultivated.

We also find that the effects of happiness on the technical efficiency of potato production are heterogeneous across educational groups, with the happiness of household heads with higher levels of education having a positive and significant impact on technical efficiency. Additional analysis reveals that happier farmers tend to achieve higher potato yields, suggesting that improved psychological states not only increase efficiency but also yield greater production.

2.6.2 Policy Implications

This study provides several policy implications for improving farmers' well-being and agricultural productivity. First, the finding that farmers' happiness enhances the technical efficiency of potato production underscores the importance of improving rural farmers' subjective well-being. In practice, governments should invest in rural public services—such as healthcare, education, and social security—to enhance farmers' overall quality of life. In addition, machine ownership is found to significantly increase farmers' happiness, suggesting that improved access to agricultural machinery can play a key role in enhancing rural farmers' subjective well-being. In practice, governments should consider improving farmers' access to machinery by subsidizing machinery purchases and promoting the development of machinery outsourcing services.

Gift expenditure is positively associated with farmers' happiness, suggesting that social participation and reciprocal relationships within rural communities play an important role in enhancing subjective well-being. In many rural areas, gift exchange reflects social connectedness, mutual assistance, and community integration. Accordingly, rural development policies should move beyond a narrow focus on economic outcomes and also support community activities and social interaction platforms that strengthen social cohesion and informal support networks. Moreover, significant regional differences in technical efficiency indicate pronounced spatial heterogeneity in production performance. This finding underscores the need for region-specific agricultural development strategies, as well as the identification and adaptation of successful practices from high-efficiency regions to enhance productivity in lagging areas.

Acknowlegement The authors gratefully acknowledge the Asian Development Bank Institute (Tokyo, Japan) and the International Potato Centre for their financial support in facilitating the data collection in India. We also acknowledge Deepa Janakiraman, a former staff member of the International Potato Centre, Delhi, India, for helping with the survey.

Data Availability Statement The data supporting this study's findings are available from Lixue Qu upon request.
Conflict of Interests There is no conflict of interest.

Appendix

See Tables 2.8 and 2.9.

Table 2.8 Falsification test of instrumental variables

Variables	Happiness	TE
IV	−0.011 (0.006)*	−0.000 (0.000)
Control Variables	Yes	Yes
Falsification test	x^2=122.51***; p-value = 0.0000	R^2= 0.075; F-value = 4.51
Observations	793	793

Notes * $p < 0.05$ and *** $p < 0.01$. Standard errors are presented in parentheses
Source Authors

Table 2.9 Results of the SPF model estimation: Translog specification

Variables	Coefficients
Ln (Pesticides)	−7.374 (7.620)
Ln (Fertilizers)	−1.218 (1.166)
Ln (Machinery)	0.605 (1.586)
Ln (Hired Labor)	1.014 (9.397)
Ln (Land)	0.135 (0.119)
Ln(Family Labor)	−0.097 (0.147)
0.5*Ln (Pesticides)^2	18.144 (22.298)
0.5*Ln (Fertilizers)^2	0.318 (2.055)
0.5*Ln (Machinery)^2	1.310 (3.245)
0.5*Ln (Hired Labor)^2	−38.130 (90.930)
0.5*Ln (Land)^2	−0.020 (0.019)
0.5*Ln (Family Labor)^2	0.036 (0.045)
Ln (Pesticides)*Ln (Fertilizers)	39.903 (26.722)
Ln (Pesticides)*Ln (Machinery)	−0.216 (35.626)
Ln (Pesticides)*Ln (Hired Labor)	−359.556 (149.492)*
Ln (Pesticides)*Ln (Land)	−0.864 (2.433)
Ln (Pesticides)*Ln (Family Labor)	2.523 (3.472)
Ln (Fertilizers)*Ln (Hired Labor)	4.255 (26.733)
Ln (Fertilizers)*Ln (Machinery)	5.018 (4.414)
Ln (Fertilizers)*Ln (Land)	0.402 (0.334)
Ln (Fertilizers)*Ln (Family Labor)	−0.212 (0.427)
Ln (Hired Labor)*Ln (Machinery)	−11.317 (46.377)
Ln (Hired Labor)*Ln (Land)	1.929 (3.538)
Ln (Hired Labor)*Ln (Family Labor)	2.916 (3.514)
Ln (Machinery)*Ln (Land)	−0.630 (0.473)
Ln (Machinery)*Ln (Family Labor)	−0.307 (0.590)
Ln (Land)*Ln (Family Labor)	−0.008 (0.040)
Constant	1.247 (0.228)***
$\sigma_{(v)}$	−3.313 (0.106)***
$\sigma_{(u)}$	−3.139 (0.241)***
Log-likelihood	47.666
Sample size	793

Note * $p < 0.10$ and *** $p < 0.01$. Standard errors are presented in parentheses
Source Authors

References

Abdul-Rahaman A., Issahaku G. and Ma W. (2023). Agrifood system participation and production efficiency among smallholder vegetable farmers in Northern Ghana, *Agribusiness* 39, 812–835.

Adhvaryu A. and Nyshadham A. (2017). Health, Enterprise, and Labor Complementarity in the Household, *Journal of Development Economics* 126, 91–111.

Ali A. and Erenstein O. (2017). Climate Risk Management Assessing farmer use of climate change adaptation practices and impacts on food security and poverty in Pakistan, *Climate Risk Management* 16, 183–194.

Andaregie A. and Astatkie T. (2020). Determinants of technical efficiency of potato farmers and effects of constraints on potato production in Northern Ethiopia, *Experimental Agriculture* 56, 699–709.

Biswas B., Mallick B., Roy A. and Sultana Z. (2021). Impact of agriculture extension services on technical efficiency of rural paddy farmers in southwest Bangladesh, *Environmental Challenges* 5, 100261.

Brew B., Inder K., Allen J., Thomas M. and Kelly B. (2016). The health and wellbeing of Australian farmers : a longitudinal cohort study, *BMC Public Health*, 1–12.

Brien M.O. (2022). Is small beautiful ? An empirical analysis of land characteristics and rural household income in Vietnam, 561–580.

Bukchin-peles S. (2022). Are positive farmers more productive ? Investigating the relationship between positivity ratio and agricultural productivity, 51, 470–481.

Casinillo L. and Seriño M.N. (2022). Econometric evidence on happiness and its determinants among rice farmers in leyte, Philippines, *Independent Journal of Management & Production* 13, 1026–1044.

Chen X. (2025). The role of modern agricultural technologies in improving agricultural productivity and land use ef fi ciency, 1–19.

DeLay N.D., Thompson N.M. and Mintert J.R. (2022). Precision agriculture technology adoption and technical efficiency, *Journal of Agricultural Economics* 73, 195–219.

Djoumessi Y., Afari-Sefa V., Kamdem C.B. and Bidogeza J.C. (2018). Socio-economic and institutional factors underlying efficiency of smallholder vegetable farms in Southwest region of Cameroon, *International Journal of Social Economics* 45, 93–106.

Đokić D., Novaković T., Tekić D., Matkovski B., Zekić S. and Milić D. (2022). Technical Efficiency of Agriculture in the European Union and Western Balkans: SFA Method, *Agriculture (Switzerland)* 12.

Duan J., Kuang N. and Cheng B. (2025). Do Entrepreneurial Village Cadres Improve Rural Subjective Well-Being ? Empirical Evidence from China, 1–22.

FAOSTAT (2025). FAOSTAT.

Feng X., Ma W., Liu M. and Qiu H. (2022). Impact of grassland transfer on technical efficiency of livestock production in Northern China, *Applied Economics* 54, 702–718.

Fikadu G. and Mulatu G. (2023). Analysis of Technical Efficiency of Potato Production: The Case of Smallholder Farmers in Welmera Woreda, *International Journal of Agricultural Economics* 8, 182–196.

Geffersa A.G., Agbola F.W. and Mahmood A. (2019). Technology adoption and technical efficiency in maize production in rural Ethiopia, *African Journal of Agricultural and Resource Economics*, 18.

González-Flores M., Bravo-Ureta B.E., Solís D. and Winters P. (2014). The impact of high value markets on smallholder productivity in the Ecuadorean Sierra: A Stochastic Production Frontier approach correcting for selectivity bias, *Food Policy* 44, 237–247.

Hanani AR N., Rahman M.S., Fahriyah F. et al. (2024). Does the climate change adaptation affect technical efficiency? Empirical evidence from potato farmers in East Java, Indonesia, *Cogent Economics and Finance* 12.

Herrera Sabillón B., Gerster-Bentaya M. and Knierim A. (2022). Measuring farmers' well-being: Influence of farm-level factors on satisfaction with work and quality of life, *Journal of Agricultural Economics* 73, 452–471.

Hossain M., Hasan M. and Naher Q. (2008). Assessment of Technical Efficiency of Potato Producers in Some Selected Areas of Bangladesh, *Journal of Agriculture & Rural Development* 6, 113–118.

Jones A.Q., Sawatzky A., Thompson R. and Hagen B.N.M. (2019). Poor mental health negatively impacts farmers personally, interpersonally, cognitively, and professionally, 1–16.

Khaled R. and Afia N. Ben (2024). EMPIRICAL ANALYSIS OF THE RELATIONSHIP BETWEEN HAPPINESS AND AGRICULTURAL PRODUCTIVITY IN AFRICAN COUNTRIES, *UTMS Journal of Economics* 15, 71–82.

Li J. and Ma W. (2025). *Alleviating Multidimensional Energy Poverty and Energy Unaffordability in Rural Areas: The Role of Renting-Out Land*. Springer Netherlands.

Li J., Ma W. and Gong B. (2023). Market participation and subjective well-being of maize farmers, *Economic Analysis and Policy* 80, 941–960.

Li J., Vatsa P. and Ma W. (2024). Internet use and household debt: insights from rural China, *Applied Economics* 00, 1–21.

Lin J., Jin S. and Guo H. (2023). Do outsourcing services provided by agricultural cooperatives affect technical efficiency? Insights from tobacco farmers in China, *Annals of Public and Cooperative Economics* 94, 781–804.

Liu Y., Chen M., Yu J. and Wang X. (2024). Being a happy farmer: Technology adoption and subjective well-being, *Journal of Economic Behavior and Organization* 221, 385–405.

Liu Y., Yan B., Wang Y. and Zhou Y. (2019). Will land transfer always increase technical efficiency in China?—A land cost perspective, *Land Use Policy* 82, 414–421.

Ma W. and Abdulai A. (2016). Does cooperative membership improve household welfare ? Evidence from apple farmers in China, *Food Policy* 58, 94–102.

Ma W., Renwick A., Yuan P. and Ratna N. (2018). Agricultural cooperative membership and technical efficiency of apple farmers in China: An analysis accounting for selectivity bias, *Food Policy* 81, 122–132.

Ma W., Vatsa P., Zhou X. and Zheng H. (2022). Happiness and farm productivity: insights from maize farmers in China, *International Journal of Social Economics* 49, 97–106.

Ma W., Zheng H., Donkor E. and Owusu V. (2023). Off-farm work and technical efficiency of wheat production: An analysis accounting for multiple dimensions of off-farm work, *International Journal of Sustainable Development and World Ecology* 30, 278–294.

Mayen C.D., Balagtas J. V. and Alexander C.E. (2010). Technology adoption and technical efficiency: Organic and conventional dairy farms in the United States, *American Journal of Agricultural Economics* 92, 181–195.

Missiame A., Nyikal R.A. and Irungu P. (2021). What is the impact of rural bank credit access on the technical efficiency of smallholder cassava farmers in Ghana? An endogenous switching regression analysis, *Heliyon* 7, e07102.

Mohamed S., Destaw H. and Seifu M. (2026). Technical efficiency of Tef production in the Wullbareg District, Silte, *Discover Sustainability* https://doi.org/10.1007/s43621-025-01233-6.

Murthy D.S., Sudha M., Hegde M.R. and Dakshinamoorthy V. (2009). Technical Efficiency and its Determinants in Tomato Production in Karnataka, India : Data Envelopment Analysis (DEA) Approach, *Agricultural Economics Research* 22, 215–224.

Muteti F.N., Akite I., Mpofu T.P. and Mugonola B. (2024). Determinants of technical efficiency among smallholder upland rice farmers in northern Uganda—a Cobb–Douglas stochastic frontier approach, *SN Business and Economics* 4, 1–20.

Njuki E., Lachaud M.A., Bravo-Ureta B.E. and Key N. (2025). Ethnic and gender disparities in U.S. agriculture: An analysis of technology and technical efficiency differentials, *American Journal of Agricultural Economics* 107, 993–1015.

Obalola O.T., Obayelu A.E., Coster A.S. and Alarima C.I. (2025). Comparing Cobb–Douglas and translog stochastic frontier models for estimating technical efficiency in rice farming in Northwestern Nigeria, *SN Business and Economics* 5, 1–23.

Rahman M.S., Toiba H., Nugroho T.W., Hartono R., Shaleh M.I., Sugiono S. and Saeri M. (2023). Does internet use make farmers happier? Evidence from Indonesia, *Cogent Social Sciences* 9.

Rajkhowa P. and Qaim M. (2021). Personalized digital extension services and agricultural performance: Evidence from smallholder farmers in India, *PLoS ONE* 16, 1–23.

Riethmuller M.L., Dzidic P.L., McEvoy P.M. and Newnham E.A. (2023). Change, connection and community: A qualitative exploration of farmers' mental health, *Journal of Rural Studies* 97, 591–600.

Selorm A., Sarpong D.B.S., Egyir I.S., Mensah Bonsu A. and An H. (2023). Does contract farming affect technical efficiency? Evidence from soybean farmers in Northern Ghana, *Agricultural and Food Economics* 11.

Shavgulidze R., Bedoshvili D. and Aurbacher J. (2017). Technical efficiency of potato and dairy farming in mountainous Kazbegi district, Georgia, *Annals of Agrarian Science* 15, 55–60.

Solís D., Bravo-Ureta B.E. and Quiroga R.E. (2009). Technical efficiency among peasant farmers participating in natural resource management programmes in Central America, *Journal of Agricultural Economics* 60, 202–219.

Sultana S., HossainI M.M. and Haque M.N. (2023). Estimating the potato farming efficiency: A comparative study between stochastic frontier analysis and data envelopment analysis, *PLoS ONE* 18, 1–15.

Wang L., Huo X. and Kabir M.S. (2013). Technical and cost efficiency of rural household apple production, *China Agricultural Economic Review* 5, 391–411.

Wang Y., Li X., Lu D. and Yan J. (2020). Land Use Policy Evaluating the impact of land fragmentation on the cost of agricultural operation in the southwest mountainous areas of China, *Land Use Policy* 99, 105099.

Wang M., Liu Z. and Ji C. (2025). Sichuan province in China, 1–10.

Waterman A.S., Schwartz S.J. and Waterman A.S. (2024). Identity Contributions to a Life Well-Lived : A Study of the Relationship of Eudaimonic Well- Being to Intrinsic Motivation for Identity-Related Activities Identity Contributions to a Life Well-Lived : A Study of the Relationship of Eudaimonic Well-Being, *Identity* 24, 1–15.

Wu L., Li C. and Gao Y. (2022). Regional agricultural cooperatives and subjective wellbeing of rural households in China, *RSPP* 14, 138–159.

Xie Y., Ke S. and Li X. (2023). Psychological Resilience and Farmers ' Homestead Withdrawal : Evidence from Traditional Agricultural Regions in China.

Xin M., Tan S., Qiu H. and Tang J. (2025). Environmental Regulations and Smallholder Farmers' Technical Efficiency: Empirical Evidence From Pastoral China, *Journal of Agricultural Economics*, 1–15.

Yekti A., Hadi D., J. J. and Hartono S. (2015). Technical Efficiency of Melon Farming in Kulon Progo: A Stochastic Frontier Approach (SFA), *International Journal of Computer Applications* 132, 15–19.

Yin F., Sun Z., You L. and Huang V.W. (2024). Technical Efficiency Versus Land-Use Efficiency: A Spatio-Temporal Efficiency Analysis of China's Crop Production, *German Journal of Agricultural Economics* 73, 1–20.

Zhang Y., Wang X., Glauben T. and Brümmer B. (2011). The impact of land reallocation on technical efficiency: Evidence from China, *Agricultural Economics* 42, 495–507.

Chapter 3
Types of Off-Farm Employment and Multidimensional Subjective Well-Being Among Wheat Farmers: Evidence from China

Ziqi Wang, Wanglin Ma, and Alan Renwick

3.1 Introduction

In many developing countries, rural development increasingly depends on diversifying livelihood strategies, most notably through off-farm employment. By earning wages through off-farm employment, rural households can improve their objective well-being, such as boosting their household income (Moro-Egido et al. 2022; Zhang 2022), smoothing household consumption of energy, food, and durable goods (Ankrah Twumasi et al. 2023; Sun et al. 2022), alleviating poverty (Addai et al. 2023; Li & Xu 2023), and reducing vulnerability to unexpected risks and uncertainties (Wang et al. 2024). Besides, off-farm employment also profoundly shapes rural residents' subjective well-being, encompassing both positive and negative affect (Das et al. 2020; Diener et al. 2018). Off-farm employment can strengthen people's subjective well-being by elevating living standards (Gansonre 2021), increasing autonomy (Clausen et al. 2022; Lips-Wiersma et al. 2022), and expanding social capital (Nugroho et al. 2022; Villalonga-Olives et al. 2022).

Extensive empirical evidence has confirmed that off-farm employment affects people's subjective well-being (Shen et al. 2022; Shen et al. 2024; Whitaker 2024; Xu et al. 2023; Ma et al. 2025). Estimating the nationally representative rural data, Shen et al. (2024) showed that only high-quality off-farm employment significantly

Z. Wang · W. Ma (✉) · A. Renwick
Department of Global Value Chains and Trade, Faculty of Agribusiness and Commerce, Lincoln University, Christchurch, New Zealand
e-mail: Wanglin.Ma@lincoln.ac.nz

Z. Wang
e-mail: Ziqi.Wang@lincolnuni.ac.nz

A. Renwick
e-mail: Alan.Renwick@lincoln.ac.nz

W. Ma et al. (eds.), *Beyond Income*, Contributions to Economics,
https://doi.org/10.1007/978-981-92-4957-2_3

improves farmers' life satisfaction. Research on rural women found that off-farm employment significantly reduces women's depressive symptoms (Shen et al. 2022). Evidence from the Chinese General Social Survey (CGSS) data demonstrated that social trust and social capital substantially enhance rural residents' life satisfaction, suggesting that employment quality and social embeddedness jointly shape their psychological well-being (Xu et al. 2023). Ma et al. (2025) estimated the effects of rural residents' different employment types on household income and their life satisfaction, finding that both pure off-farm and mixed employment significantly increase household income and household heads' life satisfaction relative to farming only.

Despite the significant research on off-farm employment, two key limitations remain. First, existing studies examining the effects of rural off-farm employment on farmers' subjective well-being (SWB) have predominantly relied on binary treatment models or simple regressions that collapse employment into "farm" versus "off-farm" categories (Marino et al. 2021; Rocchi et al. 2021), failing to distinguish between local and migrant off-farm employment. Second, existing research has focused on the relationship between off-farm employment and positive SWB outcomes, such as happiness and life satisfaction (Fang et al. 2019; Gracious & Umakrishnan 2025), with insufficient attention to negative SWB dimensions, such as anxiety, loneliness, and depression. Understanding how off-farm employment affects farmers' negative SWB outcomes is also important because psychological distress, such as anxiety, loneliness, and depression, may offset income gains and undermine the overall welfare improvements associated with labor transition.

This study examines how different types of employment affect multiple SWB dimensions among rural Chinese households and makes three contributions to the literature. First, we move beyond the simple "farm" and "off-farm" dichotomy by distinguishing three types of employment, thereby revealing their heterogeneous effects on both positive and negative aspects of SWB. Specifically, the three employment types include non-participation in off-farm work (farming only), local off-farm employment, and migrated off-farm employment. Among them, local off-farm employment refers to those employed in nearby townships or villages and can return home daily, and migrated off-farm employment refers to work in locations far from home. Second, we extend the SWB analysis by including not only farmers' positive SWB outcomes (happiness and life satisfaction), but also negative SWB outcomes (anxiety, loneliness, and depression), providing a more holistic evaluation of rural quality of life. Third, by applying the multivalued treatment effect (MVTE) model to mitigate selection bias, we obtain more credible estimates of employment effects on SWB. We analyse data collected from 648 wheat-producing farming households. The insights from this study would provide policymakers with a basis for crafting targeted interventions under China's Rural Revitalization strategy, initiatives that not only boost rural incomes but also enhance rural farmers' mental health and social cohesion.

The rest of the paper is structured as follows: Sect. 2 provides background and a literature review. Section 3 develops a conceptual framework, and Sect. 4 discusses the methodology. Section 5 presents and discusses the empirical results. The final section concludes the paper with policy recommendations.

3.2 Background and Literature Review

3.2.1 Background

China provides an interesting case to investigate the relationship between off-farm employment and farmers' SWB. The share of rural residents employed off-farm expanded markedly in China. Fig. 3.1 presents information on total rural off-farm employment in China, showing that the off-farm workforce increased from roughly 269 million in 2013 to nearly 300 million by 2024 (National Bureau of Statistics of China 2023). This upward shift reflects the large-scale absorption of rural labour into off-farm sectors, driven by market-oriented reforms and accelerated urbanization. Off-farm employment has become essential for families facing diminishing farm returns, climate variability, and shrinking landholdings, offering a pathway to greater economic security and poverty reduction (Li & Xu 2023; Zhang 2022).

During the past ten years, off-farm migration has emerged as the primary driver of rural labour transfer. Figure 3.2 presents information on rural off-farm employment in China by different types. It shows that the number of migrants from off-farm employment rose from approximately 166 million in 2013 to nearly 179 million by 2024. At the same time, local off-farm employment, in which rural residents work in township and village enterprises, service industries, or industrial parks, also expanded rapidly, reaching over 121 million positions by 2024 (National Bureau of Statistics of China 2023). This dual expansion has mitigated the social costs of family separation and enriched the social capital networks within rural communities.

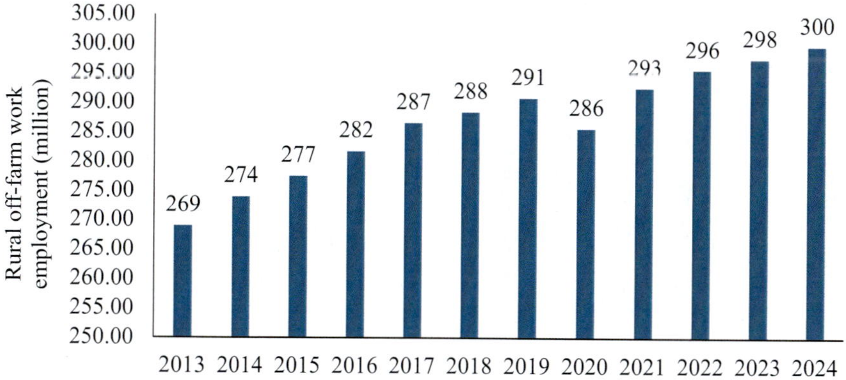

Fig. 3.1 Total rural off-farm employment in China. *Source* National bureau of statistics of China

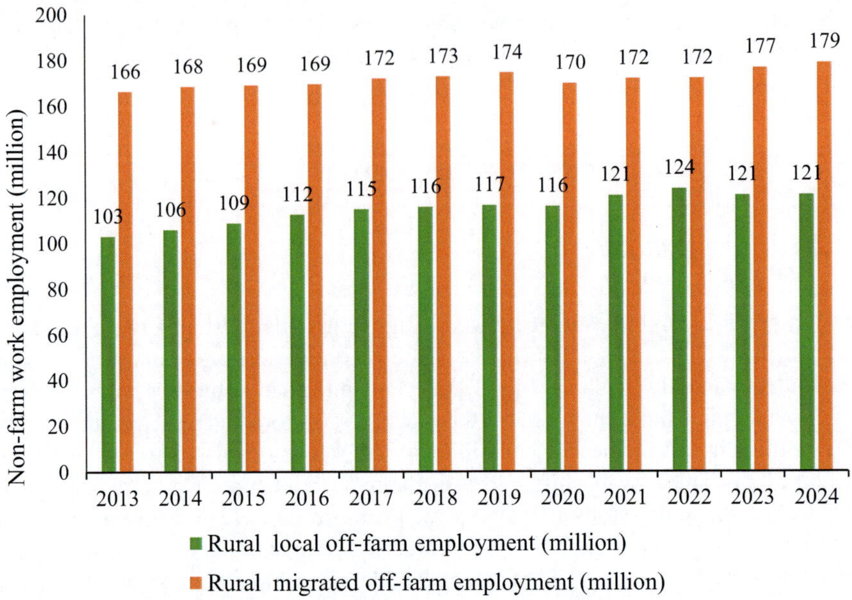

Fig. 3.2 Rural off-farm employment in China by different types. *Source* National bureau of statistics of China

Figure 3.3 demonstrates that the average monthly income for rural off-farm employment in China has roughly doubled over the past decade. The resulting boost in household remittances has markedly elevated living standards and expanded the purchasing power of families left behind.

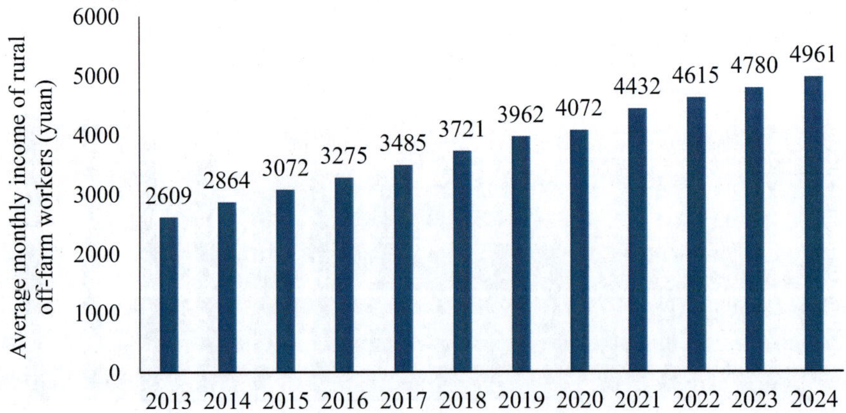

Fig. 3.3 Average monthly income for rural off-farm employment in China. *Source* National bureau of statistics of China

China's shift in rural employment has produced substantial social and mental health costs. Rural residents have higher rates of depression, anxiety, and loneliness than their urban peers (Fang et al. 2019; Shen et al. 2022). A survey found that the prevalence of depression and anxiety among rural residents in China is 4.9% and 2.9%, respectively (Tian et al. 2025). Loneliness is also highly prevalent, with studies indicating that approximately 30.6% of older women and 22% of older men experience moderate to severe loneliness (Wang et al. 2024). These deficits reflect limited access to health care and social support in isolated villages.

Migrated workers' departure for employment aggravates psychological burden. Nearly 39% of migrated off-farm employment experience depressive symptoms, while 27% exhibit anxiety symptoms (Hasan et al. 2021). In China, this "left-behind" situation affects many people. By the end of 2020, approximately 6.436 million rural children nationwide had become left-behind children (Xiong et al. 2024). These children and their left-behind family members endure prolonged loneliness and anxiety. The comprehensive analysis indicated that left-behind children experience significantly higher levels of loneliness compared to non-left-behind children (Xiong et al. 2024). Additionally, the depression rate among rural left behind women whose husbands migrate reaches 35.7%, while the anxiety rate hits 37.6% (Niu & Wang 2024). Therefore, the off-farm employment patterns in rural areas have diminished the overall SWB of rural communities and imposed significant psychological burdens.

3.2.2 *Literature Review*

3.2.2.1 Relevant Research on Subjective Well-Being

SWB has become a cornerstone of interdisciplinary research, offering a multidimensional lens for evaluating individuals' quality of life beyond traditional economic indicators. Early investigations linked people's objective welfare metrics, such as income and consumption, to their overall well-being. Until 1974, the "Easterlin Paradox" demonstrated that sustained economic growth does not guarantee rising happiness. The insight established the theoretical imperative to treat people's SWB as an autonomous research domain, distinct from traditional objective indicators. While this paradigm shift broadened welfare economics, critics argued it initially lacked rigorous conceptual and methodological coherence across cultures and populations. Pavot & Diener (1993) measured the cognitive dimensions of people's SWB; its unidimensional structure oversimplifies the complexity of subjective evaluations. Although the Satisfaction with Life Scale (SWLS) demonstrated validity across contexts (Jang et al. 2017), its reliance on self-report and cultural norms may bias comparisons, particularly across collectivist and individualist societies.

Watson et al. (1988) developed the Positive and Negative Affect Schedule (PANAS) with a 20-item inventory evenly split between positive and negative emotions. PANAS is well-suited to detect short-term mood variations in response to changing employment conditions. However, it has been critiqued for limited contextual nuance and reliance on recall accuracy. Complementing these measures, the Center for Epidemiologic Studies Depression Scale (CES-D) comprised 20-items designed to screen for depressive symptoms in the general population (Santor 2004). Similarly, the research widely used validated Chinese translations in studies of rural older adults and left-behind children, though it often conflates clinical screening with subjective affective states (Fang et al. 2019; Li et al. 2021; Ruan et al. 2024).

Recent advances in measuring people's SWB have extended the cognitive-affective framework by distinguishing life evaluation from experiential well-being (Diener et al. 2018; Martela & Ryan 2023). However, this classification remains underutilized in rural areas or among low-income groups. Drawing on Gallup World Poll data, the researchers devised a Life Evaluation Index alongside a Daily Experience Index, demonstrating that the latter more accurately tracks moment-to-moment emotional fluctuations independently (August 2023). The two indices can diverge, underscoring the importance of analysing cognitive and affective dimensions. Building on this, Kanjo et al. (2017) enhanced the PANAS framework with real-time emotion tracking via a smartphone app, confirming that high-frequency "digital experience" data enrich traditional well-being metrics and calling for future research to capture temporal dynamics in people's SWB. While real-time emotion tracking via smart devices holds promise, existing evidence is heavily weighted toward urban samples and has yet to include older adults and rural populations.

Macro-level analyses, such as those summarized in the World Happiness Report, underscore the role of social support, trust in Government, and personal freedom in shaping citizens' well-being (Rowan 2023). However, these findings glossed over intra-national disparities and informal support structures (Rowan, 2023). At the community level, social capital, particularly neighbourhood mutual aid networks, exerted a stronger influence on rural residents' happiness than purely economic transfers (Nugroho et al. 2022; Villalonga-Olives et al. 2022). Moreover, higher educational achievement bolstered farmers' life satisfaction indirectly by enhancing self-efficacy and career prospects (Yang et al. 2022), while urban study reveals that access to public services remains a critical determinant of SWB differences across modern cities (Zhou et al. 2021).

While income remains a key driver of people's SWB, its marginal utility diminished unevenly across income strata: lower-income groups exhibit greater sensitivity to income changes, whereas higher-income groups derive more of their happiness from non-material resources (Behera et al. 2024). The decline in physical function among middle-aged and older adults can lead to increased anxiety and depression; however, community participation had a positive impact on their emotional well-being, indicating that health and social interaction had a mutually reinforcing effect (Gao et al. 2023; Nugroho et al. 2022; Villalonga-Olives et al. 2022). However, current mainstream frameworks continue to underestimate the mediating role of family structures and caregiving responsibilities (Li et al. 2021; Niu & Wang 2024; Xing et al. 2021), which are precisely crucial sources of emotional resilience in collectivist cultures like China's. Therefore, future research urgently needs to deepen the dimensional decomposition of people' SWB, incorporate time-sensitive measurements, and construct theoretical models adaptable to diverse rural contexts.

3.2.2.2 Impact of Employment Types on Subjective Well-Being

Recent research has moved beyond the binary distinction between employment and unemployment to examine how job quality and work arrangements influence prople's SWB (Shen et al. 2024; Uglanova & Dettmers 2018). Although formal full-time employment is generally associated with higher personal life satisfaction and emotional well-being, some scholars pointed out that this relationship is subject to selection bias: individuals who are already happier are more likely to secure stable jobs (Lips-Wiersma et al. 2022; Zhou et al. 2024). For the informal employment and self-employment arrangements, the results are more complex. On the one hand, employment flexibility can cushion stress (Uglanova & Dettmers 2018); on the other hand, the lack of institutional safeguards can heighten insecurity (Uglanova & Dettmers 2018). Likewise, Wheatley (2017) showed that greater "work autonomy", manifested through remote work and flexible scheduling, not only boosts perople's positive affect but also mitigates their depressive symptoms, underscoring the pivotal role of job control in shaping rural residents' SWB. However, the impact of these factors on farmers' SWB has yet to be empirically examined in rural China.

In rural China's ongoing social transformation, farm and off-farm employment exert contrasting influences on farmers' SWB (Chen & Hu 2024; Herrera Sabillón et al. 2022; Ma et al. 2025; Watema et al. 2025). Farm labour offered deep community embeddedness and social support but yields lower incomes, whereas off-farm employment delivers a substantial wage premium at the cost of weaker local ties (Ma et al. 2025; Watema et al. 2025). Empirically, off-farm employment exerted a markedly larger effect on farmers material living standards and cognitive life evaluations (Shen et al. 2024; Zhang 2022). Conversely, the long-standing community roots and collective participation inherent in farm work more effectively buffer against farmers' negative emotions, particularly among women and older people (Chen & Hu 2024; Herrera Sabillón et al. 2022). Nevertheless, most current research remains focused on income improvements while failing to adequately examine the emotional toll of off-farm transformation, particularly overlooking the high dependence of women and older people on local social connections (Shen et al. 2024; Watema et al. 2025; Zhang 2022).

Pure farm employment, pure off-farm employment, and mixed employment exert markedly different effects on rural residents' SWB (Ma et al. 2025; Wang et al. 2024). Farmers, who are purely engaged in farming, experience high income volatility and incomplete social protection, resulting in lower SWB than those in off-farm employment (Ma et al. 2025). Agricultural households are doubly vulnerable to natural shocks and price fluctuations, which reduce incomes and heighten psychological stress (Wang et al. 2024). However, this conclusion often overlooks the positive role of cultural resilience and informal mutual aid networks inherent in agricultural life. Moreover, rural social security and public services gaps, especially in health care and elder support, further depress life satisfaction among farming families (Ding et al. 2023). Yet migrated off-farm employment incurs "urban integration costs"; newcomers contend with housing challenges (Sen et al. 2021), diminished community ties (Ma et al. 2025; Watema et al. 2025), and identity pressures (Li & Xu 2023; Sen et al. 2021) that can counterbalance income gains.

Mixed-employment households, those who combine farm and off-farm employment, consistently report the highest SWB (Gracious & Umakrishnan 2025; Ma et al. 2025; Sen et al. 2021; Villalonga-Olives et al. 2022). By retaining land-based security while diversifying income sources, these households achieved greater income stability and risk dispersion (Ma et al. 2025). Simultaneously, they leverage dual social networks across rural and urban settings to reinforce social capital, enhanced identity recognition, and psychological belonging beyond what single-mode workers experience (Gracious & Umakrishnan 2025; Sen et al. 2021; Villalonga-Olives et al. 2022). However, existing research has rarely examined the heterogeneity within off-farm employment. Most empirical studies continue to treat "off-farm employment" as a unified category (Marino et al. 2021; Rocchi et al. 2021), overlooking the fundamental differences between "local off-farm employment" and "migrated off-farm employment" in terms of social support (Li & Xu 2023; Shen et al. 2022), family structure (Chen & Hu 2024), and exposure to migration pressures (Sen et al. 2021). This binary classification tends to obscure the true impact of different employment types on farmers' SWB, particularly their influence on negative emotions such as anxiety, loneliness, and depression. These emotions often more accurately reflect the psychological costs borne by vulnerable rural populations during employment transitions.

The existing literature highlights several critical research gaps. First, there is a lack of identification of how different employment types of farmers affect their multidimensional SWB outcomes, including positive and negative emotions. Second, most existing methodologies fail to adequately control for endogeneity biases in employment choices, leading to systematic distortions in the relationship between rural residents' employment types and SWB. To address these gaps, this study employs an MVTE model to systematically estimate the effects of the three employment types on five dimensions of farmers' SWB. This approach not only helps determine whether off-farm employment enhances farmers' SWB but also reveals under which employment arrangements and for which groups it may impose potential psychological burdens.

3.3 Conceptual Framework

Understanding how different employment types (non-participation in off-farm work, local off-farm employment, and migrated off-farm employment) shape farmers' positive SWB (happiness and life satisfaction) and negative SWB (anxiety, loneliness, and depression) requires a multidimensional conceptual framework. Drawing on established theories in psychology, sociology, and labor economics (Behera et al.

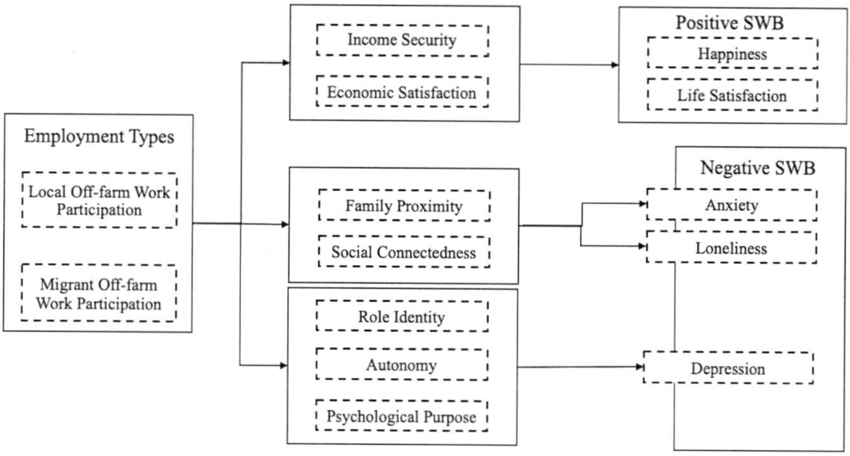

Fig. 3.4 Conceptual framework illustrating the relationship between employment types and farmers' SWB. *Source* authors' own

2024; Ma et al. 2025; Shen et al. 2022), this study proposes a conceptual framework linking employment types to five core dimensions of farmers' SWB (see Fig. 3.4). Each employment form entails distinct experiential, relational, and psychological implications, which we organize into three empirically grounded and theoretically informed pathways.

The first pathway shows that off-farm employment, both local and migrated, influences farmers' positive SWB outcomes (happiness and life satisfaction) through income security and economic satisfaction. Empirical evidence consistently demonstrates that off-farm employment, particularly formal or migrated jobs, provides higher and more stable income than farming only labor (Ma et al. 2025). This pathway aligns with income-based theories of perple's SWB, which posit that material resources satisfy basic and psychological needs, enhancing their happiness and life satisfaction (Behera et al. 2024). However, the marginal utility of income varies: low-income individuals gain more positive SWB per unit of income, while high-income individuals may experience status anxiety instead (Behera et al. 2024). Farmers' happiness and life satisfaction are particularly sensitive to income levels, making them the primary SWB dimensions affected via this channel.

The second pathway shows that migrating off-farm employment affects farmers' negative SWB outcomes (anxiety and loneliness) by reshaping family proximity and social connectedness. Whereas local off-farm employment helps maintain household cohesion and enables active participation in community life, migrant off-farm employment often involves geographic separation, fragmented caregiving, and reduced daily interaction (Chen & Hu 2024). These conditions erode emotional intimacy and heighten the risk of loneliness and depression for farmers (Chen & Hu 2024). This dynamic posits that disruptions in intimate social ties compromise psychological resilience. Consequently, farmers' loneliness and depression are particularly responsive to variations in familial and social embeddedness, with rural women and elderly left-behind populations most affected (Li & Xu 2023; Shen et al. 2022).

The third pathway shows that migrated off-farm employment influences farmers' negative SWB (depression) through role identity, autonomy, and psychological purpose. Beyond material and relational aspects, employment types affect how individuals perceive themselves within their social context (Uglanova & Dettmers 2018; Wheatley 2017). Local off-farm employment can enhance community status and self-worth, whereas migrated off-farm employment may induce role conflict, identity fragmentation, and cultural alienation (Sen et al. 2021). These conditions often manifest as anxiety and emotional fatigue, particularly when workers struggle to reconcile external labor demands with internal expectations for identity coherence (Uglanova & Dettmers 2018). This perspective aligns with theories of role strain and rural residents' SWB (Uglanova & Dettmers 2018; Wheatley 2017), which emphasizes the psychological costs of dissonant social roles.

Taken together, these three pathways form an integrated framework for understanding how employment types shape farmers' multi-dimensional SWB outcomes in rural China. Rather than assuming a uniform effect of off-farm employment, this study disaggregates the influence across both employment types and farmers' SWB. The conceptual framework, thus, sets the stage for robust empirical identification using MVTE models, enabling a nuanced assessment of rural labor diversification and its psychosocial consequences.

3.4 Methodology

3.4.1 Estimation Strategy

3.4.1.1 Model Selection

Accurately estimating the impact of a multi-category treatment variable, such as employment types, hinges on selecting an appropriate measurement model. Commonly employed methods include propensity score matching (PSM), endogenous treatment regression (ETR), endogenous switching regression (ESR), and MVTE models. While PSM and ESR are well-suited to binary treatments, such as farm employment versus off-farm employment, applying them to a three-variable (0 = non-participation in off-farm work, 1 = local off-farm employment, 2 = migrated off-farm employment) requires pairwise comparisons that necessarily drop one category. This practice reduces sample efficiency and can introduce bias by omitting important contrasts (Ma et al. 2025). In contrast, the MVTE framework accommodates all three treatment states simultaneously, enabling a unified estimation of each status's effect and yielding a more systematic and comprehensive identification of relationships under multivalued treatments.

ETR and ESR both rely on valid instrumental variables to correct for selection bias, but identifying multiple, category-specific instruments becomes increasingly difficult as the number of treatment states grows (Zheng et al. 2023). Furthermore, these models are often sensitive to distributional assumptions and specification choices, which can introduce identification bias. In contrast, the MVTE framework shifts the burden from instruments to generalized propensity scores (GPS), enabling nonparametric covariate balancing and enhancing robustness (Imbens 2000). While the multinomial endogenous switching regression (MESR) approach can also accommodate multi-state Selection, its structural complexity, high computational cost, and sensitivity to variable and distributional assumptions limit its practicality, particularly in applications with many control variables (Ma et al. 2025), making MVTE the more operationally feasible and interpretable choice.

Imbens (2000) introduced the MVTE model for settings with more than two treatment categories, which extends the traditional propensity-score framework by incorporating GPS. GPS balances covariate distributions across all treatment groups, after which treatment effects are estimated via weighted regressions. Unlike binary-treatment approaches, MVTE naturally accommodates multiple treatment states within a single estimation, ensuring covariate balance through GPS and improving the precision and credibility of estimates (Cattaneo et al. 2013). By enabling the simultaneous estimation of effects for non-participation in off-farm work, local off-farm employment, and migrated off-farm employment, MVTE offers a comprehensive lens for uncovering how distinct employment types influence rural residents' SWB.

3.4.1.2 Modelling and Estimation Process

High-dimensional pre-treatment covariates X_i complicate the direct estimation of treatment effects under an MVTE framework. We employ GPS to provide a tractable solution (Imbens 2000). This study estimates GPS via a multinomial logit (MNL) model, allowing us to balance covariates across all treatment categories. The treatment variable T_i is defined as three mutually exclusive employment types, including non-participation in off-farm work, local off-farm employment, and migrated off-farm employment, with values $t = 0, 1, 2$. For each observed individual i, given its characteristic variables X_i, the probability of selecting a specific employment type t can be expressed as:

$$r(j, x) \equiv \Pr\left[T_i = j|X_i = x\right] \quad (1)$$

where $r(j, x)$ is GPS. T_i is a multivalued treatment variable indicating different types of employment, taking integer values between 0, 1, and 2. The maximum likelihood method is used to estimate the MNL model above, and the GPS of each individual under the three treatment conditions is derived accordingly.

After obtaining GPS, this paper uses it for sample weighting or covariate adjustment to eliminate observable differences in features across employment types and achieve balance in covariates between treatment statuses. This process lays the foundation for subsequent effect estimation.

We can estimate the GPS using the MNL model. Specifically, it is specified as follows:

$$\Pr\left[T_i = j\right] = \frac{\exp\left(\beta_j X_i\right)}{\sum_{j=1}^{M} \exp(\beta_m X_i)}, \ j \leq M \tag{2}$$

where $Pr[T_i = j]$ denotes the probability that farmer i chooses employment type j from the available options M. X_i is the vector of explanatory variables that are expected to influence a farmer's choice of employment type j; β_j and β_m are the corresponding coefficient vectors, which can be estimated by a maximum likelihood estimator.

The GPS obtained from the MNL model estimation can be used to balance the observations, creating a sample in which the covariates are balanced across all treatment groups. It allows for the calculation of the average results of these treatments. Under the selected covariate X_i, the expected potential outcomes of treatment level j and k ($j \neq k$) can be expressed as:

$$E\Big(Y_{ij} \mid X_i] = E\left[Y_i | T_i = j, X_i\right] = \beta_{0j} + X_i' \beta_{1j} \tag{3a}$$

$$E\Big(Y_{ik} \mid X_i] = E[Y_i | T_i = k, X_i] = \beta_{0k} + X_i' \beta_{1k} \tag{3b}$$

where β_{0j} and β_{0k} are constants. β_{1j} and β_{1k} are the corresponding parameters to be estimated. After estimating the parameters in Eqs. (3a) and (3b), the average treatment effect (ATE) of treatment j relative to treatment k ($j \neq k$) over the whole population, ATE_{jk}, can be consistently estimated as follows:

$$ATE_{jk} = \left(\beta_{0j} - \beta_{0k}\right) + \frac{1}{N} \sum_{i=1}^{N} X_i' \left(\beta_{1j} - \beta_{1k}\right) \tag{4}$$

where N refers to the total number of observations that participate in the treatment $T_i = j$ and $T_i = k$; $j, k \in \{0, 1, 2\}$.

The identification of consistent and unbiased estimates for Eq. (4) is grounded in two fundamental assumptions: the conditional independence (CI) assumption and the overlap assumption (Imbens 2000). The CI assumption requires that, after conditioning on a set of observable covariates, the potential outcomes are statistically independent of the treatment assignment. To enhance the plausibility of this assumption, we incorporate an extensive range of control variables in X_i. The overlap assumption further requires that each observational unit has a strictly positive probability of receiving any treatment status. In practice, this assumption is ensured by restricting the sample to observations whose estimated treatment probabilities fall within the admissible range.

3.4.2 Data and Key Variable Measurements

3.4.2.1 Data

This study utilizes primary cross-sectional survey data collected between 2022 and 2023 in China's three major wheat-producing regions: Henan Province, Shandong Province, and Hebei Province (China Rural Statistical Yearbook 2023). These regions are in the North China Plain, the core area for wheat cultivation in China, accounting for over half of the country's total wheat production, with large rural populations, making them broadly representative of China's agricultural economy. Each province also has a huge rural labor force and high off-farm employment. Henan, the most populous inland province, had a rural population of about 42.38 million in 2022 (Gu et al. 2025). Its urbanization rate of 57.1% is well below the national average of 65.2%, indicating a large residual rural population and a large number of migrant workers (Gu et al. 2025). Shandong and Hebei similarly have large rural populations and are major labor-exporting provinces. In sum, these three provinces combine very large rural populations with significant engagement in off-farm work, mirroring national rural labor-force patterns.

Within each province, we employed multistage stratified sampling based on local economic development. First, we collected the latest official statistics for 2022 and 2023 from sources such as provincial statistical yearbooks and the National Bureau of Statistics of China (NBS) bulletins on indicators including per-capita rural income, county gross domestic product (GDP), and agricultural output. Using such data, we sorted counties into high, medium, and low development strata. Counties with the highest per-capita income formed the "high" stratum, and similarly for mid and low strata. From each stratum, we randomly selected sample counties, and within each selected county, we randomly selected villages. By stratifying on these official development indicators, the sample captures variation in county-level prosperity, agricultural scale, and off-farm employment. Then, the survey employed a multi-stage stratified sampling method, randomly selecting survey participants from typical agricultural counties and conducting on-site interviews with rural residents engaged in wheat production in the local area, ultimately obtaining 648 valid samples.

3.4.2.2 Key Variable Measurements

The key treatment variable in this study is employment types, which classifies rural respondents into three categories based on their off-farm employment status and work locations: non-participation in off-farm work, local off-farm employment, and migrated off-farm employment. Specifically, individuals who do not engage in any off-farm work are categorized as non-participants. Local off-farm employment refers to rural laborers engaged in off-farm work within their township or nearby villages (such as township enterprises, service sectors, and industrial parks), allowing them to return home daily and interact with family members. Migrated off-farm employment, by contrast, denotes off-farm work undertaken in locations geographically distant from the household, which is typically outside the home county or in urban centers, which requires prolonged residence away from home and results in sustained spatial separation from family members.

The outcome variables include two positive SWB outcomes (happiness and life satisfaction) and three negative SWB outcomes (anxiety, loneliness, and depression). To measure positive SWB outcomes, we included two questions in our survey questionnaire, *"To what extent do you feel happy with your current life?" and "To what extent are you satisfied with your current life*", each measured on a 5-point Likert scale ranging from 1 = very unhappy/very unsatisfied to 5 = very happy/very satisfied. Similarly, to measure negative SWB outcomes, we included three questions in our survey questionnaire: "*To what extent do you feel Anxiety about your current life?*" "*To what extent do you feel lonely with the current life?*" and "*To what extent do you feel depressed about the current life?*" The answers to those three questions are also measured on a 5-point Likert scale ranging from 1 = not anxious at all/not lonely at all/very undepressed to 5 = very anxious/very lonely/very depressed.

Unlike objective indicators of quality of life, such as income or consumption, SWB captures people's subjective feelings and psychological experiences, thereby addressing the limitations of income-based measures. For farmers' happiness and life satisfaction, higher values indicate better subjective outcomes, while for their anxiety, loneliness, and depression, higher values represent more severe negative emotions. This multidimensional approach enables a more comprehensive understanding of how different employment arrangements influence both positive and negative aspects of farmers' SWB.

3.4.2.3 Selection of Control Variables

To address potential confounding and omitted variable bias, the model controls for a comprehensive set of individual, household, agricultural, and regional characteristics. These controls were selected based on extensive prior literature that links socioeconomic background to both employment types and farmers' SWB outcomes (Hasan et al. 2021; Ma et al. 2025; Tov et al. 2022; Yang et al. 2022). Specifically, age, marriage status, and education capture life cycle status and human capital endowment, which influence both employment capacity and emotional states (Gracious & Umakrishnan 2025; Hasan et al. 2021; Ma et al. 2025). Farming experience, household size, and farm size are included to reflect production capacity and social structure, factors that prior work links to job choice and residents' SWB in rural settings (Behera et al. 2024; Yang et al. 2022). Asset variables like tractor ownership, receipt of living allowances, and participation in farm insurance proxy for financial security and institutional support (Tov et al. 2022; Yang et al. 2022). Finally, regional dummies for Henan, Shandong, and Hebei control for unobserved province-level differences in policies, labor markets, and welfare access.

3.4.3 Descriptive Statistics

Table 3.1 provides the definitions, measurements, and summary statistics of the main variables used in the empirical analysis. The outcome variables cover five key dimensions of farmers' SWB, including happiness, life satisfaction, anxiety, loneliness, and depression, which are all self-reported on a 1 to 5 scale. The average scores for respondents' happiness and life satisfaction are 4.25 and 4.04, respectively, and are relatively high, indicating that the samples generally report a satisfactory emotional state. In contrast, the mean values for respondents' anxiety, loneliness, and depression are notably low, which are 1.92, 1.87, and 1.82, respectively, suggesting that severe psychological distress is not widespread in the sample population.

For the key treatment variables, the employment types are defined in three groups (0 = non-participation in off-farm work, 1 = local off-farm employment, 2 = migrated off-farm employment), with a mean value of 1.05 and a standard deviation of 0.89. The mean slightly above 1 suggests that off-farm employment participation is prevalent in the sample, with local off-farm employment accounting for a substantial share. The relatively large standard deviation indicates considerable dispersion across the three employment categories, reflecting substantial heterogeneity in labor allocation strategies. Specifically, 37% of the sample are non-participants in off-farm work, 21% of the respondents engage in local off-farm employment, and 42% of the observations are migrants to off-farm employment.

Regarding the control variables, the average age of the household head is 42.5 years. Approximately 91% of the respondents are married. The mean years of education around the sample is 10.5 years, roughly equivalent to junior high school completion, and the average household size is 2.87 persons. The mean farm size of the observations is 7.4 acres, with a standard deviation of 15.76 acres, indicating substantial variation across households. About 12% of households own a tractor, and around 25% of the sample report having purchased farm insurance. Regional distribution is relatively balanced: Henan accounts for 39% of the sample, Hebei for 36%, and Shandong for 25%. These figures align with the stratified sampling design and reinforce the sample's heterogeneity and external validity.

Table 3.2 reports the mean differences for key variables by employment type, along with the corresponding F-test results. These comparisons offer initial insight into the relationship between employment types and farmers' SWB, as well as the observable heterogeneity in socioeconomic attributes. Migrants' off-farm employment exhibits the most favourable SWB profile, with the highest happiness score of 4.49 and overall life satisfaction score of 4.07, alongside the lowest mean levels of anxiety of 1.70, loneliness of 1.77, and depression of 1.62. These values imply a superior emotional profile compared to their counterparts, suggesting that long-distance migration may yield psychological benefits, possibly due to higher income,

Table 3.1 Variable definitions and summary statistics

Variables	Measurements	Mean (S.D.)
Outcome variables		
Happiness	Self-reported: From 1 = very unhappy to 5 = very happy	4.25 (0.97)
Life satisfaction	Self-reported: From 1 = very unsatisfied to 5 = very satisfied	4.04 (0.85)
Anxiety	Self-reported: From 1 = very un-anxious to 5 = very anxious	1.92 (0.82)
Loneliness	Self-reported: From 1 = very un-lonely to 5 = very lonely	1.87 (0.93)
Depression	Self-reported: From 1 = very un-depressed to 5 = very depressed	1.82 (0.94)
Treatment variables		
Employment types	Types of employment of head of household: 0 = non-participation in off-farm work; 1 = local off-farm employment; 2 = migrated off-farm employment	1.05 (0.89)
Non-participation in off-farm work	1 if household head did not participate in off-farm work, 0 otherwise	0.37 (0.48)
Local off-farm employment	1 if the head of household participates in local off-farm work, 0 otherwise	0.21 (0.41)
Migrated off-farm employment	1 if the head of household participates in migrated off-farm work, 0 otherwise	0.42 (0.50)
Control variables		
Age	Age of household head (years)	42.5 (10.84)
Marriage status	Marriage status of respondent, 1if respondent is married, 0 = otherwise	0.91 (0.28)
Education	Farmer's maximal education level (years)	10.46 (3.14)
Farming experience	The time of household head experience in agricultural production (years)	12.66 (9.09)
Household size	Number of people residing in a household (persons)	2.87 (1.23)
Tractor ownership	1 if the household owns a tractor, 0 otherwise	0.12 (0.34)
Living allowance	1 if the household receives a subsistence allowance from the government, 0 otherwise.	0.29 (0.45)
Farm size	Total size of operated arable land (acres)	7.40 (15.76)
Soil conditions	1 if the household's soil is fertile, 0 otherwise.	0.98 (0.15)

(continued)

Table 3.1 (continued)

Variables	Measurements	Mean (S.D.)
Distance to arable land	Distance from home to arable land (km)	0.97 (0.69)
Farm insurance	1 if the household participates in farm insurance, 0 otherwise	0.25 (0.44)
Shandong	1 if household resides in Shandong, 0 otherwise	0.25 (0.43)
Henan	1 if household resides in Henan, 0 otherwise	0.39 (0.49)
Hebei	1 if household resides in Hebei, 0 otherwise	0.36 (0.48)
Observations		648

[a]Yuan is Chinese currency (1USD = 7.26 yuan in 2024)

stronger role identity, or urban exposure. In contrast, non-participation in off-farm work is associated with substantially lower SWB among farmers across both positive and negative dimensions, underscoring the profound impact of employment choice on rural residents' mental health.

With respect to demographic characteristics, non-participating off-farm workers have a mean age of 38.17 years, while off-farm workers engaged in migration have a mean age of 48.28 years. The mean years of education are 9.86 years among migrants from off-farm employment. Local off-farm employment has the largest household size, averaging 3.21 persons. Landholding differs substantially across groups. Non-participation in off-farm work is associated with the largest farm size, averaging 11.11 acres. Tractor ownership is highest among those who do not participate in off-farm work at 18%. The F-value indicates that most of these differences are statistically significant, suggesting systematic variation in observable characteristics across employment types.

3.5 Empirical Results

3.5.1 Factors Influencing Farmers' Decisions to Choose Different Employment Types

Table 3.3 reports marginal effects of selected control variables on different employment types from MNL regressions, pinpointing the individual and household characteristics that significantly shape the likelihood of non-participation in off-farm work, local off-farm employment, and migrated off-farm employment.

Table 3.2 Mean differences in the selected variables between different employment types

	Non-participation in off-farm work	Local off-farm employment	Migrated off-farm employment	*F*-value
Happiness	4.00 (1.26)	4.22 (0.68)	4.49 (0.71)	16.93^{***}
Life satisfaction	3.93 (1.20)	4.19 (0.58)	4.07 (0.49)	4.52^{*}
Anxiety	2.18 (1.06)	1.89 (0.54)	1.70 (0.59)	23.92^{***}
Loneliness	2.10 (1.17)	1.66 (0.60)	1.77 (0.77)	13.08^{***}
Depression	2.12 (1.25)	1.67 (0.65)	1.62 (0.62)	21.28^{***}
Age	38.17 (10.26)	38.49 (11.23)	48.28 (8.16)	84.67^{***}
Marriage status	0.82 (0.38)	0.99 (0.09)	0.95 (0.21)	21.75^{***}
Education	10.57 (4.47)	11.50 (1.63)	9.86 (1.90)	34.95^{***}
Farming experience	14.99 (9.16)	17.67 (6.88)	8.15 (7.85)	76.25^{***}
Household size	2.59 (1.04)	3.21 (1.37)	2.96 (1.27)	12.72^{***}
Tractor ownership	0.18 (0.43)	0.10 (0.31)	0.07 (0.25)	7.09^{***}
Living allowance	0.22 (0.42)	0.72 (0.45)	0.14 (0.35)	99.47^{***}
Farm size	11.11 (21.66)	5.74 (2.44)	4.93 (12.44)	11.10^{***}
Soil conditions	0.95 (0.21)	0.99 (0.09)	0.99 (0.10)	4.36^{*}
Distance to arable land	1.15 (0.83)	1.04 (0.21)	0.78 (0.65)	20.94^{***}
Farm insurance	0.17 (0.38)	0.22 (0.41)	0.34 (0.48)	10.70^{***}
Henan	0.44 (0.50)	0.38 (0.49)	0.36 (0.48)	1.49
Hebei	0.23 (0.42)	0.46 (0.50)	0.42 (0.49)	12.74^{***}
Shandong	0.34 (0.47)	0.16 (0.36)	0.22 (0.41)	8.73^{***}

Note $^{***}p < 0.01$, $^{**}p < 0.05$, $^{*}p < 0.10$

Age is positively and significantly associated with off-farm employment. A one-year increase in age raises the probability of selecting migrated off-farm employment by 1.9%, while reducing engagement in local off-farm employment and non-participation in off-farm work by 1.2% and 0.7%, respectively. This pattern indicates that older rural residents are more likely to engage in long-distance migration than in other forms of employment. One possible explanation is that accumulated household responsibilities and financial pressures may increase the incentive for migration at later stages of life. This finding is consistent with Gracious & Umakrishnan (2025), emphasizing that migration decisions are closely tied to household economic burdens and stage-specific financial pressures.

Education shows a statistically significant positive effect only for local off-farm employment. Each additional year of schooling increases the probability of engaging in local off-farm employment by 1.1%, while its effects on migrated off-farm employment and non-participation in off-farm work are not statistically significant. This suggests that education strengthens access to nearby labor markets and mixed employment strategies (Ma et al. 2025), rather than necessarily promoting

Table 3.3 Marginal effects of selected control variables on different employment types: MLOGIT model

Variables	Non-participation in off-farm work	Local off-farm employment	Migrated off-farm employment
Age	−0.007 (0.002)***	−0.012 (0.002)***	0.019 (0.001)***
Marriage statue	−0.295 (0.080)***	0.217 (0.076)	0.078 (0.103)
Education	−0.006 (0.006)	0.011 (0.006)**	−0.005 (0.006)
Farming experience	0.007 (0.002)***	0.015 (0.003)***	−0.022 (0.002)***
Household size	−0.047 (0.013)***	0.022 (0.011)**	0.025 (0.012)**
Tractor ownership	0.066 (0.052)	−0.010 (0.043)	−0.010 (0.043)
Living allowance	−0.183 (0.038)***	0.218 (0.026)***	−0.035 (0.039)
Farm size	0.010 (0.002)***	−0.011 (0.003)***	0.001 (0.002)
Soil conditions	−0.031 (0.119)	−0.009 (0.112)	0.040 (0.126)
Distance to arable land	−0.053 (0.037)	0.046 (0.033)	0.007 (0.036)
Farm insurance	0.007 (0.036)	0.154 (0.042)***	−0.021 (0.042)
Henan	−0.054 (0.040)	−0.020 (0.038)	0.074 (0.039)*
Hebei	−0.147 (0.043)***	−0.002 (0.041)	0.149 (0.041)***

Note $^{***}p < 0.01$, $^{**}p < 0.05$, $^{*}p < 0.10$; Standard errors in parenthesis; Shandong is reference province

distant migration. A plausible reason is that local off-farm employment may require moderate skill levels and information access that are more directly enhanced by schooling.

Farming experience significantly increases the probability of remaining in agriculture by 0.7% and of local off-farm employment by 1.5%, while decreasing the probability of migrated off-farm employment by 2.2%. These findings imply that longer agricultural engagement reduces the long-distance relocation, and stronger agricultural dependence lowers the probability of transitioning into distant off-farm employment (Sen et al. 2021). This pattern may reflect occupational specialization and land attachment accumulated through farming experience.

Larger household size increases the probability of both local and migrated off-farm employment, by 2.2% and 2.5%, respectively, while decreasing non-participation in off-farm work by 4.7%. This may reflect labor supply effects that households with more working-age members have a greater capacity to engage in diversified employment strategies. A living allowance receipt decreases the probability of non-participation in off-farm work by 18.3%. It increases engagement in local off-farm employment by 21.8%, suggesting that social assistance may lower entry barriers for vulnerable groups. Having farm insurance increases the probability of local off-farm employment by 15.4%, potentially reflecting access to financial risk mitigation that encourages moderate employment diversification. This facilitating role of institutional support is consistent with Li & Xu (1), who argue that risk-reducing mechanisms enhance households' willingness to reallocate labor toward off-farm employment.

Moreover, regional dummies reveal that, relative to Shandong, rural residents in Hebei are 14.9% more likely to migrate and 14.7% less likely to remain in non-participation in off-farm work, while Henan shows a weaker but similar pattern. These results may be due to Hebei provinceis proximity to modern cities such as Beijing and Tianjin, and the differences may reflect variation in local labor market saturation, policy implementation, or out-migration culture (Gu et al. 2025; Xing et al. 2022).

3.5.2 *Treatment Effects of Employment Types on Farmers' Subjective Well-Being*

Table 3.4 presents estimates from our MVTE model across five SWB outcomes: happiness, life satisfaction, anxiety, loneliness, and depression. The coefficients represent ATEs comparing local and migrated off-farm employment with the reference group (non-participation in off-farm work), as well as direct comparisons between migrated and local off-farm employment. Both absolute and percentage changes are reported to contextualize the magnitude of effects.

3.5.2.1 Average Treatment Effects on Farmers' Positive Subjective Well-Being

Part (a) of Table 3.4 presents the results estimating the impact of types of off-farm employment on farmers' positive subjective well-being outcomes. The ATEs indicate that shifting from non-participation in off-farm work to local off-farm employment reduces farmers' happiness by 1.106 units, corresponding to a 26.7% decline, and reduces their life satisfaction by 0.970 units, equivalent to a 24.7% decrease. A plausible interpretation is that local off-farm employment may not yield sufficient improvements in perceived living conditions to offset increased time pressure or role strain. Therefore, employment quality, rather than work participation, determines farmers' positive SWB outcomes (Shen et al. 2024), and informal employment arrangements may undermine their SWB (Zhou et al. 2024).

The most pronounced differences emerge when comparing migrated with local off-farm employment. Migrated off-farm employment increases farmers' happiness by 1.243 units relative to local off-farm employment, representing a 41.0% improvement, and raises their life satisfaction by 1.054 units, equivalent to a 35.5% increase. These magnitudes are comparable to the losses observed for local off-farm employment relative to non-participation in off-farm work. This indicates that the key distinction is between different types of off-farm employment. Ma et al. (2025) and also emphasize that different employment categories generate distinct welfare outcomes.

Table 3.4 Treatment effects of employment types on farmers' SWB: MVTE estimator

	ATE estimates			Percentage changes in ATE	
	Coefficients	*z*-value		Coefficients	*z*-value
Part (a): Positive SWB outcomes					
Happiness					
Local VS non	−1.106 (0.187) ***	−5.92		−0.267 (0.043) ***	−6.18
Migrated VS non	0.137 (0.105)	1.30		0.033 (0.026)	1.28
Migrated VS local	1.243 (0.185) ***	6.72		0.410 (0.083) ***	4.97
Life satisfaction					
Local VS non	−0.970 (0.183) ***	−5.29		−0.247 (0.045) ***	−5.48
Migrated VS non	0.084 (0.084)	1.00		0.021 (0.022)	0.98
Migrated VS local	1.054 (0.174) ***	6.05		0.355 (0.079) ***	4.53
Part (b): Negative SWB outcomes					
Anxiety					
Local VS non	0.560 (0.117) ***	4.79		0.270 (0.060) ***	4.48
Migrated VS non	−0.194 (0.082) *	−2.38		−0.094 (0.038) *	−2.49
Migrated VS local	−0.754 (0.118) ***	−6.39		−0.286 (0.036) ***	−8.06
Loneliness					
Local VS non	0.976 (0.143) ***	6.80		0.503 (0.087) ***	5.77
Migrated VS non	−0.226 (0.103) *	−2.20		−0.042 (0.053)	−0.79
Migrated VS local	−1.202 (0.137) ***	−8.80		−0.412 (0.033) ***	−12.39
Depression					
Local VS non	0.922 (0.166) ***	5.55		0.458 (0.095) ***	4.81
Migrated VS non	−0.243 (0.105) *	−2.32		−0.120 (0.047) *	−2.54
Migrated VS local	−1.165 (0.147) ***	−7.94		−0.397 (0.033) ***	−11.97

Note $^{***}p < 0.01$, $^{**}p < 0.05$, $^{*}p < 0.10$; Robust standard errors in parenthesis; Non means non-participation in off-farm work, Local means local off-farm employment, Migrated means migrated off-farm employment

A possible mechanism is that migrated off-farm employment may provide clearer income trajectories, stronger perceptions of upward mobility, and reduced exposure to local social pressures. Migrant workers who live and work in more modern cities maintain optimistic expectations about their future economic prospects and living conditions, while larger cities facilitate family immigration, strengthening emotional connection, which both positively impact their current sense of happiness and life satisfaction (Xing et al. 2022).

3.5.2.2 Average Treatment Effects on Farmers' Negative Subjective Well-Being

Part (b) of Table 3.4 presents the results estimating the impact of types of off-farm employment on farmers' negative subjective well-being outcomes. The results show that relative to non-participation in off-farm work, local off-farm employment generates statistically significant and economically meaningful increases in all three negative SWB indicators. The estimated ATEs imply that, on average, individuals who transition from non-participation in off-farm work to local off-farm employment would experience an increase of 0.560 units in anxiety (27.0%), 0.976 units in loneliness (50.3%), and 0.922 units in depression (45.8%), holding observable characteristics constant. The magnitudes of the percentage changes, particularly the 50.3% increase in loneliness and the 45.8% rise in depression, indicate that local off-farm employment is associated with a substantial deterioration in emotional health across multiple distress dimensions, rather than a marginal or isolated psychological response. A plausible explanation is that local off-farm employment may expose individuals to unstable earnings, stronger local social comparison, and persistent household responsibilities, which consequently increase their anxiety, loneliness, and depression. Shen et al. (2022) demonstrated that rural Chinese female farmers who migrate for off-farm work experience pronounced declines in depressive symptoms, consistent with our finding of significantly lower depression levels among migrated off-farm employees.

In contrast, migrating off-farm employment significantly reduces farmers' negative SWB outcomes relative to non-participation in off-farm work. Individuals who shift from non-participation in off-farm work to migrated off-farm employment would experience a decline of 0.194 units in anxiety and 0.243 units in their depression. The uniform reduction across multiple distress outcomes suggests that migration alleviates psychological strain broadly. Therefore, improved income stability and risk mitigation associated with certain forms of off-farm employment can enhance household welfare and psychological resilience (Li & Xu 2023).

The largest differences again emerge when comparing migrated with local off-farm employment. The estimated ATEs indicate that transitioning from migrated to local off-farm employment is associated with statistically significant reductions in all farmers' three distress outcomes, implying proportional declines of 28.6% for anxiety, 41.2% for loneliness, and 39.7% for depression. These results indicate that migrating for off-farm employment is associated with substantially better emotional outcomes than remaining in local off-farm employment. Although international meta-evidence suggests elevated mental health risks among migrant workers (Hasan et al. 2021), the present result identifies average differences within a comparable rural sample. In this context, migrating from off-farm employment appears to yield net psychological benefits relative to both local off-farm employment and non-participation in off-farm work. A potential reason is that off-farm employment that has been migrated may offer better income stability and distance from local stressors that intensify negative emotions.

3.6 Conclusion and Policy Recommendations

3.6.1 Conclusion

As China's rural labour force diversifies, off-farm employment increasingly spans a spectrum of distinct patterns. Moving beyond the traditional farm-off-farm dichotomy, this study adopts an interdisciplinary lens to examine 648 survey responses from households in China's leading wheat-producing provinces, bridging rural revitalization and farmers' SWB. Employing an MVTE model, we systematically estimate the impacts of three employment types (non-participation in off-farm work, local off-farm employment, and migrated off-farm employment) on five dimensions of rural residents' SWB (happiness, life satisfaction, anxiety, loneliness, and depression).

The findings also show that education, farming experience, household size, living allowance, and farm insurance are the main factors driving farmers' decisions to participate in local off-farm employment, while age and household size determine their participation in migrated off-farm employment. In contrast, age, tractor ownership, and farm size are the main factors that discourage farmers from engaging in local off-farm employment, whereas farming experience is the primary factor discouraging farmers from migrating for off-farm work.

The study further finds that the impacts of off-farm employment on farmers' subjective well-being vary substantially across employment types. Specifically, compared with non-participation in off-farm work, local off-farm employment reduces farmers' happiness and life satisfaction while increasing their anxiety, loneliness, and depression. In contrast, migrated off-farm employment does not significantly affect farmers' happiness or life satisfaction relative to non-participation in off-farm work, but it significantly reduces their anxiety, loneliness, and depression. Finally, compared with local off-farm employment, migrated off-farm employment significantly increases farmers' happiness and life satisfaction while reducing their anxiety, loneliness, and depression.

3.6.2 Policy Recommendations

The findings of this study offer several implications for rural employment and SWB policies in China. The findings of this study provide several important implications for rural labour and well-being policies in China. The evidence indicates that local off-farm employment significantly reduces farmers' happiness and life satisfaction while increasing their anxiety, loneliness, and depression, highlighting the need to improve job stability, working conditions, and income prospects in local rural labour markets. Enhancing labour protection, providing skills training, and promoting higher-quality non-farm industries in rural areas could help mitigate the psychological costs of local off-farm employment. Given that migrated off-farm employment significantly reduces farmers' anxiety, loneliness, and depression and performs better than local off-farm employment across most well-being indicators, policies should facilitate orderly rural–urban labour mobility. Reducing institutional barriers to migration, improving access to urban public services, and strengthening social protection for migrant workers can help rural households better capture the economic and psychological benefits of migration.

Turning to the factors that affect farmers' off-farm employment, we find that education significantly increases the likelihood of participating in local off-farm employment. The findings suggest that policymakers should strengthen rural education and vocational training programs to enhance farmers' skills and improve their access to nearby non-farm labour markets. Expanding technical training and adult education initiatives could help rural workers transition more effectively into diversified employment opportunities. The positive role of household size in both local and migrated off-farm employment suggests that labour availability within households facilitates employment diversification. Policies that promote rural labour mobility, such as improved transportation infrastructure and better labour market information systems, could further help households allocate labour efficiently across farm and non-farm activities. The findings indicate that institutional support mechanisms, including living allowances and farm insurance, significantly encourage participation in local off-farm employment. Thus, strengthening social protection programs and expanding agricultural insurance coverage may reduce risk exposure and enable rural households to pursue more diversified livelihood strategies.

Data Availability Statement The data supporting this study's findings are available from Ziqi Wang upon request.

References

2023 China Rural Statistical Yearbook. (n.d.).

Addai, K. N., Ng'ombe, J. N., & Lu, W. (2023). Disaggregated impacts of off-farm work participation on household vulnerability to food poverty in Ghana. *The Journal of Economic Inequality, 21*(1), 83–104. doi:https://doi.org/10.1007/s10888-022-09543-9

Ankrah Twumasi, M., Zheng, H., Asante, I. O., Ntiamoah, E. B., & Amo-Ntim, G. (2023). The off-farm income and organic food expenditure nexus: Empirical evidence from rural Ghana. *Cogent Food and Agriculture, 9*(1). doi:https://doi.org/10.1080/23311932.2023.2258845

August, U. (2023). *Worldwide Research Methodology and Codebook.*

Behera, D. K., Rahut, D. B., Padmaja, M., & Dash, A. K. (2024). Socioeconomic determinants of happiness: Empirical evidence from developed and developing countries. *Journal of Behavioral and Experimental Economics, 109*, 102187. doi:https://doi.org/10.1016/j.socec.2024.102187

Cattaneo, M. D., Drukker, D. M., & Holland, A. D. (2013). Estimation of multivalued treatment effects under conditional independence. *The Stata Journal, 13*(3), 407–450. doi:https://doi.org/10.1177/1536867X1301300301

Chen, X., & Hu, X. (2024). Crossing the rice–wheat border: Income, gender role attitudes and female subjective well-being. *Asian Journal of Social Psychology, 27*(4), 779–791. https://doi.org/10.1111/ajsp.12637

Clausen, T., Pedersen, L. R. M., Andersen, M. F., Theorell, T., & Madsen, I. E. H. (2022). Job autonomy and psychological well-being: A linear or a non-linear association? *European Journal of Work and Organizational Psychology, 31*(3), 395–405. doi:https://doi.org/10.1080/1359432X.2021.1972973

Das, K. V., Jones-Harrell, C., Fan, Y., Ramaswami, A., Orlove, B., & Botchwey, N. (2020). Understanding subjective well-being: perspectives from psychology and public health. *Public Health Reviews, 41*(1), 1–32. doi:https://doi.org/10.1186/s40985-020-00142-5

Diener, E., Oishi, S., & Tay, L. (2018). Advances in subjective well-being research. *Nature Human Behaviour, 2*(4), 253–260. doi:https://doi.org/10.1038/s41562-018-0307-6

Ding, X., Lu, Q., Li, L., Sarkar, A., & Li, H. (2023). Evaluating the impact of institutional performance and government trust on farmers' subjective well-Being: A case of urban–rural welfare gap perception and family economic status in Shanxi, Sichuan and Anhui, China. *International Journal of Environmental Research and Public Health, 20*(1), 710. doi:https://doi.org/10.3390/ijerph20010710

Fang, M., Mirutse, G., Guo, L., & Ma, X. (2019). Role of socioeconomic status and housing conditions in geriatric depression in rural China: A cross-sectional study. *BMJ Open, 9*(5), 1–8. doi:https://doi.org/10.1136/bmjopen-2018-024046

Gansonre, S. (2021). Welfare impacts of non-farm employment in semi-arid areas: evidence from Burkina Faso. *Heliyon, 7*(10). doi:https://doi.org/10.1016/j.heliyon.2021.e08080

Gao, Y., Jia, Z., Zhao, L., & Han, S. (2023). The effect of activity participation in middle-aged and older people on the trajectory of depression in later life: National cohort study. *JMIR Public Health and Surveillance, 9*(1), e44682. doi:https://doi.org/10.2196/44682

Gracious, N., & Umakrishnan, K. (2025). Rural-urban migration and the well-being of the migrant-sending households: An impact evaluation study. *South African Journal of Economic and Management Sciences, 25*(1), 4120. doi:https://doi.org/10.4102/sajems.v25i1.4120

Gu, H., Li, Y., Wan, S., & Wang, Y. (2025). Spatial patterns and driving factors of interprovincial elderly migration in China. *Progress in Geography, 44*(3), 534–550. https://doi.org/10.18306/dlkxjz.2025.03.008

Hasan, S. I., Yee, A., Rinaldi, A., Azham, A. A., Mohd Hairi, F., & Amer Nordin, A. S. (2021). Prevalence of common mental health issues among migrant workers: A systematic review and meta-analysis. *PLOS ONE, 16*(12), e0260221. doi:https://doi.org/10.1371/journal.pone.0260221

Imbens, G. W. (2000). The role of the propensity score in estimating dose-response functions. *Biometrika, 87*(3), 706–710. doi:https://doi.org/10.1093/biomet/87.3.706

Jang, S., Kim, E. S., Cao, C., Allen, T. D., Cooper, C. L., Lapierre, L. M., O'Driscoll, M. P., Sanchez, J. I., Spector, P. E., Poelmans, S. A. Y., Abarca, N., Alexandrova, M., Antoniou, A.-S., Beham, B., Brough, P., Carikci, I., Ferreiro, P., Fraile, G., Geurts, S., … Woo, J.-M. (2017). Measurement invariance of the satisfaction with life scale across 26 countries. *Journal of Cross-Cultural Psychology, 48*(4), 560–576. doi:https://doi.org/10.1177/0022022117697844

Kanjo, E., Kuss, D. J., & Ang, C. S. (2017). Noti Mind: Utilizing responses to smart phone notifications as affective sensors. *IEEE Access, 5*, 22023–22035. doi:https://doi.org/10.1109/ACCESS.2017.2755661

Leung, S.-O. (2011). A comparison of psychometric properties and normality in 4-, 5-, 6-, and 11-Point Likert Scales. *Journal of Social Service Research, 37*(4), 412–421. doi:https://doi.org/10.1080/01488376.2011.580697

Li, L., Ma, M., Peng, H., Yan, Z., Wang, M., Hu, M., Liu, J., & Zhenhai, Z. (2021). Prevalence and associated factors of depressive symptoms in China's rural elderly. *BMC Geriatrics, 24*, 3432–3438.

Li, Y., & Xu, Y. (2023). Does off-farm work alleviate rural households' energy poverty in China? Comparative analysis based on livelihood patterns. *Journal of Cleaner Production, 427*(October), 139144. doi:https://doi.org/10.1016/j.jclepro.2023.139144

Lips-Wiersma, M., Haar, J., & Cooper–Thomas, H. D. (2022). Is meaningful work always a resource toward wellbeing? The effect of autonomy, security and multiple dimensions of subjective meaningful work on wellbeing. *Personnel Review*, *52*(1), 321–341. doi:https://doi.org/10.1108/PR-10-2020-0754

Ma, W., Zheng, H., Boansi, D., Horlu, G. S. A. K., & Owusu, V. (2025). Types of employment and well-being of rural residents: A multinomial endogenous switching regression application. *Economic Modelling*, *147*, 107047. https://doi.org/10.1016/j.econmod.2025.107047

Marino, M., Rocchi, B., & Severini, S. (2021). Conditional income disparity between farm and non-farm households in the european union: A longitudinal analysis. *Journal of Agricultural Economics*, *72*(2), 589–606. https://doi.org/10.1111/1477-9552.12420

Martela, F., & Ryan, R. M. (2023). Clarifying eudaimonia and psychological functioning to complement evaluative and experiential well-being: Why basic psychological needs should be measured in national accounts of well-being. *Perspectives on Psychological Science*, *18*(5), 1121–1135. doi:https://doi.org/10.1177/17456916221141099

Moro-Egido, A. L., Navarro, M., & Sánchez, A. (2022). Changes in Subjective Well-Being Over Time: Economic and Social Resources do Matter. *Journal of Happiness Studies*, *23*(5), 2009–2038. doi:https://doi.org/10.1007/s10902-021-00473-3

National Bureau of Statistics of China. (2023). *National Economy Withstood Pressure and Reached a New Level in 2022*. National Bureau of Statistics of China. https://www.stats.gov.cn/english/PressRelease/202301/t20230117_1892094.html#:~:text=,1 percent

Niu, F., & Wang, X. (2024). Psychological well-being of rural left-behind women in Northwest China and its associated factors: a regional, population-based study. *Frontiers in Public Health*, *12*(December), 1–11. doi:https://doi.org/10.3389/fpubh.2024.1395996

Nugroho, T. W., Hanani, N., Toiba, H., & Sujarwo, S. (2022). Promoting Subjective Well-Being among Rural and Urban Residents in Indonesia: Does Social Capital Matter? *Sustainability (Switzerland)*, *14*(4). doi:https://doi.org/10.3390/su14042375

Pavot, W., & Diener, E. (1993). Review of the Satisfaction With Life Scale. *Psychological Assessment*, *5*(2), 164–172. doi:https://doi.org/10.1207/s15327752jpa4901

Rocchi, B., Marino, M., & Severini, S. (2021). Does an Income Gap between Farm and Nonfarm Households Still Exist? The Case of the European Union. *Applied Economic Perspectives and Policy*, *43*(4), 1672–1697. https://doi.org/10.1002/aepp.13116

Rowan, A. N. (2023). *World Happiness Report 2023* (Vol. 5, Issue 3).

Ruan, Q. N., Shen, G. H., Xu, S., Xu, D., & Yan, W. J. (2024). Depressive symptoms among rural left-behind children and adolescents in China: A large-scale cross-sectional study. *BMC Public Health*, *24*(1). doi:https://doi.org/10.1186/s12889-024-20699-z

Santor, D. A.. (2004). Center For epidemiologic studies depression scale. *Applied Psychological Measurement*, *1*(3), 385–401. doi:https://doi.org/10.1037/10517-024

Sen, B., Dorosh, P., & Ahmed, M. (2021). Moving out of agriculture in Bangladesh: The role of farm, non-farm and mixed households. *World Development*, *144*, 105479. doi:https://doi.org/10.1016/j.worlddev.2021.105479

Shen, Z., Fang, X., & Zheng, X. (2022). The impact of women's off-farm employment on depressive symptoms: Evidence from rural China. *Social Science & Medicine*, *311*, 115309. https://doi.org/10.1016/j.socscimed.2022.115309

Shen, Z., Shen, Y., Brown, D. S., & Li, J. (2024). Quality of non-farm employment and subjective well-being in rural China. *Current Psychology*, *43*(39), 30556–30570. doi:https://doi.org/10.1007/s12144-024-06678-y

Sun, D., Yang, X., & Qiu, H. (2022). Off-farm work and rural residential energy transition: a farm-household model and empirical evidence from China. *China Agricultural Economic Review*, *14*(4), 816–831. doi:https://doi.org/10.1108/CAER-09-2021-0188

Tian, W., Yan, G., Zhang, X., Shui, D., Liu, T., Yang, J., Li, Z., Hou, H., Zhang, P., Hu, C., Hao, T., Bao, M., Ye, P., Jiang, W., Xiong, S., Yan, L. L., Tian, W., Zhang, J., Ding, D., … Tian, M. (2025). The prevalence, risk factors, awareness and treatment of depression and anxiety among adults aged 30 years and older in rural China: a cross-sectional study. *Journal of Affective Disorders*, *387*, 119516. doi:https://doi.org/10.1016/j.jad.2025.119516

Tov, W., Keh, J. S., Tan, Y. Q., Tan, Q. Y. J., & Aziz, I. A. S. Bin. (2022). Assessing subjective well-being: A review of common measures. *Handbook of Positive Psychology Assessment*. https://ink.library.smu.edu.sg/soss_research/3729

Uglanova, E., & Dettmers, J. (2018). Sustained effects of flexible working time arrangements on subjective well-being. *Journal of Happiness Studies*, *19*(6), 1727–1748. doi:https://doi.org/10.1007/s10902-017-9894-6

Villalonga-Olives, E., Wind, T. R., Armand, A. O., Yirefu, M., Smith, R., & Aldrich, D. P. (2022). Social-capital-based mental health interventions for refugees: A systematic review. *Social Science and Medicine*, *301*(November 2021), 114787. doi:https://doi.org/10.1016/j.socscimed.2022.114787

Wang, Y., Li, S., Zou, X., Ni, Y., Xu, L., Liao, S., Cao, L., Bao, J., Li, Y., & Xi, Y. (2024). Exploration of subgroups and predictors of loneliness among older adults in rural China: A latent profile analysis. *BMC Geriatrics*, *24*(1), 1–10. doi:https://doi.org/10.1186/s12877-024-04812-w

Wang, Z., Zhao, Q., & Ji, Y. (2024). The Impact of Off-Farm Employment Recession and Land on Farmers' Mental Health: Empirical Evidence from Rural China. *Land*, *13*(6), 837. doi:https://doi.org/10.3390/land13060837

Watema, J. R. A., Siele, R. K., & Kimitei, E. (2025). Non-farm income and household welfare: Empirical evidence from a developing economy. *Wellbeing, Space and Society*, *8*, 100232. https://doi.org/10.1016/j.wss.2024.100232

Watson, D., Clark, L. A., & Tellegen, A. (1988). Development and validation of brief measures of positive and negative affect: The PANAS scales. *Journal of Personality and Social Psychology*, *54*(6), 1063–1070. doi:https://doi.org/10.1037/0022-3514.54.6.1063

Wheatley, D. (2017). Autonomy in paid work and employee subjective well-being. *Work and Occupations*, *44*(3), 296–328. doi:https://doi.org/10.1177/0730888417697232

Xing, C., Yuan, X., & Zhang, J. (2022). City size, family migration, and gender wage gap: Evidence from rural–urban migrants in China. *Regional Science and Urban Economics*, *97*, 103834. https://doi.org/10.1016/j.regsciurbeco.2022.103834

Xiong, Y., Li, X., Li, H., Qu, C., Liu, M., Lu, C., & Dong, W. (2024). A meta-analysis of loneliness among left-behind children in China. *Current Psychology*, *43*(12), 10660–10668. doi:https://doi.org/10.1007/s12144-023-04882-w

Xu, H., Zhang, C., & Huang, Y. (2023). Social trust, social capital, and subjective well-being of rural residents: micro-empirical evidence based on the Chinese General Social Survey (CGSS). *Humanities and Social Sciences Communications*, *10*(1). doi:https://doi.org/10.1057/s41599-023-01532-1

Yang, D., Zheng, G., Wang, H., & Li, M. (2022). Education, income, and happiness: Evidence from China. *Frontiers in Public Health*, *10*, 1–10. doi:https://doi.org/10.3389/fpubh.2022.855327

Zhang, W. (2022). Social capital, income and subjective well-being: Evidence in rural China. *Heliyon*, *8*(1). doi:https://doi.org/10.1016/j.heliyon.2021.e08705

Zheng, H., Zhou, Y., & Rahut, D. B. (2023). Smartphone use, off-farm employment, and women's decision-making power: Evidence from rural China. *Review of Development Economics*, *27*(3), 1327–1353. https://doi.org/10.1111/rode.12966

Zhou, X., Chen, S., Chen, L., & Li, L. (2021). Social class identity, public service satisfaction, and happiness of residents: The mediating role of social trust. *Frontiers in Psychology*, *12*, 1–14. doi:https://doi.org/10.3389/fpsyg.2021.659657

Zhou, D., Zhang, Q., & Li, J. (2024). Impact of informal employment on individuals' psychological well-being: microevidence from China. *International Journal of Mental Health Systems*, *18*(1), 29. doi:https://doi.org/10.1186/s13033-024-00648-4

Wanglin Ma is a Full Professor of Applied Economics at the Department of Global Value Chains and Trade, Faculty of Agribusiness and Commerce, Lincoln University, New Zealand. His research spans agricultural and development economics, with a strong emphasis on identifying strategies that enhance farm performance, strengthen the sustainability of the agrifood systems, improve household welfare and farmers' subjective well-being, and promote sustainable rural and agricultural development. He earned his PhD in Agricultural Economics from the University of Kiel, Germany, and has authored more than 160 articles in leading international journals.

Chapter 4
Clean Energy Use for Heating and Rural Subjective Well-Being in China: Implications for Energy Transition

Xiance Sang, Xiaofeng Luo, Hongyun Zheng, and Wanglin Ma

4.1 Introduction

In many developing and transition economies, household heating—especially in rural and cold regions—continues to rely heavily on non-clean fuels (e.g., coal, biomass, and firewood). Globally, more than two billion people still rely on non-clean fuels for residential energy use, with heating accounting for a considerable share of demand in cold-climate areas (IEA, IRENA, UNSD, World Bank, WHO 2025). This persistent reliance has severe public health consequences, leading to an estimated 3.2 million premature deaths each year through increased exposure to household air pollution, which is closely associated with major non-communicable diseases, including stroke, ischemic heart disease, chronic obstructive pulmonary disease, and lung cancer (Li et al. 2024a, b). Beyond health impacts, the widespread use of carbon-intensive fuels also poses a significant challenge to the decarbonization of residential energy systems, particularly in some transition economies such as Kazakhstan (Kapsalyamova et al. 2025), Mongolia (Namkhainyam et al. 2024), and China (Huang et al. 2025).

X. Sang
College of Economics and Management, Zhejiang A&F University, Hangzhou, China
e-mail: sangxiance@zafu.edu.cn

X. Luo (✉) · H. Zheng
College of Economics and Management, Huazhong Agricultural University, Wuhan, China
e-mail: luoxiaofeng@mail.hzau.edu.cn

H. Zheng
e-mail: Hongyun.Zheng@mail.hzau.edu.cn

W. Ma
Department of Global Value Chains and Trade, Faculty of Agribusiness and Commerce, Lincoln University, Christchurch, New Zealand
e-mail: Wanglin.Ma@lincoln.ac.nz

W. Ma et al. (eds.), *Beyond Income*, Contributions to Economics,
https://doi.org/10.1007/978-981-92-4957-2_4

Existing studies have documented a range of observable gains from clean heating energy transitions, including reductions in air pollution (Salvo et al. 2024) and carbon emissions (Hao and Qiao 2025), as well as improvements in physical health (Liao et al. 2025). Meanwhile, some evidence suggests potential adverse effects, notably higher heating costs, which may offset the benefits of clean energy use and place additional financial pressure (Xie et al. 2022; Zhu et al. 2025). These cost-related concerns highlight the burden of uneven welfare outcomes under clean heating energy transitions (Fan et al. 2022; Xie et al. 2022; Meng et al. 2023). Despite the increased visible costs, many households continue to use clean energy for heating, suggesting potential unrecognized benefits. For example, subjective well-being, though invisible, captures individuals' overall life satisfaction and lived experiences (Li and Hu 2026; Nakagomi et al. 2026). Focusing on the impact of clean energy use on subjective well-being is therefore beneficial for understanding the broader influences of energy transitions on rural households.

A small but growing body of research has explored the relationship between household energy transitions and subjective well-being. Focusing on heating energy, Barrington-Leigh et al. (2019) showed that replacing coal with electric heating improves life satisfaction among rural households in China. Building on this evidence, Xie and Zhou (2021) demonstrated that improvements in indoor temperature, affordability, and convenience play a key role in shaping Chinese residents' subjective evaluations of clean heating programs. Turning to cooking energy, Ma et al. (2022) found that using clean cooking fuels significantly enhances the happiness and life satisfaction of rural residents in China. Further Liu et al. (2024a, b) quantified the happiness benefits of the cooking energy transition, showing that these positive effects are more noticeable among females, rural residents, and low-income households in China. Nduka and Jimoh (2024) documented that access to clean cooking energy is positively associated with women's happiness and life satisfaction in Nigeria. These studies suggest that transitioning to clean energy can improve subjective well-being. However, research specifically focusing on clean energy use for heating remains limited.

Another potential source of inconsistency arises from the simplified treatment of clean energy use for heating as a binary decision (Chen and Wang 2026; Xu et al. 2026). In reality, rural households often undergo partial or incomplete transitions, combining clean and non-clean heating energy sources (Villafranca et al. 2025; Zheng et al. 2025; Mao et al. 2026). Failing to account for this heterogeneity may obscure essential differences in households' experiences, potentially explaining the mixed findings in the existing literature. Thus, distinguishing between partial and complete clean energy transition is also crucial for gaining a more accurate understanding of the impacts on household well-being.

Therefore, this study aims: (a) to evaluate the impacts of clean energy use for heating on subjective well-being, measured by happiness and life satisfaction, using an endogenous switching regression (ESR) model; and (b) to explore the heterogeneity in outcomes by distinguishing between partial and complete transitions to clean energy using a multivalued treatment effects (MVTE) framework. We use household survey data collected in China for empirical analysis.

This study makes three contributions to the literature. First, it provides novel micro-level evidence on how the use of clean energy for heating affects the subjective well-being of rural residents, complementing existing studies that have primarily emphasized environmental or technical outcomes (Wang and Wei 2024; Yan et al. 2025). Second, this study distinguishes between partial and complete transitions to clean energy. The partial transition involves using both clean and non-clean energy sources, whereas the complete transition involves using only clean energy sources. This addresses the limitations of previous research, which treated clean energy adoption for heating as a binary decision (Xie and Zhou 2021; Uribe et al. 2023). Third, we examine the potential mechanisms through which clean energy use for heating influences subjective well-being, including the benefits of improved indoor temperature and health versus the increased heating energy cost (Barrington-Leigh et al. 2019; Wang et al. 2025).

China provides a critical context for examining household heating energy transitions, particularly given the country's heavy reliance on coal and other non-renewable fuels such as firewood, especially in its northern regions (Su and Tan 2023). The widespread use of solid fuels for residential heating produces harmful emissions that severely impact air quality and public health (Niu et al. 2024; Shen and Sun 2025). Severe winter smog episodes have become common in northern China, posing significant challenges to sustainable development (Han et al. 2024; Wang et al. 2024). Rural households in northern China face high heating costs and health risks from using polluting heating sources (Jin et al. 2026; Yan 2026). Examining subjective well-being, therefore, offers a more comprehensive view of how these changes affect daily life.

The remainder of the paper is structured as follows. Section 4.2 develops the conceptual framework and outlines the estimation strategies. Section 4.3 describes the data and presents the descriptive statistics. Section 4.4 reports the empirical findings. Section 4.5 concludes with key policy implications.

4.2 Conceptual Framework and Empirical Strategies

4.2.1 Conceptual Framework

This study conceptualizes three pathways through which clean energy use for heating affects subjective well-being: health status, indoor temperature, and heating energy cost. Figure 4.1 illustrates these pathways and their influence on rural residents' subjective well-being.

The first pathway indicates that clean energy use for heating can improve health outcomes, which, in turn, enhance subjective well-being. The use of solid fuels, such as coal and biomass, for heating generates indoor air pollution, exposing residents to harmful pollutants that increase the risk of respiratory and cardiovascular diseases

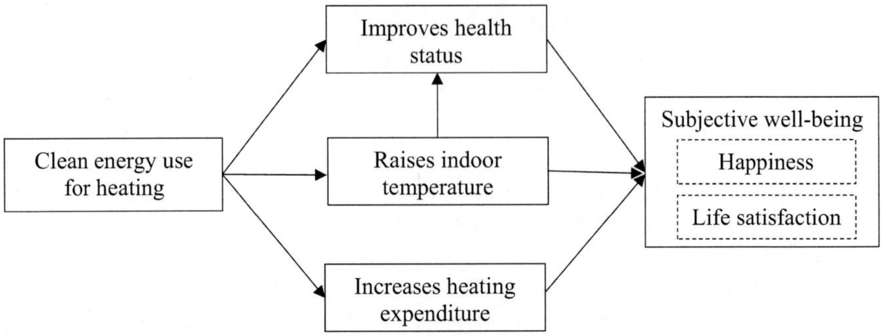

Fig. 4.1 The relationship between clean energy use for heating and subjective well-being. *Source* Authors

(Pei et al. 2026; Wu et al. 2026). Using clean energy for heating reduces these emissions, improving indoor air quality and supporting better physical health (Pillarisetti et al. 2022; Yang et al. 2024). Given that health is a crucial determinant of subjective well-being, improvements in health are a key mechanism through which clean energy use for heating enhances subjective well-being (Nie et al. 2021; Li et al. 2024a, b).

The second pathway demonstrates that clean energy use for heating can enhance subjective well-being by improving indoor temperature. Clean heating energy sources, such as electricity or natural gas, provide more stable, controllable heat than traditional solid fuels. This allows households to maintain higher and more consistent indoor temperatures, which improves thermal comfort, reduces cold-related health risks, and enhances daily living conditions (Chen et al. 2023; Janssen et al. 2023; Yao et al. 2024). Grimes et al. (2024) demonstrated that increases in indoor temperature significantly improve people's happiness and life satisfaction, while thermal discomfort reduces overall well-being in New Zealand. Furthermore, a recent systematic review confirms that cold indoor environments harm multiple dimensions of well-being (Janssen et al. 2023). Thus, better indoor warmth is expected to contribute to higher levels of subjective well-being (Grimes et al. 2024).

The third pathway suggests that higher heating costs associated with clean energy use may negatively affect subjective well-being. Clean energy sources, such as electricity and natural gas, tend to be more expensive than non-clean sources like coal, which can lead to higher heating costs. For low-income or financially constrained households, this added financial strain may induce energy-related stress and limit other essential consumption, thereby reducing subjective well-being. This mechanism aligns with the energy poverty literature, which suggests that high energy costs can offset the benefits of improved indoor conditions and health, ultimately harming subjective well-being (Welsch and Biermann 2017; Qiu et al. 2024).

The magnitude of these mechanisms may be influenced by the degree of clean energy transition. Households that fully transition to clean energy for heating are likely to experience more significant improvements in indoor temperature and health outcomes. In contrast, those employing partial or mixed heating strategies may see limited benefits. However, exclusive reliance on clean energy may also intensify financial pressure due to higher heating costs. These heterogeneous effects underscore the importance of distinguishing between different levels of clean energy use.

4.2.2 Estimation Strategies

4.2.2.1 Endogenous Switching Regression Model

The first objective of this study is to assess the impact of clean energy use for heating on the subjective well-being of rural residents. However, rural residents decide for themselves whether to use clean energy for heating. This self-selection induces endogeneity of the clean energy use variable. To address this endogeneity issue, we employ the endogenous switching regression (ESR) model, which effectively accounts for both observed and unobserved factors that may influence utilization decisions (Zheng and Ma 2024; Miao et al. 2026).

The ESR model framework consists of one selection equation and two outcome equations. As outlined by Lokshin and Sajaia (2004), the model for rural households' clean energy use for heating can be specified as follows:

$$P_i^* = \alpha Z_i + \mu_i, withP_i = \begin{cases} 1, if\ P_i^* > 0 \\ 0, otherwise \end{cases} \tag{4.1}$$

where P_i^* is an unobserved latent variable representing the propensity of the household i to use clean energy for heating. The observed variable P_i takes the value of one for users and zero for non-users; Z_i denotes a set of exogenous explanatory variables that influence households' decisions to use clean energy for heating; and μ_i is an error term.

In this study, we control for a set of household head, household, housing, and regional characteristics for Z_i. Household head characteristics include age, gender, and education, capturing demographic attributes and human capital (Ren et al. 2025; Stahlmann-Brown et al. 2025). Household-level controls comprise household size, dependency ratio, household income, and car ownership, reflecting family composition, economic capacity, and asset endowment (Mohetaer et al. 2025; Zhang et al. 2025). We also account for housing characteristics, including housing age, housing area, and housing structure, which are closely related to heating demand and energy efficiency (Wang and Xie 2023). Finally, city dummy variables are included to control for unobserved regional heterogeneity associated with climatic conditions, energy infrastructure, and local policy environments (Zheng and Zhou 2025).

In the second stage, we specify two separate outcome equations: one for households that have used clean energy for heating and another for those that have not.

$$Y_{1i} = \alpha_1 X_{1i} + \varepsilon_{1i} \text{ if } P = 1 \quad (4.2a)$$

$$Y_{0i} = \alpha_0 X_{0i} + \varepsilon_{0i} \text{ if } P = 0 \quad (4.2b)$$

where Y_{1i} and Y_{0i} represent the subjective well-being outcomes (e.g., happiness or life satisfaction) for clean energy users and non-users, respectively. X_i is a vector of variables expected to influence the outcome variables; α_1 and α_0 are vectors of unknown parameters; and ε_{1i} and ε_{0i} are the random error terms.

The ESR model addresses selection bias arising from unobservable factors by calculating inverse Mills ratios (IMRs) after estimating the selection Eq. (4.1) and including them in the outcome Eqs. (4.2a) and (4.2b). Intuitively, the IMR accounts for the fact that clean energy users and non-users are not randomly drawn from the population. Unobservable characteristics—such as households' risk preferences, attitudes toward new heating technologies, or expectations about future heating costs—can influence both the decision to use clean energy and subjective well-being. The IMR term captures this non-random selection and adjusts the outcome equations accordingly, ensuring that these unobserved factors do not confound any differences in subjective well-being between users and non-users (Lokshin and Sajaia 2004; Ahmadzai and Morrissey 2025). Equations (4.2a) and (4.2b) are, therefore, rewritten as follows:

$$Y_{1i} = \alpha_1 X_{1i} + \sigma_{u\varepsilon_1}\lambda_{1i} + \varepsilon_{1i} \text{ if } P = 1 \quad (4.3a)$$

$$Y_{0i} = \alpha_0 X_{0i} + \sigma_{u\varepsilon_0}\lambda_{0i} + \varepsilon_{0i} \text{ if } P = 0 \quad (4.3b)$$

where λ_{1i} and λ_{0i} are the inverse Mills ratios, which capture the selection bias arising from unobservable factors; $\sigma_{u\varepsilon_1}$ and $\sigma_{u\varepsilon_0}$ are the covariance terms, defined as $\sigma_{u\varepsilon_1} = \text{cov}(\mu_i, \varepsilon_{1i})$ and $\sigma_{u\varepsilon_0} = \text{cov}(\mu_i, \varepsilon_{0i})$, respectively; and ε_{1i} and ε_{0i} are error terms. The selection Eq. (4.1) and the outcome Eqs. (4.3a) and (4.3b) are estimated simultaneously using the full information maximum likelihood (FIML) estimator. The ESR estimation process generates correlation coefficients, $\rho_{u\varepsilon_1}$ and $\rho_{u\varepsilon_0}$, to identify the existence of selection bias from unobservable factors. Specifically, selection bias exists if $\rho_{u\varepsilon_1}$ or $\rho_{u\varepsilon_0}$ is statistically significant.

The regression results from the ESR model reveal the differential effects of various factors on the subjective well-being of clean energy users and non-users. Based on these estimates, a counterfactual analysis framework is used to compare subjective well-being across the actual and counterfactual scenarios. The expected subjective well-being in the observed scenario and the expected outcome in the counterfactual scenario (i.e., the expected subjective well-being of users had they not used) are predicted as follows:

$$E(Y_{1i}|P = 1) = \alpha_1 X_{1i} + \sigma_{u\varepsilon_1}\lambda_{1i} \quad (4.4a)$$

$$E(Y_{0i}|P = 1) = \alpha_0 X_{1i} + \sigma_{u\varepsilon_0}\lambda_{1i} \tag{4.4b}$$

This allows for the estimation of the average treatment effect on the treated (ATT). The ATT can be expressed as the difference between Eq. (4.4a) and Eq. (4.4b):

$$ATT = E(Y_{1i}|P = 1) - E(Y_{0i}|P = 1) = X_{1i}(\alpha_1 - \alpha_0) + \lambda_{1i}(\sigma_{u\varepsilon_1} - \sigma_{u\varepsilon_0}) \tag{4.5}$$

For model identification, at least one instrumental variable (IV) should be included in Eq. (4.1) but excluded from Eqs. (4.2a) and (4.2b). A valid IV should be correlated with clean energy use for heating while remaining uncorrelated with subjective well-being. Following prior studies (Guta et al. 2024; Feng 2025), this paper uses the village-level utilization rate of clean energy for heating as the IV. This variable reflects the diffusion of clean energy for heating within the community. It is unlikely to directly affect subjective well-being, as residents' well-being is primarily influenced by their own heating choices rather than by other households' decisions in the village. The strong correlation between the IV and the endogenous variable is theoretically supported by previous research, such as Zhu et al. (2022), which highlights the significant role of peer effects in influencing households' energy use and technology adoption decisions in rural China. To validate the selected IV, we conducted a falsification test following Di Falco et al. (2011). The falsification test results reported in the Appendix indicate that the IV has a positive and significant effect on clean energy use for heating. Furthermore, the IV does not have a statistically significant impact on happiness or life satisfaction among non-users.

4.2.2.2 Multivalued Treatment Effects Model

The second objective is to estimate the impact of different levels of clean heating energy transition—no transition, partial transition, and complete transition—on the subjective well-being of rural households. Since the treatment variable involves more than two options, binary treatment models are inadequate for capturing the heterogeneity across multiple transition levels. To overcome this limitation, we draw on recent studies that use multivalued treatment frameworks and apply the multivalued treatment effects (MVTE) model to estimate the impact of varying transition intensities (Ma et al. 2024; Rahman et al. 2025).

We assume that each household chooses one of the three mutually exclusive transition levels to maximize its expected utility from heating. Household decisions to adopt a particular clean heating energy transition level are modeled using a multinomial logit (MNL) model, as follows:

$$P_{ij} = \frac{exp(Z_i\beta_j)}{\sum_{j=1}^{3} exp(Z_i\beta_j)} \tag{4.6}$$

where P_{ij} represents the probability that household i chooses the energy transition type j, with $j = 1$ for no transition, $j = 2$ for partial transition, and $j = 3$ for complete transition; Z_i denotes a set of household head, household, housing, and regional characteristics; and β_j represents the corresponding parameters. The parameters of the MNL model, as presented in Eq. (4.6), are estimated using a maximum likelihood method. At this stage, the generalized propensity (GP) scores are calculated.

In the second stage, the GP scores from the MNL model are used to assign weights to observations, creating a sample in which covariates are balanced across all treatment groups. The MVTE model then estimates the treatment effects of different levels of clean heating energy transition on subjective well-being. Conditional on the selected covariates Z_i, the ATT for households receiving the transition level j is specified as follows:

$$ATT_j = E\left[(Y_j - Y_0)|Z_i\right] \tag{4.7}$$

where Y_0 represents the potential outcome for the control group (i.e., households with no transition), and Y_j denotes the potential outcome for the treated group (i.e., households experiencing partial or complete transition). In this study, we employ the Inverse-Probability-Weighted Regression Adjustment (IPWRA) estimator to estimate Eq. (4.7). The IPWRA estimator is double-robust, meaning that the estimated treatment effects remain consistent and unbiased as long as either the treatment model or the outcome model is correctly specified (Zhou and Ma 2022).

4.3 Data Collection, Variables, and Descriptive Statistics

4.3.1 Data Collection

The data used in this study were obtained from a field survey conducted in China between May and June 2024. A stratified random sampling strategy was employed. In the first stage, four cities—Jinan and Dezhou in Shandong Province, Yangquan in Shanxi Province, and Anyang in Henan Province—were purposively selected. In China, using clean energy for heating has been progressively elevated to a national policy priority. The Plan for Clean Winter Heating in Northern Regions (2017–2021) provided a unified framework for policy implementation, leading to the rapid adoption of clean heating technologies. Jinan was among the first batch of national clean-heating pilot cities designated in 2017, while Yangquan, Dezhou, and Anyang were included in the second batch in 2018. In the second stage, one to two counties were purposively chosen within each city, followed by the random selection of one to four townships per county. Subsequently, one to five villages were randomly sampled within each township, and 20–30 households were randomly selected for interview in each village.

To ensure the reliability and accuracy of the information collected, all interviews were conducted face-to-face by trained enumerators using a structured questionnaire. The household financial manager was identified as the primary respondent, as this individual was most knowledgeable about household energy use and socio-economic conditions. A total of 945 observations were valid after excluding households that used centralized heating and cases with missing key information.

4.3.2 Variable Measurements

4.3.2.1 Subjective Well-Being Outcomes

Following prior studies (Gao et al. 2025; Zheng and Zhou 2025), this study employs two widely used outcomes of subjective well-being: happiness and life satisfaction. Happiness is measured using the question: "*Overall, to what extent do you think you are happy?*" Respondents rate their happiness on a 1–10 scale, with higher values indicating greater happiness. Life satisfaction is measured through the question: "*Overall, how satisfied are you with your current life?*" using the same 1–10 scale, where higher scores denote higher satisfaction. The two variables capture different dimensions of well-being. Happiness reflects the affective or emotional dimension, capturing short-term feelings and momentary affective states (Diener et al. 2003; Neve and Oswald 2012). In contrast, life satisfaction represents the cognitive dimension of well-being, defined as individuals' deliberate, evaluative judgment of their overall quality of life, which is more stable and long-term in nature (Chui and Wong 2016; Zhang et al. 2017).

4.3.2.2 Clean Energy Use for Heating

We consider two treatment variables. The first treatment variable is a binary indicator equal to one if a household primarily uses clean fuels for heating (either jointly uses clean and non-clean fuels or uses clean fuels only), and zero if a household relies exclusively on non-clean fuels. The clean energy used for heating in this study includes electricity, natural gas, or methanol. Non-clean energy sources include firewood, charcoal, and coal.

The second treatment variable is a multivalued variable that captures variation in the degree of clean energy transition. We refine clean energy users by distinguishing among samples that combine clean and non-clean fuels and those that use only clean fuels. This yields three categories: no transition (use only non-clean fuels), partial transition (jointly use clean and non-clean fuels), and complete transition to clean energy (use only clean fuels).

4.3.3 Descriptive Statistics

Table 4.1 reports the descriptive statistics for the variables used in the analysis. On average, respondents report a happiness score of 7.61 and a life satisfaction score of 7.54. Clean energy use for heating is prevalent in the sample, with 83.6% of households primarily relying on clean fuels. Household heads are, on average, 61 years old, 56.6% are male, and they have completed 7.5 years of schooling. Households consist of four members with a dependency ratio of 0.72, and the mean per capita income is 18,319 yuan. About 41.3% of households own a car. The average housing age is 26 years, the mean housing area is 134.6 m^2 (log-transformed value = 4.789), and 10.7% of residences are reinforced-concrete structures. City-level shares indicate that 21.9, 27.7, 20.9, and 29.5% of sampled households reside in Yangquan, Jinan, Dezhou, and Anyang, respectively.

Table 4.2 compares the characteristics of households that primarily use clean energy for heating with those that do not. Significant differences emerge across multiple dimensions. Clean-energy users report higher levels of happiness and life satisfaction and tend to be younger and better educated than non-users. They also have larger households, lower dependency ratios, higher per capita income, and a greater likelihood of owning a car. In terms of housing conditions, users are more likely to reside in reinforced-concrete dwellings, though housing age and housing area do not differ significantly between the two groups. Overall, the descriptive differences indicate systematic variation, underscoring the need to account for potential selection bias in the empirical analysis.

4.4 Empirical Results

4.4.1 Treatment Effects of Clean Energy Use for Heating on Subjective Well-Being

The first objective of this study is to assess the impact of clean energy use for heating on rural residents' subjective well-being. This estimate is based on the ESR model, which simultaneously identifies the determinants of clean energy use and the factors influencing subjective well-being among both users and non-users. The estimated coefficients from both the selection and outcome equations are reported in the Appendix. For brevity, we do not discuss each coefficient individually. Notably, the statistically significant estimates of $\rho_{u\varepsilon_1}$ indicate the presence of unobserved selection bias, thereby validating the use of the ESR framework (Zhao et al. 2025; Zhang et al. 2026).

Table 4.3 reports the average treatment effects on the treated (ATTs) of clean energy use for heating on subjective well-being. The estimated ATT for happiness is 0.456, implying that using clean energy for heating increases happiness by 6.27% relative to the counterfactual group without it. For life satisfaction, the ATT is 0.584.

Table 4.1 Variable definitions and descriptive statistics

Variables	Definition	Mean (S.D.)
Dependent variables		
Happiness	Happiness level at the 10-point scale: from 1 = very unhappy to 10 = very happy	7.611 (1.367)
Life satisfaction	Life satisfaction at the 10-point scale: from 1 = very unsatisfied to 10 = very satisfied	7.540 (1.377)
Binary Treatment variable		
Clean energy use for heating	1 if household primarily uses clean fuels (e.g., electricity, natural gas, and methanol) for heating; 0 otherwise	0.836 (0.370)
Multivalued treatment variables		
No transition	1 = Household only uses non-clean fuels for heating, 0 = otherwise	0.164 (0.370)
Partial transition	1 = Household jointly uses clean and non-clean fuels for heating, 0 = otherwise	0.083 (0.275)
Complete transition	1 = Household only uses clean fuels for heating, 0 = otherwise	0.753 (0.431)
Control variables		
Age	Age of household head (HH) (years)	60.914 (11.852)
Gender	1 if the HH is male, 0 otherwise	0.566 (0.496)
Education	Education experience of HH (years)	7.512 (3.763)
Household size	Number of members in a household (persons)	4.172 (2.157)
Dependency ratio	Ratio of the number of members aged under 14 and over 65 to the number of members aged 15 to 64	0.719 (0.648)
Household income	Total household income (1000 yuan/capita)[a]	18.319 (27.095)
Car ownership	1 if household owns a car, 0 otherwise	0.413 (0.493)
Housing age	Housing age (years)	26.026 (14.584)
Housing area	Housing area (square meters), log	4.789 (0.477)
Housing structure	1 if housing load-bearing structure is reinforced concrete, 0 otherwise	0.107 (0.309)
Yangquan	1 if household lives in Yangquan city, 0 otherwise	0.219 (0.414)
Jinan	1 if household lives in Jinan city, 0 otherwise	0.277 (0.448)

(continued)

Table 4.1 (continued)

Variables	Definition	Mean (S.D.)
Dezhou	1 if household lives in Dezhou city, 0 otherwise	0.209 (0.406)
Anyang	1 if household lives in Anyang city, 0 otherwise	0.295 (0.456)
Instrumental variable		
IV	Proportion of households primarily using clean energy for heating among surveyed samples within the village	0.836 (0.201)
Variables used for mediation analysis		
Health status	Health status at the 5-point scale: from 1 = very unhealthy to 5 = very healthy	3.421 (1.053)
Indoor temperature	Average indoor temperature during the 2023–2024 heating season (°C)	17.670 (3.042)
Heating energy cost	Expenditure on heating during the 2023–2024 heating season (1000 yuan)	1.770 (1.267)

Note S.D. refers to the standard deviation
Source Authors
[a]yuan is a Chinese currency (1 USD = 7.13 yuan in 2023)

The finding suggests that using clean energy increases rural residents' life satisfaction by 8.25%. These results are consistent with existing evidence indicating that transitions from solid to clean household energy improve well-being (Liu et al. 2024a, b; Nduka and Jimoh 2024).

We also find that the treatment effects of using clean energy for heating are larger for life satisfaction than for happiness. The larger effect size for life satisfaction compared with happiness aligns with the conceptual distinction between the two indicators: happiness reflects short-term affective states, whereas life satisfaction captures more stable, long-term cognitive evaluations of overall life quality (Diener et al. 2003; Neve and Oswald 2012). Clean energy use for heating may exert a greater influence on residents' broader assessments of living conditions than on their immediate emotional experiences.

Three reasons can explain the positive relationship between clean energy use and rural residents' subjective well-being. First, clean energy sources (e.g., electricity, natural gas, and methanol) substantially reduce indoor air pollution compared with traditional solid fuels such as coal or firewood (Xu et al. 2026). Lower exposure to smoke and particulate matter alleviates respiratory discomfort, headaches, eye irritation, and fatigue (Dida and Abuom 2022; Bisui et al. 2024; Radbel et al. 2024), which directly improves daily physical well-being. Better health and thermal comfort are closely linked to higher reported happiness and life satisfaction, especially in rural households that use heating intensively during cold seasons. Second, traditional heating fuels often require time-consuming collection, transportation, and handling (Alnour et al. 2026; Liao et al. 2026). Clean energy

Table 4.2 Mean differences in selected variables between users and non-users of clean energy for heating

Variables	Users	Non-users	Mean difference
Happiness	7.730	7.000	0.730***
Life satisfaction	7.662	6.916	0.746***
Age	60.171	64.703	−4.532***
Gender	0.576	0.516	0.060
Education	7.711	6.497	1.215***
Household size	4.246	3.800	0.446**
Dependency ratio	0.693	0.849	−0.156***
Household income	18.987	14.920	4.067*
Car ownership	0.430	0.323	0.108**
Housing age	25.966	26.335	−0.370
Housing area	4.799	4.737	0.062
Housing structure	0.119	0.045	0.074***
Yangquan	0.237	0.129	0.108***
Jinan	0.251	0.413	−0.162***
Dezhou	0.185	0.329	−0.144***
Anyang	0.328	0.129	0.199***
IV	0.884	0.590	0.294***
Health status	3.523	2.903	0.620***
Indoor temperature	17.967	16.155	1.812***
Heating energy cost	1.798	1.626	0.172

Note *** $p < 0.01$, ** $p < 0.05$, * $p < 0.10$
Source Authors

Table 4.3 ATTs of clean energy use for heating on happiness and life satisfaction: ESR model estimates

Variables	Mean outcomes		ATT	Change (%)
	Actual	Counterfactual		
Happiness	7.729	7.273	0.456***	6.27
Life satisfaction	7.663	7.079	0.584***	8.25

Note *** $p < 0.01$. ATT refers to average treatment effects on the treated
Source Authors

systems are typically more convenient, reliable, and less physically demanding. By reducing the drudgery associated with fuel use, clean energy frees time and energy for leisure, social interaction, or income-generating activities—factors that are well known to enhance subjective well-being. Third, clean energy provides more stable and predictable heating. This reduces uncertainty related to fuel shortages, price volatility, or weather-dependent fuel collection. Lower energy-related stress improves emotional well-being, contributing to both short-term happiness and longer-term life satisfaction.

4.4.2 Robustness Check

To verify the robustness of our results in Table 4.3, we re-estimated the ATTs using an alternative instrumental variable: neighbors' utilization of clean energy for heating, collected through a question asking whether nearby households had used clean energy for heating. Peer behavior is theoretically relevant for decisions of using clean energy for heating in rural settings and does not directly affect respondents' subjective well-being, thereby satisfying both relevance and exogeneity conditions (Gu 2022). The corresponding ATT estimates reported in the Appendix show that using clean energy for heating increases rural residents' happiness and life satisfaction by 9.97% and 9.49%, respectively. These findings confirm the robustness of our estimates in Table 4.3.

4.4.3 Mediation Analysis

While the findings above establish that clean energy use for heating improves rural residents' subjective well-being, understanding the underlying transmission channels remains essential. As outlined earlier, we consider three potential mechanisms: health status, indoor temperature, and heating energy cost. The definitions of these three variables are presented in the lower part of Table 4.1. To quantify their mediating roles, we estimate a generalized structural equation (GSE) model with 5000 bootstrap replications. The GSE framework is well-suited for our setting because it allows the three mediators to be estimated jointly and does not require the outcome variable to be normally distributed (Li et al. 2025). This specification enables us to decompose the total effect into direct and indirect components associated with each transmission channel.

The results for happiness are reported in the upper panel of Table 4.4. The estimates indicate that the coefficients for the direct and total effects of clean energy use are 0.271 and 0.577, respectively, implying that clean energy adoption for heating explains approximately 47% of the total improvement in happiness. Put differently, 53% of the happiness gains associated with clean energy use are transmitted through the mediating channels of health status, indoor temperature, and heating energy costs. Specifically, the estimated coefficients for health status and indoor temperature are 0.205 and 0.121, respectively, suggesting that clean energy use improves rural residents' health and indoor thermal comfort, contributing 36% and 21%, respectively, to the overall increase in happiness. By contrast, the coefficient for heating energy cost is −0.020 and statistically significant, indicating that clean energy use is associated with higher heating expenditures, which partially offsets the positive effects on happiness.

The results for life satisfaction are presented in the lower panel of Table 4.4. The coefficients for the direct and total effects of clean energy use are 0.306 and 0.593, respectively, indicating that clean energy adoption accounts for approximately 52% of the total gains in life satisfaction. Consequently, the remaining 48% of the improvement in life satisfaction is mediated through health status, indoor temperature, and heating energy costs. More specifically, the coefficients for health status and indoor temperature are 0.196 and 0.110, respectively, suggesting that improvements in health and indoor thermal conditions contribute 33 and 19%, respectively, to the observed increase in life satisfaction. Similar to the happiness results, the coefficient for heating energy cost is negative (−0.019) and statistically significant, implying that higher heating costs associated with clean energy use dampen, but do not outweigh, its overall positive effect on life satisfaction.

Taken together, these results suggest that clean energy adoption improves rural well-being primarily by enhancing health and living conditions, while higher energy costs act as a modest countervailing force. The coexistence of strong positive health and comfort effects with a weaker negative cost effect explains why the net impact on happiness and life satisfaction remains positive and significant. This nuanced mechanism underscores the importance of complementary policies—such as targeted

Table 4.4 Mediation analysis

Mediators	Coefficient	Bootstrapped SE	95% confidence intervals	
			Lower	Upper
Outcome = Happiness				
Direct effects	0.271**	0.113	0.050	0.493
Total indirect effects	0.306***	0.055	0.199	0.413
Health status	0.205***	0.048	0.111	0.299
Indoor temperature	0.121***	0.031	0.060	0.181
Heating energy cost	-0.020*	0.011	-0.041	0.001
Total effects	0.577***	0.124	0.335	0.820
Outcome = Life satisfaction				
Direct effects	0.306***	0.115	0.080	0.531
Total indirect effects	0.287***	0.053	0.184	0.391
Health status	0.196***	0.046	0.105	0.287
Indoor temperature	0.110***	0.029	0.054	0.167
Heating energy cost	-0.019*	0.011	-0.054	0.002
Total effects	0.593***	0.127	0.345	0.841

Note *** $p < 0.01$, ** $p < 0.05$, * $p < 0.10$
Source Authors

subsidies or pricing support—to ease cost burdens and maximize the well-being returns of clean energy transitions.

4.4.4 *Treatment Effects of Energy Transitions on Subjective Well-Being*

The second objective of this study is to estimate the effects of energy transition on the subjective well-being of rural residents. The ATT estimates from the MVTE model reported in Table 4.5 indicate that only a complete transition to clean energy leads to statistically significant improvements in both happiness and life satisfaction. Specifically, switching from non-clean to clean energy (i.e., complete transition) increases happiness and life satisfaction by 8.4% and 8.94%, respectively. However, the partial transition to clean energy (i.e., switching from non-clean to mixed clean and non-clean energy) does not significantly affect rural residents' happiness and life satisfaction. This pattern is consistent with evidence from Ma et al. (2022), who found that well-being gains emerge primarily when households fully substitute traditional fuels with clean alternatives rather than relying on mixed-use strategies.

The health and comfort benefits of using clean energy arise mainly from substantially reducing indoor air pollution. Partial adoption—where households continue to use solid fuels alongside clean energy—often fails to reduce pollution levels below the threshold needed to generate noticeable health improvements. Continued exposure to smoke and particulate matter can offset the potential benefits of clean energy, resulting in no statistically detectable gains in well-being. In contrast, a complete transition eliminates most pollution sources, leading to clear improvements in physical comfort and health, which directly translate into higher happiness and life satisfaction. Besides, households that partially adopt clean energy may reserve it for limited uses or emergencies, continuing to rely on traditional fuels for routine heating. As

Table 4.5 ATTs of clean energy use for heating on happiness and life satisfaction: MVTE model estimates

Transition level	Mean outcomes		ATT	Change (%)
	Actual	Counterfactual		
Outcome = Happiness				
Partial transition to clean energy	7.192	7.000	0.192 (0.162)	2.74
Complete transition to clean energy	7.789	7.185	0.604 (0.132)***	8.40
Outcome = Life satisfaction				
Partial transition to clean energy	7.179	6.925	0.254 (0.164)	3.67
Complete transition to clean energy	7.715	7.082	0.633 (0.135)***	8.94

Note *** $p < 0.01$. ATT refers to average treatment effects on the treated. The reference group is no transition
Source Authors

a result, actual exposure, comfort, and convenience do not change enough to affect well-being. Full adopters, on the other hand, adjust their behavior and daily routines to take advantage of clean energy, allowing its benefits to be fully realized.

4.5 Conclusions and Policy Implications

Household heating is a critical issue in rural areas, and transitioning to clean energy can improve residents' subjective well-being. This study examines the impact of clean energy use for heating on the subjective well-being of rural residents, as measured by happiness and life satisfaction. We employ the endogenous switching regression (ESR) model to address potential self-selection bias and the multivalued treatment effects (MVTE) framework to capture heterogeneity across varying levels of clean energy adoption. The analysis is based on household survey data collected in 2024 from four national clean-heating pilot cities in northern China.

Three key findings emerge from this study. First, clean energy use for heating significantly improves subjective well-being: households using clean energy report higher levels of happiness and life satisfaction than those relying on non-clean energy. Second, heterogeneity analysis reveals that only households fully transitioning to clean energy experience substantial, statistically significant improvements in subjective well-being, whereas partial transitions yield limited or insignificant effects. Third, mechanism analysis shows that the primary drivers of these improvements are better health status and higher indoor temperatures, while increased heating costs slightly offset these gains.

The findings of this study offer several important policy implications for promoting clean energy adoption for heating while enhancing rural well-being. First, given that clean energy use significantly improves happiness and life satisfaction—primarily through better health and indoor thermal comfort—policies should frame clean energy not only as an environmental intervention but also as a public health and welfare–enhancing strategy. Integrating clean heating into rural health and social welfare programmes can help broaden policy support and improve implementation effectiveness. Second, the heterogeneity results highlight that only a complete transition to clean energy delivers substantial well-being gains, whereas partial adoption yields limited benefits. This implies that policies encouraging incremental or mixed energy use may be insufficient. Policymakers should therefore prioritize measures that enable full substitution away from non-clean energy. This includes targeted financial support—such as subsidies, concessional loans, or energy vouchers—for low-income households to offset higher upfront and operating costs, thereby reducing financial barriers to complete adoption and ensuring equitable access to the well-being benefits of clean energy.

Third, the mechanism analysis underscores the importance of complementary investments. Expanding clean energy supply alone is not enough; improvements in housing quality and energy efficiency, such as home insulation and heating-system upgrades, are essential to fully realize health and thermal comfort gains. At the same

Table 4.6 Falsification test of IV

Variables	Statistics
Clean energy use for heating	χ^2= 132.39***; p-value = 0.000
Happiness	F-value = 1.00; p-value = 0.320
Life satisfaction	F-value = 0.47; p-value = 0.494

Note *** $p < 0.01$
Source Authors

time, the negative cost channel suggests a need for pricing and support policies that mitigate short-term expenditure pressures during the transition. Finally, education and awareness campaigns can play a critical role in accelerating full adoption. By clearly communicating the health, comfort, and long-term economic benefits of clean energy—alongside available financial support—policymakers can help rural households overcome uncertainty and make informed decisions.

Acknowledgements Xiaofeng Luo acknowledges financial support from the National Natural Science Foundation of China (grant 72573066). Hongyun Zheng acknowledges the financial support from the National Natural Science Foundation of China (72303076).

Data Availability Statement The data that support the findings of this study are available from Xiance Sang upon request.
Conflict of Interests There is no conflict of interest.

Appendix

See Tables 4.6, 4.7, and 4.8

Table 4.7 Impact of clean energy use for heating on happiness and life satisfaction: ESR model estimates

Variables	Selection equation	Happiness		Selection equation	Life satisfaction	
		Users	Non-users		Users	Non-users
Age	−0.009 (0.006)	0.003 (0.005)	−0.015 (0.013)	−0.009 (0.006)	0.005 (0.005)	−0.012 (0.013)
Gender	0.208 (0.123)*	−0.294 (0.099)***	−0.171 (0.212)	0.214 (0.124)*	−0.222 (0.099)**	−0.183 (0.219)
Education	−0.003 (0.018)	0.073 (0.015)***	0.011 (0.034)	−0.002 (0.018)	0.070 (0.015)***	0.015 (0.036)
Household size	0.009 (0.031)	0.066 (0.025)***	0.085 (0.051)*	0.010 (0.031)	0.093 (0.025)***	0.107 (0.053)**
Dependency ratio	−0.168 (0.097)*	0.012 (0.077)	0.063 (0.179)	−0.152 (0.098)	0.042 (0.077)	0.032 (0.185)
Household income	0.013 (0.005)**	0.004 (0.002)**	0.011 (0.009)	0.011 (0.005)**	0.004 (0.002)**	0.005 (0.010)
Car ownership	0.195 (0.140)	0.271 (0.105)**	0.235 (0.261)	0.194 (0.140)	0.256 (0.105)**	0.219 (0.269)
Housing age	0.008 (0.005)*	0.000 (0.004)	0.005 (0.009)	0.009 (0.005)*	0.001 (0.004)	0.004 (0.009)
Housing area	0.399 (0.127)***	−0.018 (0.109)	0.042 (0.232)	0.428 (0.129)***	−0.000 (0.109)	0.005 (0.240)
Housing structure	0.847 (0.277)***	−0.036 (0.171)	−0.604 (0.546)	0.786 (0.276)***	0.048 (0.172)	−0.540 (0.561)
Yangquan	−0.046 (0.216)	0.223 (0.148)	−0.663 (0.454)	−0.012 (0.218)	0.397 (0.148)***	−0.600 (0.470)
Jinan	−0.301 (0.170)*	0.161 (0.137)	−0.152 (0.340)	−0.319 (0.174)*	0.247 (0.138)*	−0.015 (0.353)
Dezhou	−0.278 (0.194)	0.242 (0.156)	0.003 (0.420)	−0.235 (0.196)	0.264 (0.157)*	0.087 (0.433)
IV	4.025 (0.420)***			4.130 (0.431)***		
Constant	−3.890 (0.881)***	6.820 (0.630)***	7.377 (1.511)***	−4.158 (0.889)***	6.281 (0.629)***	7.176 (1.559)***
$\rho_{u\varepsilon_0}$		0.133 (0.154)			0.084 (0.154)	
$\rho_{u\varepsilon_1}$			−0.722 (0.082)***			−0.692 (0.099)***
Sample size	945			945		

Note *** $p < 0.01$, ** $p < 0.05$, * $p < 0.10$; Robust standard errors are presented in parentheses; The reference city is Anyang

Source Authors

Table 4.8 Robustness check: changing IV as neighbors' clean energy use for heating

Variables	Mean outcomes		ATT	Change (%)
	Actual	Counterfactual		
Happiness	7.730	7.029	0.701***	9.97
Life satisfaction	7.662	6.953	0.660***	9.49

Note *** $p < 0.01$. ATT refers to average treatment effects on the treated
Source Authors

References

Ahmadzai H. and Morrissey O. (2025). Climate shocks, household food security and welfare in Afghanistan, *Food Policy* 134, 102910.

Alnour M., Bilgili F. and Khan K. (2026). Spatial Dimensions of Energy Poverty Alleviation and Socioeconomic Sustainability in Sub-Saharan Africa, *Sustainable Development*, 1–27.

Barrington-Leigh C., Baumgartner J., Carter E., Robinson B.E., Tao S. and Zhang Y. (2019). An evaluation of air quality, home heating and well-being under Beijing's programme to eliminate household coal use, *Nature Energy* 4, 416–423.

Bisui S., Hasanuzzaman M., Sing J., Midya S. and Shit P.K. (2024). Exploring the cooking energy biomass and its impact on women's health and quality of life in rural households: a micro-environmental study from West Bengal in India, *Environmental Monitoring and Assessment* 196, 1184.

Chen Y., Li M., Lu J. and Chen B. (2023). Influence of residential indoor environment on quality of life in China, *Building and Environment* 232, 110068.

Chen L. and Wang Y. (2026). Does targeted poverty alleviation promote the adoption of clean cooking fuels? Evidence from a quasi-experimental study in China, *Energy Policy* 211, 115084.

Chui W.H. and Wong M.Y.H. (2016). Gender differences in happiness and life satisfaction among adolescents in Hong Kong: Relationships and self-concept, *Social Indicators Research* 125, 1035–1051.

Dida G.O. and Abuom P.O. (2022). Factors predisposing women and children to indoor air pollution in Trans Nzoia County, Kenya, *Archives of Public Health* 80, 46.

Diener E., Oishi S. and Lucas R.E. (2003). Personality, culture, and subjective well-being: Emotional and cognitive evaluations of life, *Annual review of psychology* 54, 403–425.

Di Falco S., Veronesi M. and Yesuf M. (2011). Does adaptation to climate change provide food security? A micro-perspective from Ethiopia, *American Journal of Agricultural Economics* 93, 825–842.

Fan S., Zha S., Zhao C., Sizheng F. and Li M. (2022). Using energy vulnerability to measure distributive injustice in rural heating energy reform: A case study of natural gas replacing bulk coal for heating in Gaocheng District, Hebei Province, China, *Ecological Economics* 197, 107456.

Feng H. (2025). Using clean fuels promotes diverse diets and health in Chinese households, *Food Security* 17, 1207–1222.

Gao S., Zhou P., Zhang H. and Yang S. (2025). Evaluating socio-economic and subjective well-being impacts of coal power phaseout in China, *Nature Communications* 16, 2320.

Grimes A., Smith C., O'Sullivan K., Howden-Chapman P., Le Gros L. and Dohig R.K. (2024). Housing Tenure and Subjective Wellbeing: The Importance of Public Housing, *Applied Research in Quality of Life*, 1–24.

Gu J. (2022). Importance of neighbors in rural households' conversion to cleaner cooking fuels: The impact and mechanisms of peer effects, *Journal of Cleaner Production* 379, 134776.

Guta D., Zerriffi H., Baumgartner J. *et al.* (2024). The impact of LPG consumption on cooking energy efficiency : Evidence from rural Indian household panel data, *World Development Perspectives* 36, 100627.

Han D., Yan S. and Sun X. (2024). Research on the air pollution reduction effect of winter clean heating policy, *Urban Climate* 53, 101760.

Hao J. and Qiao L. (2025). Carbon emissions in the building sector: the effect of clean heating policy in China's "2 + 26" cities, *Energy and Buildings* 348, 116393.

Huang H., Chen J., Sun Y. and Zhai S. (2025). Reduction of air pollution and carbon emission in response to clean heating policies in northern China, *Urban Climate* 64, 102705.

IEA, IRENA, UNSD, World Bank, WHO. (2025). *Tracking SDG 7: The Energy Progress Report.*

Janssen H., Ford K., Gascoyne B., Hill R., Roberts M., Bellis M.A. and Azam S. (2023). Cold indoor temperatures and their association with health and well-being: a systematic literature review, *Public Health* 224, 185–194.

Jin B., Zhou C., Zhao M., Zhang C. and Tian Z. (2026). Pensions as hidden green levers: The impact of China's new rural pension scheme on household energy transition, *Energy Policy* 210, 115022.

Kapsalyamova Z., Juatova S. and Azhgaliyeva D. (2025). Measuring energy poverty by estimating the income elasticity of energy demand : An application to Kazakhstan, *Utilities Policy* 95, 101901.

Li R. and Hu Y. (2026). Identifying Key Predictors of Subjective Well-Being across 92 Countries : A Machine Learning Approach, *Journal of Happiness Studies* 27, 16.

Li C., Lao W. and Wang S. (2024a). Risk assessment of unclean cooking energy usage from the perspective of subjective wellbeing: The mediating role of perceived physical and mental health, *Ecotoxicology and Environmental Safety* 281, 116603.

Li H., Li Y., Zheng G. and Zhou Y. (2024b). Interaction between household energy consumption and health : A systematic review, *Renewable and Sustainable Energy Reviews* 189, 113859.

Li J., Vatsa P. and Ma W. (2025). Internet use and household debt: Insights from rural China, *Applied Economics* 57, 10256–10276.

Liao H., Chen J., Tang X., Zhu L. and Ma C. (2026). Children's extracurricular learning participation under household energy transition: Evidence from China, *International Journal of Educational Development* 120, 103486.

Liao L., Kong S. and Du M. (2025). The effect of clean heating policy on individual health: Evidence from China, *China Economic Review* 89, 102309.

Liu Y., Chen M., Yu J. and Wang X. (2024). Being a happy farmer: Technology adoption and subjective well-being, *Journal of Economic Behavior and Organization* 221, 385–405.

Liu P., Han C., Liu X. and Meng L. (2024). From smoke to smiles: Quantifying the happiness benefits of household cooking energy transition, *Journal of Environmental Management* 368, 122203.

Lokshin M. and Sajaia Z. (2004). Maximum likelihood estimation of endogenous switching regression models, *The Stata Journal* 4, 282–289.

Ma W., Vatsa P. and Zheng H. (2022). Cooking fuel choices and subjective well-being in rural China: Implications for a complete energy transition, *Energy Policy* 165, 112992.

Ma W., Zhou X., Boansi D., Horlu G.S.A. and Owusu V. (2024). Adoption and intensity of agricultural mechanization and their impact on non-farm employment of rural women, *World Development* 173, 106434.

Mao H., Shi C., Tang H. and Dai C. (2026). Risk preferences and rural energy transition in China: based on experimental data analyses, *China Agricultural Economic Review*, 1–21.

Meng W., Zhu L., Liang Z. *et al.* (2023). Significant but inequitable cost-effective benefits of a clean heating campaign in Northern China, *Environmental Science and Technology* 57, 8467–8475.

Miao S., Huang W. and Li X. (2026). The Beneficial Role of Farmers' Digital Economy Participation in Reducing Chemical Fertilizer Use: Evidence from China, *Information Technology for Development* 32, 1–31.

Mohetaer Y., Han C., Meng L. and Shangguan Y. (2025). From Flush to Fulfillment: Unveiling the Influence of Upgraded Sanitation on Subjective Well-Being, *Social Indicators Research* 178, 335–370.
Nakagomi A., Akutsu Y., Yasuoka M., Abe N., Ihara S., Teroh T. and Tabuchi T. (2026). AI companions and subjective well-being: Moderation by social connectedness and loneliness, *Technology in Society* 85, 103229.
Namkhainyam T., Ovgor B., Jargal D. and Malley C.S. (2024). Modelling long-term greenhouse gas mitigation pathways for Mongolia Modelling long-term greenhouse gas mitigation pathways for Mongolia, *Environmental Research Communications* 6, 125010.
Nduka E. and Jimoh M. (2024). Cooking energy, health, and happiness of women in Nigeria, *The Energy Journal* 45, 1–29.
Neve J. De and Oswald A.J. (2012). Estimating the influence of life satisfaction and positive affect on later income using sibling fixed effects, *Proceedings of the National Academy of Sciences* 109, 19953–19958.
Nie P., Li Q. and Sousa-Poza A. (2021). Energy poverty and subjective well-being in China: New evidence from the China Family Panel Studies, *Energy Economics* 103, 105548.
Niu J., Chen X. and Sun S. (2024). China's Coal Ban policy: Clearing skies, challenging growth, *Journal of Environmental Management* 349, 119420.
Pei J., Li L., Duan M., Xia H., Yang J. and Zhang Y. (2026). Low-cost trap: The multidimensional health risks and burdens of household pollutive fuels, *Energy Policy* 208, 114946.
Pillarisetti A., Ye W. and Chowdhury S. (2022). Indoor Air Pollution and Health: Bridging Perspectives from Developing and Developed Countries, *Annual Review of Environment and Resources* 47, 197–229.
Qiu H., Sha Y. and Zhang Y. (2024). Energy affordability and subjective well-being in China : Causal inference, heterogeneity, and the mediating role of disaster risk, *Energy Economics* 129, 107180.
Radbel J., Rebuli M.E., Kipen H. and Brigham E. (2024). Indoor air pollution and airway health, *Journal of Allergy and Clinical Immunology* 154, 835–846.
Rahman M.S., Sujarwoto S., Toiba H., Nugroho T.W., Fahriyah F., Shaleh M.I., Purwanti T.S. and Andrianto B. (2025). Exploring the Impact of Cooking Fuel Choices on Household Food Security and Healthy Food Consumption in Indonesia, *Review of Development Economics*, 2242–2257.
Ren Z., Shahbaz M. and Zhong K. (2025). Social networks, Internet use, and farmers' participation in clean heating, *Energy* 320, 135300.
Salvo A., Tang Q., Yang J., Yin P. and Zhou M. (2024). Fine-particulate air pollution and behaviorally inclusive mortality impacts of China's winter heating policy, 2013–2018, *Journal of Environmental Economics and Management* 124, 102945.
Shen Y. and Sun W. (2025). The winter depression: coal heating and mental health in China, *Journal of Population Economics* 38, 8.
Stahlmann-Brown P., Milfont T.L., Norriss H. and Wesselbaum D. (2025). Perceived personal control and subjective well-being among farmers, *Journal of Rural Studies* 113, 103487.
Su X. and Tan J. (2023). Regional energy transition path and the role of government support and resource endowment in China, *Renewable and Sustainable Energy Reviews* 174, 113150.
Uribe A., Chávez C., Gómez W., Jaime M. and Bluffstone R. (2023). Private benefits from ambient air pollution reduction policies: Evidence from the household heating stove replacement program in Chile, *Energy for Sustainable Development* 77, 101323.
Villafranca M.S. De, Numminen S. and Hyysalo S. (2025). Characterizing hybrid heating in the households: Diverse configurational arrangements premised on citizen's agency and peer-support, *Environmental Innovation and Societal Transitions* 55, 100958.
Wang S., Bleil C., Souza D. and Golubchikov O. (2025). Recent advances in decarbonising heating in rural China : A review, *Renewable and Sustainable Energy Reviews* 210, 115282.
Wang M. and Wei C. (2024). Toward sustainable heating: Assessment of the carbon mitigation potential from residential heating in northern rural China, *Energy Policy* 190, 114141.

Wang M. and Xie L. (2023). Households' participation in energy transition and sustained use of clean energy: Evidence from China's clean heating program, *China Economic Review* 80, 102005.

Wang H., Zhou S. and Zhang P. (2024). Clean heating and clean air: Evidence from the coal-to-gas program in China, *China Economic Review* 85, 102179.

Welsch H. and Biermann P. (2017). Energy Affordability and Subjective Well-Being: Evidence for European Countries, *The Energy Journal* 38, 159–176.

Wu X., Xiao Y., Xie Y., Lan Y., Li J., Zhao Y. and Xu M. (2026). Uncovering the indoor health co-benefits of rural residential energy transition in Northern China, *Sustainable Production and Consumption* 63, 1–18.

Xie L., Hu X., Zhang X. and Zhang X.B. (2022). Who suffers from energy poverty in household energy transition? Evidence from clean heating program in rural China, *Energy Economics* 106, 105795.

Xie L. and Zhou O. (2021). What improves subjective welfare during energy transition? Evidence from the clean heating program in China, *Energy and Buildings* 253, 111500.

Xu H., Wang X. and Zhang D. (2026). Internet use propels cleaner cooking adoption and health gains in rural China, *Energy Policy* 210, 115082.

Yan H. (2026). A pathway towards energy transition: Urbanization and clean fuel adoption in Chinese homes, *Energy Economics* 154, 109153.

Yan W., Chen Y. and Wang Y. (2025). Efficiency improvement effect of clean energy transformation—A quasi-natural experiment based on China's clean heating policy, *Energy* 334, 137798.

Yang J., Lin Z. and Shi S. (2024). Household air pollution and attributable burden of disease in rural China: A literature review and a modelling study, *Journal of Hazardous Materials* 470, 134159.

Yao J., Zhang L., Hu Z. and Xie Y. (2024). Creating energy poverty by an anti-energy poverty policy? An analysis of the impact of the "coal-to-gas" policy in Northern China, *World Development Sustainability* 4, 100154.

Zhang C., Chen J., Xue L. and Han Q. (2026). Understanding the Effect of Agricultural Irrigation Infrastructure Failures on Cropland Abandonment in Rural China, *Review of Development Economics* 30, 588–602.

Zhang S., Sang X., Yang W. and Luo X. (2025). Empowering household energy transition: The impact of digital economy on clean energy use in rural China, *Energy* 324, 136016.

Zhang X., Zhang X. and Chen X. (2017). Happiness in the air: How does a dirty sky affect mental health and subjective well-being?, *Journal of Environmental Economics and Management* 85, 81–94.

Zhao L., Min S., Wang X. and Yu X. (2025). Unintended effect of refrigerator usage on household food waste: Evidence from rural China, *Resources, Conservation and Recycling* 219, 108274.

Zheng H. and Ma W. (2024). Economic benefits of internet use for smallholder wheat farmers, *Applied Economics* 56, 398–413.

Zheng H., Ma W. and Bahadur D. (2025). Fuel choices for cooking and heating and gender empowerment : Implications for promoting gender equality and sustainable rural development, *Energy Economics* 141, 108104.

Zheng X. and Zhou Y. (2025). Earlier move, greater joy: Migration timing and subjective well-being among rural migrants in China, *Economic Modelling* 145, 107011.

Zhou X. and Ma W. (2022). Agricultural mechanization and land productivity in China, *International Journal of Sustainable Development and World Ecology* 29, 530–542.

Zhu M., Huang Y. and Wei C. (2022). Role of Peer Effects in China's Energy Transition: Evidence from Rural Beijing, *Environmental Science and Technology* 56, 16094–16103.

Zhu Y., Liu Z. and Hermann D. (2025). How an energy policy prevents child migration: A natural experiment of the coal-to-gas policy in China, *Energy Policy* 198, 114487.

Chapter 5
Improved Sanitation Through Flush Toilet Use and Rural Subjective Well-Being in China

Junpeng Li, Wanglin Ma, Dil B. Rahut, and Quan He

5.1 Introduction

It is widely observed that an unsanitary environment has become a significant obstacle to improving the quality of life of rural residents in the developing world (Cameron et al. 2021; Cao and Li 2025). For instance, the mismanagement of human feces leads to severe contamination of drinking water and food, which accounts for 80% of human infectious diseases (e.g., Cholera, Hepatitis A, and COVID-19) (Park et al. 2021). Consequently, rural residents' lives are degraded by poor sanitary conditions, which substantially slow the development of rural society (Zhang et al. 2020). Thus, great significance attaches to improving rural sanitary conditions.

Flush toilets, a typical sanitary facility, have been consistently shown to improve rural living conditions, thereby enhancing rural residents' health status and economic performance and promoting long-term rural development (Li et al. 2024; Nguyen et al. 2025; Stopnitzky 2017). Duflo et al. (2015) found that the use of sanitary toilets can help reduce treated diarrhea episodes by 30–50% in India. Li et al. (2024) suggested that the use of flush toilets plays a pivotal role in improving rural residents' physical health and, in turn, reducing their healthcare expenditures in China. Nguyen

J. Li (✉)
Business School, Huaiyin Normal University, Huai'an, China
e-mail: junpeng.li_ae@outlook.com

W. Ma
e-mail: Wanglin.Ma@lincoln.ac.nz

W. Ma · Q. He
Department of Global Value Chains and Trade, Faculty of Agribusiness and Commerce, Lincoln University, Christchurch, New Zealand
e-mail: Mccree.He@lincolnuni.ac.nz

D. B. Rahut
Asian Development Bank Institute, Tokyo, Japan
e-mail: drahut@adbi.org

W. Ma et al. (eds.), *Beyond Income*, Contributions to Economics,
https://doi.org/10.1007/978-981-92-4957-2_5

et al. (2025) found that the use of flush toilets can significantly reduce the incidence of stunting, wasting, and underweight among children in Thailand and Vietnam. Moreover, Wang and Shen (2022) found that the use of flush toilets improves rural residents' economic performance by increasing their labor supply in China. Li et al. (2025) also documented a positive association between flush toilet use and improved off-farm performance of Chinese rural residents. Evidently, advancing the use of flush toilets can be an effective strategy to improve rural sanitation, enhance rural residents' lives, and support rural development. However, the flush toilet penetration rate in rural areas of the developing world remains low. Estimates indicate that fewer than 50% of rural residents in India and Cambodia have access to flush toilets, respectively (Tiwari et al. 2022; Yamada and Vu 2024). More effort should be made to promote the use of flush toilets among rural residents in developing countries.

One should note that one of the ultimate goals of accelerating rural development is uplifting rural residents' subjective well-being (Zhang et al. 2023). Correspondingly, a growing body of literature has focused on pathways to improving rural residents' subjective well-being. Generally, they have discussed how rural residents' subjective well-being is influenced by rural informatization (Rahman et al. 2023; Zheng and Ma 2021), income generation (Dufhues et al. 2022; Tauseef 2022), consumption (Ma et al. 2022; Nie et al. 2021), and social capital (Minh and Anh 2022; Schlossarek et al. 2024). For instance, Zheng and Ma (2021) found that online shopping significantly increases farmers' happiness and life satisfaction in China. Tauseef (2022) found that higher earnings improve farmers' subjective well-being in Bangladesh. Minh and Anh (2022) argued that social capital exists as a critical determinant of farmers' subjective well-being in Vietnam.

As discussed above, flush toilet use tends to influence farmers' health and economic performance, which, in turn, may be associated with their subjective well-being. For instance, flush toilet use has been shown to improve labor productivity, thereby increasing household income and enabling more diversified consumption (Li et al. 2024). Consequently, the subjective well-being of rural residents who use flush toilets may improve. However, empirical evidence on the relationship between flush toilet use and rural residents' subjective well-being remains limited. It is worth noting that Mohetaer et al. (2025) conducted a pioneering work and found that flush toilet use improves rural residents' subjective well-being. However, this study only considered the past and present dimensions of subjective well-being (i.e., happiness and life satisfaction) and neglected the future dimension. The existing literature has concluded that people's perceptions of their future directly influence the quality of their current lives and economic performance (Li et al. 2023; Pleeging et al. 2021). Thus, it is necessary to include the future dimension in the measurement of rural residents' subjective well-being. Given this, the association between flush toilet use and rural residents' subjective well-being warrants further empirical investigation.

This study aims to investigate in depth the impact of flush toilet use on rural residents' subjective well-being, using data collected from China. The present study adds to the literature on three fronts. First, this study measures rural residents' subjective well-being by including the future dimension. The measurement of subjective well-being in existing studies includes only the past and present dimensions, using indicators of happiness and life satisfaction, respectively, but ignores the future dimension (e.g., Mohetaer et al. 2025; Zheng and Ma 2021). Our study jointly considers the dimensions of the past, present, and future, thereby providing a comprehensive evaluation of rural residents' subjective well-being. Second, this study explores the impact of flush toilet use on multiple dimensions of rural residents' subjective well-being. By integrating the future-oriented dimension, this study advances a more nuanced and comprehensive account of the relationship between flush toilet use and the subjective well-being of rural residents. Third, we also disaggregate the impact of flush toilet use on rural subjective well-being by age, gender, and education levels. This provides deeper insight into the mechanisms through which flush toilet use affects rural residents' subjective well-being.

We chose China as the case. China's representativeness in unveiling the association between flush toilet use and rural subjective well-being comes from two aspects. First, the Chinese government has historically attached great importance to the use of flush toilets in constructing a favourable rural living environment (Cheng et al. 2018). For instance, since the launch of the "Rural Toilet Revolution" in 2015, China has been installing flush toilets in its rural areas. Evidently, the living environment in rural China has been substantially improved (Li et al. 2024). However, the adoption ratio of flush toilets among rural residents in China remains relatively low. In particular, 25% of rural households nationwide are still considered flush toilet non-users (NSBC 2023). Second, enhancing rural residents' subjective well-being has long been a sustained policy imperative for the Chinese government (Zheng and Ma 2021). However, the large rural population (over 510 million) suggests that improving rural residents' subjective well-being is a challenging task. For instance, the suicide rate among rural residents was almost twice that of urban residents in China (NHCC 2022). Thus, China is expected to place greater emphasis on promoting the subjective well-being of its rural residents. In sum, China provides a suitable case to unlock the impact of flush toilet use on rural residents' subjective well-being.

Using the inverse probability-weighted regression adjustment (IPWRA) model to analyse rural household data collected from Jiangsu, Hubei, and Yunnan provinces in China, the present study confirms that using flush toilets significantly improves rural residents' subjective well-being, as measured by happiness, life satisfaction, and confidence about the future. Our results also suggest that rural residents categorized as young, female, and low educated tend to experience greater subjective well-being improvement from using flush toilets than their counterparts.

The rest of the paper is arranged as follows: Sect. 2 presents a conceptual framework. Section 3 introduces data, variable definitions, and descriptive statistics. Section 4 outlines the empirical methods, followed by the results discussion in Sect. 5. The final section concludes the paper and proposes policy implications.

5.2 Conceptual Framework

It is widely agreed that improved sanitary facilities, such as flush toilets, can enhance the hygiene of rural residents' living environments, thereby improving health and economic performance (Dar and Vellakkal 2025; Li et al. 2025; Wang and Shen 2022). Building on this premise, the use of flush toilets may further improve rural residents' subjective well-being. Drawing on the existing literature (Duflo et al. 2015; Li et al. 2025; Mohetaer et al. 2025; Wang and Shen 2022), our study examines the mechanisms linking flush toilet use to rural residents' subjective well-being, as illustrated in Fig. 1.

The first channel, as shown in Fig. 1, suggests that using a flush toilet can enhance rural residents' subjective well-being by upgrading sanitary conditions. This channel is manifested in two specific pathways. One of them is the health improvement mechanism. That is, flush toilets improve households' sanitary conditions, which, in turn, enhances rural residents' health and ultimately raises their subjective well-being. Evidently, using flush toilets can effectively isolate food and drinking water from fecal pollution, thereby improving rural residents' health (Duflo et al. 2015; Li et al. 2024; Zhao et al. 2025). Previous studies have confirmed that using sanitary toilets significantly reduces the incidence of gastrointestinal infection (e.g., diarrhea and cholera) (Duflo et al. 2015). Good health conditions can directly make people happier and more satisfied with their lives (Ngamaba et al. 2017). More importantly, good health conditions help reduce the medical burden and allow rural residents to maintain a relaxed budget for consumption (Li et al. 2024). This can lead rural flush toilet users to a higher level of subjective well-being.

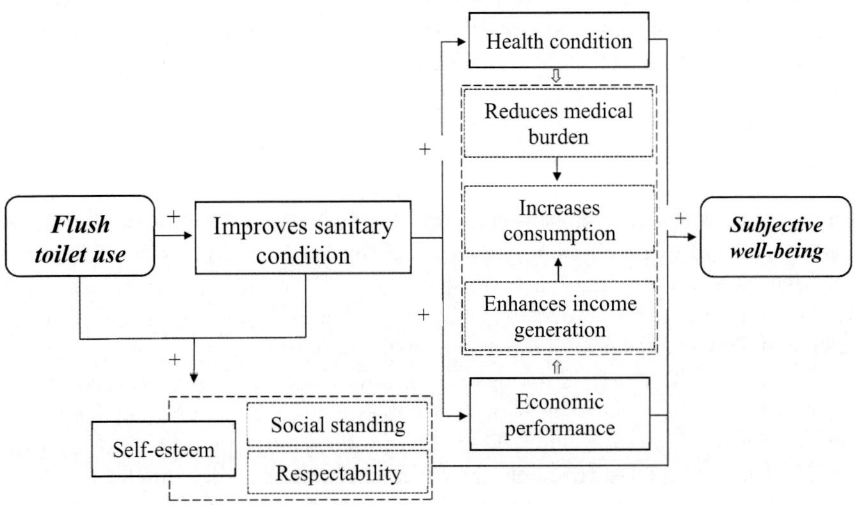

Fig. 1 Influencing mechanisms between flush toilet use and rural residents' subjective well-being *Source* Authors

Another specific channel suggests that flush toilet use boosts economic performance and, ultimately, subjective well-being, with improved household sanitation as a key pathway. On the one hand, people's productivity strongly depends on the environmental quality (Kunn et al. 2023). A sound living environment can invigorate individuals, thereby enhancing their productivity and economic performance. Since the use of flush toilets improves rural residents' sanitary conditions, it is easy to link it to improved economic performance (Wang and Shen 2022). On the other hand, good health is a critical prerequisite for strong economic performance, as it determines people's labor supply and productivity (Smith and Ehrenberg 2016). As discussed above, flushing toilets are beneficial for the health of rural residents. Thus, flush toilet use can further drive rural residents' economic performance. Good economic performance yields good income and diversified consumption, which is essential for a positive evaluation of life (García-Rodríguez et al. 2025; Zheng and Ma 2021). Therefore, flush toilet use can improve rural residents' subjective well-being through reinforcing their economic performance.

The second mechanism suggests that flush toilet use and improvements in subjective well-being can be linked through rural residents' self-esteem. Installing flush toilets is a novelty in rural areas of developing countries (Li et al. 2024). It represents the rural residents' pursuit of modern life. The installation of flush toilets enables rural households to enjoy a more modern, convenient lifestyle than households without them. This can effectively enhance rural residents' self-esteem (Mohetaer et al. 2025), making them happier and more confident about their future. Figure 1 also shows that the enhancement of self-esteem can be partially explained by the channel of improved sanitary conditions. In rural areas, household cleanliness is widely seen as a marker of respectability and, to a considerable extent, shapes a household's social standing within the village (Pakhtigian et al. 2022). By substantially improving household sanitary conditions, the use of flush toilets can bolster rural residents' self-esteem, thereby enhancing their subjective well-being.

Overall, our conceptual framework suggests that flush toilet use tends to correlate positively with rural residents' subjective well-being. In what follows, we will apply appropriate econometric methods to empirically investigate this association.

5.3 Data, Variable Definitions, and Descriptive Statistics

5.3.1 Data

The data used in our study were derived from a rural household survey in eastern, central, and western China. A team of scholars and students from local universities conducted the survey. It was carried out between December 2023 and January 2024. Thus, the collected information pertains to 2023. Using a multi-stage sampling method, the survey gathered samples in six steps. First, three provinces, including Jiangsu, Hubei, and Yunnan provinces, were randomly selected from eastern, central, and western China, respectively. Second, two prefecture-level cities within each selected province were randomly chosen. They are Huai'an, Yancheng, and Suqian in Jiangsu Province; Jingmen, Xiaogan, and Huanggang in Hubei Province; and Chuxiong, Honghe, and Lincang in Yunnan Province. In the following two steps, two counties and two towns were randomly selected from each sampled city and county, respectively. Next, with the help of local statistical bureaus, two villages were picked out from each sampled town. Then, 10–15 households from each village were randomly selected for face-to-face interviews. As a result, the survey yields 1577 rural household samples.

Using a detailed and structured questionnaire, the survey collected rich data to portray the social and economic lives of rural households. In particular, the dataset contains multiple indicators reflecting rural households' demographic characteristics, living conditions, employment, agricultural production, and spatial locations. More importantly, the dataset contains rich information on flush toilet use and subjective well-being, making it well-suited for studying the topic of our primary interest.

Before conducting the empirical analysis, we followed rigorous data-cleaning procedures. First, we dropped 15 samples that reported abnormal or missing values for the subjective well-being variables. Second, 4 samples containing missing values in the flush toilet use variable were purposively deleted. Third, we also excluded 18 samples with abnormal and/or missing values in control variables. As a result, 1540 samples were analyzed in our study.

5.3.2 Variable Definitions

5.3.2.1 Subjective Well-Being

Variables reflecting rural residents' subjective well-being are regarded as the dependent variables in our study. Following previous studies (Li et al. 2023; Mohetaer et al. 2025; Tauseef 2022), we use happiness and life satisfaction to measure rural residents' subjective well-being. Among them, happiness captures the short-run hedonic well-being of rural residents (Zheng and Ma 2021), while life satisfaction reflects rural residents' long-term views of life (Nie et al. 2021). As can be seen, these two indicators capture people's subjective well-being only in the past and present, neglecting the future dimension. It is well recognized that people's confidence in their future heavily determines their present performance and long-term development (Pleeging et al. 2021). To comprehensively measure rural residents' subjective well-being, we also include their confidence about the future as a dependent variable. Rural residents' happiness, life satisfaction, and confidence about the future were measured using a 5-point Likert scale from 1 = very unhappy/unsatisfied/unconfident to 5 = very happy/satisfied/confident.

5.3.2.2 Flush Toilet Use

Flush toilet use serves as our treatment variable. Since people's decisions to use improved facilities are dichotomous, we adopt the strategy of Wang and Shen (2022) and Mohetaer et al. (2025) and use a dummy variable to measure flush toilet use. In particular, the variable equals one if the sampled rural household uses a flush toilet and zero otherwise.

5.3.2.3 Control Variables

Our study also applies a vector of exogenous variables as controls. In particular, we use household heads' age, gender, and education, household size, and elderly ratio as proxies of rural households' demographic characteristics. Following Li et al. (2023) and Vatsa et al. (2023), the variables for credit access and asset ownership are used to capture the impact of rural households' economic status. To control the impact of unexpected shocks, the variable for natural disasters is included. Convenient traffic conditions ease people's shopping (Verma et al. 2025), which is helpful for toilet upgrading and enhances their subjective well-being. Thus, we include supermarket access as a control variable. Existing literature (Johnsson and Moon 2021; Tong and Zhu 2020) has confirmed that farmers' adoption of improved practices is influenced by their peers. Accordingly, we use the variable for neighbors' flush toilet use as a control variable. Additionally, to capture the impact of unobserved spatial disparities, our study also includes three location dummies representing Jiangsu, Hubei, and Yunnan provinces as control variables. The specific definitions of the selected variables are presented in Table 1.

5.3.3 Descriptive Statistics

Table 1 also illustrates the descriptive statistics of the selected variables. It shows that the mean values for rural residents' happiness, life satisfaction, and confidence about the future were 3.86, 3.88, and 4.01, respectively, on a 5-point Likert scale. This suggests rural residents in our sample tend to enjoy a relatively high level of subjective well-being. Approximately 86% of the sampled rural households use flush toilets, suggesting that this sanitary facility is well penetrated in rural areas of China. This is due to the "Rural Toilet Revolution" launched by the Chinese central government in 2015. However, as shown, there is still room for the adoption of flush toilets in rural China.

Table 1 also indicates that our sample is dominated by relatively old, male, poorly educated rural residents. The mean household size was 5.04, of which 18% were elderly. On average, 36%, 18%, and 86% of rural households in our sample owned air conditioners, had experienced natural disasters, and had neighbors using flush

Table 1 Definitions and descriptive statistics of selected variables

Variables	Definition	Mean	S.D.
Outcome variables			
Happiness	Self-reported happiness: From 1 = very unhappy to 5 = very happy	3.86	0.89
Life satisfaction	Self-reported life satisfaction: From 1 = very unsatisfied to 5 = very satisfied	3.88	0.86
Confidence about the future	Self-reported confidence about the future: From 1 = very unconfident to 5 = very confident	4.01	0.99
Treatment variable			
Flush toilet use	1 if household uses a flush toilet, 0 otherwise	0.86	0.35
Control variables			
Age	Age of household head (HH) (years)	57.91	12.06
Gender	1 if HH is male, 0 otherwise	0.68	0.47
Education	Education level of HH (years)	7.36	4.04
Household size	Number of people residing in a rural household	5.04	2.10
Elderly ratio	Ratio of the number of family members aged over 65 years to household size	0.18	0.25
Credit access	1 if households have access to credit from formal financial institutions, 0 otherwise		
Asset ownership	1 if household owns an air conditioner, 0 otherwise	0.36	0.48
Natural disaster	1 if a respondent experiences natural disasters (e.g., flood and pest infection), 0 otherwise	0.18	0.39
Supermarket access	1 if the supermarket is easy to access, 0 otherwise	0.81	0.39
Neighbor's flush toilet use	1 if the respondent has a neighbor using a flush toilet, 0 otherwise	0.86	0.35
Jiangsu province	1 if household is located in Jiangsu province, 0 otherwise	0.33	0.47
Hubei province	1 if household is located in Hubei province, 0 otherwise	0.32	0.47
Yunnan province	1 if household is located in Yunnan province, 0 otherwise	0.35	0.48
Observations		1540	

Note S.D. refers to standard deviation. *Source* Authors

toilets, respectively. Additionally, 81% of our respondents report convenient access to supermarkets.

Table 2 reports the mean differences in the selected variables between flush toilet users and non-users. Compared with non-users, flush toilet users are more likely to report higher levels of happiness, life satisfaction, and confidence about the future. Meanwhile, rural households with flush toilets tend to be larger, have a smaller proportion of older people, and are more likely to have younger heads than those without flush toilets. Compared with non-users, flush toilet users are more likely to own assets, have access to credit, live close to supermarkets, and have neighbors who use flush toilets.

The statistics presented in Table 2 suggest that flush toilet users and non-users differ systematically in terms of demographic characteristics, economic conditions, and spatial location. Nevertheless, this cannot be considered as the impact of flush toilet use on rural residents' subjective well-being, as it does not control for other factors. Therefore, we will use appropriate econometric methods to investigate the association between flush toilet use and rural residents' subjective well-being.

Table 2 Differences in the mean values of selected variables between flush toilet users and non-users

Variables	Flush toilets		Mean differences	*t* values
	Users	Non-users		
Happiness	3.894	3.647	0.248 (0.065)***	3.825
Life satisfaction	3.914	3.684	0.230 (0.063)***	3.659
Confidence about the future	4.043	3.823	0.220 (0.073)***	3.023
Age	57.395	61.116	−3.722 (0.882)***	−4.221
Gender	0.678	0.660	0.017 (0.034)	0.501
Education	7.387	7.195	0.192 (0.297)	0.646
Household size	5.082	4.819	0.263 (0.154)**	1.702
Elderly ratio	0.175	0.232	−0.057 (0.018)***	−3.150
Asset ownership	0.370	0.274	0.095 (0.035)***	2.714
Credit access	0.133	0.047	0.086 (0.024)***	3.616
Natural disaster	0.186	0.163	0.023 (0.028)	0.805
Supermarket access	0.823	0.744	0.079 (0.029)***	2.764
Neighbor's flush toilet use	0.913	0.516	0.397 (0.024)***	16.806
Constant	0.370	0.195	0.174 (0.035)***	5.028
Observations	1325	215	1540	

Note Standard errors are in parentheses. *** < 0.01, ** < 0.05, and * < 0.10. *Source* Authors

5.4 Empirical Methods

Although rural toilet renovation is policy-oriented (Cheng et al. 2018), flush toilet use is not randomly assigned among rural residents. In particular, rural residents' use of flush toilets is influenced by multiple factors, including demographic characteristics, economic conditions, and even managerial abilities (Li et al. 2025). This can lead to endogeneity issues with our treatment variable, flush toilet use. Without addressing them, the impact of flush toilet use on rural residents' subjective well-being can be overestimated or underestimated. Thus, it is critical to address endogeneity in flush toilet use when assessing its impact on subjective well-being.

For the case of cross-sectional data, empirical methods like the propensity score matching (PSM) model (dos Santos et al. 2023), the inverse probability weights (IPW) model (Adeel et al. 2026), the IPWRA model (Chigusiwa et al. 2023), and the conditional mixed process (CMP) model (Shen et al. 2025) are widely used to address the endogeneity issues associated with the treatment variable. Among them, the CMP model's effectiveness in addressing endogeneity issues deeply relies on a valid instrumental variable (IV) (Li 2025; Mallapragada et al. 2016). However, our dataset lacks an indicator that can serve as an IV for flush toilet use. Thus, the CMP model is unfavourable for our study. In comparison, the PSM, IPW, and IPWRA models can address endogeneity issues in flush toilet use without requiring an IV (Chigusiwa et al. 2023; dos Santos et al. 2023). This suggests the three models are suitable for the present study.

The estimation process for the PSM, IPW, and IPWRA models consists of two steps. The first step estimates the determinants of rural residents' flush toilet use using a Probit model. The second step of these models assesses the impact of flush toilet use on subjective well-being. It is worth noting that the PSM and IPW models require the equations for both steps to be appropriately specified, whereas the IPWRA model relaxes this restriction and allows the equations for either the first or the second step to be correctly specified (Chigusiwa et al. 2023). Thus, the IPWRA model possesses double robustness compared with the PSM and IPW models (Hörner and Wollni 2021). Accordingly, the IPWRA model is preferred by the present study.

Suggested by Wossen et al. (2017) and Ma et al. (2025), the IPWRA model can be specified as follows:

Step one:

$$P(X) = \Pr(T_i = 1) = f(X_i; \alpha) \tag{1}$$

Step two:

$$Y_i^n = f([X_i]; \beta) + \mu_i, \quad n = 1, 2, 3 \tag{2}$$

where $P(X)$ indicates the probability of a rural household i using flush toilets. T_i refers to the treatment variable, flush toilet use ($T_i = 1$ for flush toilet users and $T_i = 0$ for non-users). Y_i^n indicates a specific indicator measuring subjective well-being, where Y_i^1, Y_i^2, and Y_i^3 refers to happiness, life satisfaction, and confidence about the future, respectively. X_i is the vector of variables influencing flush toilet use and subjective well-being, respectively.

Using the inverse-probability weights calculated in step one, the IPWRA model can then estimate the average treatment effect (ATE) of flush toilet use on variables of subjective well-being. This can be treated as the assessment of the impact of flush toilet use on rural residents' subjective well-being. In the case of our study, the ATE can be calculated by the following equation:

$$ATE_{IPWRA} = E\left(Y_{1i}^n - Y_{0i}^n\right) \tag{3}$$

where Y_{1i}^n and Y_{0i}^n refer to a specific indicator of the subjective well-being of flush toilet users and non-users, respectively. $E\left(Y_{1i}^n - Y_{0i}^n\right)$ measures the expectation of the difference in a specific indicator of subjective well-being between flush toilet users and non-users.

5.5 Results

This section discusses our empirical findings. In what follows, we first discuss the determinants of rural residents' use of flush toilets. Then, we discuss the ATEs of flush toilet use on rural residents' subjective well-being, as measured by happiness, life satisfaction, and confidence about the future. Finally, we discuss the disaggregated impacts of flush toilet use on rural residents' subjective well-being by specific categories, including age, gender, and education levels.

5.5.1 *Determinants of Flush Toilet Use*

Table 3 presents estimates of the determinants of rural residents' flush toilet use, estimated using a Probit model. Since the Probit model estimates cannot be directly interpreted, we also calculated the marginal effects of the selected variables (see Column 3 in Table 3). The results suggest that the household size variable has a positive and significant impact on flush toilet use. In particular, having one more household member increases the likelihood of farmers using flush toilets by 0.7%. This is understandable as large households increase the need for fecal management (Li et al. 2024). This finding is mirrored by the work of Nguyen et al. (2025) on Thailand and Vietnam. The variables for asset ownership and credit access are positively and significantly associated with flush toilet use, suggesting that good economic status can encourage rural residents to use the facility. In fact, installing flush toilets is cost-intensive (Cheng et al. 2018). Good economic conditions enhance rural residents' ability to afford the costs associated with toilet upgrades and thus encourage them to use this sanitary facility.

Table 3 Predictors of flush toilet use: Probit model

Variables	Coefficients	Marginal effects
Age	−0.004 (0.005)	−0.001 (0.001)
Gender	−0.002 (0.101)	−0.000 (0.018)
Education	−0.013 (0.014)	−0.002 (0.003)
Household size	0.039 (0.022)*	0.007 (0.004)*
Elderly ratio	−0.156 (0.181)	−0.028 (0.033)
Asset ownership	0.182 (0.102)*	0.033 (0.018)*
Credit access	0.382 (0.174)**	0.069 (0.032)**
Natural disaster	−0.102 (0.119)	−0.019 (0.022)
Supermarket access	0.347 (0.111)***	0.063 (0.020)***
Neighbor's flush toilet use	1.263 (0.103)***	0.230 (0.017)***
Jiangsu province	−0.253 (0.138)*	−0.046 (0.025)*
Hubei province	−0.245 (0.132)*	−0.044 (0.024)*
Yunnan province	0.127 (0.325)	
Observations	1540	1540

Note Robust standard errors are in parentheses. The reference region is Yunnan province. *** < 0.01, ** < 0.05, and * < 0.10.
Source Authors

As expected, the supermarket access variable positively and significantly impacts rural residents' flush toilet use. In particular, convenient access to supermarkets increases the likelihood that farmers use flush toilets by 6.3%. Additionally, the neighbor's flush toilet use variable is positively and significantly associated with rural residents' flush toilet use. Specifically, rural residents with neighbors using flush toilets are 23% more likely to use this facility than those without. This finding provides new evidence that farmers' adoption of improved facilities and practices depends on their peers' behavior (Eilers et al. 2022; Sampson and Perry 2019).

5.5.2 ATEs of Flush Toilet Use on Rural Residents' Subjective Well-Being

Table 4 illustrates the ATEs of flush toilet use on rural residents' happiness, life satisfaction, and confidence about the future. Generally, estimates of ATEs suggest that flush toilet use has a positive and significant impact on rural residents' happiness, life satisfaction, and confidence about the future. More specifically, the results in Table 4 suggest that using flush toilets is associated with statistically significant increases in rural residents' happiness, life satisfaction, and confidence about the future by 0.263, 0.257, and 0.273 points, respectively, on a 5-point Likert scale. This finding confirms the positive association between flush toilet use and rural residents' subjective well-being. As we discussed in the conceptual framework, using

Table 4 Average treatment effects of flush toilet use on rural residents' subjective well-being

Variables	ATE	z-value
Happiness	0.263 (0.082)***	3.21
Life satisfaction	0.257 (0.081)***	3.15
Confidence about the future	0.273 (0.109)**	2.51

Note Robust standard errors are in parentheses. ATE refers to the average treatment effect. *** < 0.01 and ** < 0.05. *Source* Authors

flush toilets improves rural residents' sanitary conditions, thereby boosting their self-esteem and enhancing their health and economic performance (Li et al. 2024; Wang and Shen 2022), which consequently improves rural residents' happiness, life satisfaction, and confidence about the future. As shown, this finding not only confirms the positive impact of flush toilet use on farmers' happiness and life satisfaction documented by Mohetaer et al. (2025) but also cements our understanding of the facility's role by revealing its impact on farmers' confidence in their future. In sum, the results in Table 4 confirm that flush toilet use is an effective strategy for improving rural residents' subjective well-being.

5.5.3 Disaggregated Impacts of Flush Toilet Use on Subjective Well-Being

To solidify our understanding of the flush toilet's role in determining rural residents' subjective well-being, we also disaggregate its impact by age, gender, and education levels. Table 5 presents the disaggregated impacts of flush toilet use on subjective well-being by rural residents' age, gender, and education levels.

The upper part of Table 5 shows the estimates for the age groups. It shows that flush toilet use has a positive and significant impact on happiness, life satisfaction, and confidence about the future among rural residents aged under 65. In contrast, its impact on those aged 65 and older is insignificant. This finding suggests that young rural residents are the main beneficiaries of improvements in subjective well-being from the use of flush toilets. Older people often adhere to traditional habits, which makes them less inclined to embrace new things (Moore et al. 2021). Meanwhile, older people are more likely to lack the skills and labor force to fix flush toilets (Li et al. 2024). This can diminish elderly people's favorable perception of flush toilets, thereby offsetting the positive effects of flush toilet use on their subjective well-being. In comparison, young people tend to carve out new things and have a higher demand for environmental sanitation. This can reinforce their positive feelings about using flush toilets and thus help strengthen the positive impact of flush toilet use on their subjective well-being.

The middle part of Table 5 presents estimates for the gender category. The results show that flush toilet use positively and significantly affects the happiness and life

Table 5 Disaggregated impacts of flush toilet use on subjective well-being by age, gender, and education levels

Categories	Variables	ATE	*z*-value
By age			
Age≥65	Happiness	0.075 (0.105)	0.72
	Life satisfaction	0.030 (0.104)	0.29
	Confidence about the future	0.132 (0.112)	1.18
Age<65	Happiness	0.297 (0.124)**	2.39
	Life satisfaction	0.337 (0.125)***	2.69
	Confidence about the future	0.275 (0.138)**	1.98
By gender			
Males	Happiness	0.237 (0.092)**	2.58
	Life satisfaction	0.211 (0.089)**	2.37
	Confidence about the future	0.196 (0.133)	1.48
Females	Happiness	0.280 (0.158)*	1.78
	Life satisfaction	0.365 (0.163)**	2.24
	Confidence about the future	0.508 (0.195)***	2.60
By education levels			
Illiterate	Happiness	0.514 (0.141)***	3.64
	Life satisfaction	0.400 (0.115)***	3.48
	Confidence about the future	0.127 (0.190)	0.67
Primary school	Happiness	0.192 (0.120)	1.61
	Life satisfaction	0.245 (0.116)**	2.12
	Confidence about the future	0.407 (0.155)***	2.63
Junior high school	Happiness	0.254 (0.158)	1.61
	Life satisfaction	0.229 (0.154)	1.49
	Confidence about the future	0.011 (0.153)	0.07
High school or above	Happiness	0.111 (0.140)	0.80
	Life satisfaction	0.073 (0.129)	0.56
	Confidence about the future	0.003 (0.122)	0.03

Note Robust standard errors are in parentheses. ATE refers to the average treatment effect. *** < 0.01, ** < 0.05, and * < 0.10. *Source* Authors

satisfaction of male and female farmers. However, using flush toilets only significantly improves female farmers' confidence about the future, while posing no benefit to males. Accordingly, female farmers receive a major part of the subjective well-being improvement from using flush toilets. This finding can be explained by two main reasons. First, in most East Asian countries, rural females are the primary undertakers of household chores (Zhou and Turvey 2018). Using flush toilets improves household sanitary conditions, reducing the need for heavy housework. This allows them to participate in entertaining activities and improves their subjective well-being.

Second, women's unique physiological structure requires a sanitary toilet environment to avoid urinary tract infections (O'Connell et al. 2023). The use of flush toilets improves household sanitary conditions, isolates females from urinary tract infections, and uplifts their subjective well-being.

The lower part of Table 5 shows the impact of flush toilet use on subjective well-being disaggregated by rural residents' education levels. The results show that the use of flush toilets has a positive and significant effect only on the happiness and life satisfaction of illiterate rural residents and the life satisfaction and confidence about the future of those with a primary school education. Accordingly, flush toilet use is more likely to improve the subjective well-being of rural residents with low levels of education. This is plausible, as poorly educated farmers tend to be in poor economic conditions (Smith and Ehrenberg 2016), which hinders their ability to obtain the tools and services needed to improve their sanitation. Accordingly, a low level of education can amplify the positive impact of flush toilet use on rural residents' subjective well-being.

5.6 Conclusions and Implications

Improving rural sanitation conditions and rural residents' subjective well-being are two critical, pressing tasks for developing nations to achieve long-term rural development. Due to its effectiveness in improving household sanitary conditions, rural residents' health and economic performance, and self-esteem, flush toilet use, a promising strategy to improve rural sanitary conditions, has the potential to enhance rural residents' subjective well-being. Accordingly, our study attempts to bridge the linkage between flush toilet use and rural residents' subjective well-being.

Using data from a rural household survey in eastern, central, and western China, this study provides a comprehensive measure of rural residents' subjective well-being by using variables for happiness, life satisfaction, and confidence about the future. The IPWRA model was applied to address endogeneity in the treatment variable, flush toilet use, and to estimate its impact on subjective well-being variables. Our empirical results suggest that flush toilet use improves rural residents' happiness, life satisfaction, and confidence about the future by 0.263, 0.257, and 0.273 points on a 5-point Likert scale, respectively. Disaggregated analysis indicates that young, female, and low-educated rural residents tend to experience the greatest improvement in subjective well-being from using flush toilets. Moreover, our results suggest that rural residents' flush toilet use is significantly driven by household size, asset ownership, credit access, supermarket access, and neighbors' flush toilet use.

Several significant policy implications can be summarized from our empirical findings. Our study confirms a positive association between flush toilet use and rural residents' subjective well-being. This highlights that the government should prioritize toilet upgrades in its efforts to improve rural subjective well-being. Regarding the positive impact of asset ownership and credit access on rural residents' use of flush toilets, the government is expected to take steps to improve rural residents' financial conditions. In particular, the government should consider providing employment and agricultural production training to improve farmers' economic performance. Meanwhile, strategies that can simplify the loan process should also appear on the list of policymakers. Importantly, the positive impact of neighbors' flush toilet use on respondents' flush toilet use suggests that the government should give great attention to peer effects among farmers. For instance, targeted subsidies and rewards should be provided to positive responders to toilet renovation; this can inspire more adopters. Last but not least, our disaggregated analysis suggests the impact of flush toilet use on subjective well-being is heterogeneous across age, gender, and education levels. This reminds us that policymakers should formulate policy instruments that are targeted at specific populations.

Acknowledgments Junpeng Li acknowledges the financial support from the Ministry of Education of China Project of Humanities and Social Sciences (Project No. 21YJC630062), the National Statistical Science Research Project (Project No.: 2023LY033), the Jiangsu Provincial Department of Education (Project No.: 2020SJA1763), and the 2024 Jiangsu Higher Education "Qinglan Project".

Data Availability Statement The data supporting this study's findings are available from Junpeng Li upon request.

Conflict of Interests There is no conflict of interest.

Ethics Statement Not applicable.

References

Adeel, M., Khattak, A.J., Usman, S.M., Moradloo, N., 2026. Are we ready for highly automated vehicles? Evaluating automated driving systems' safety and reliability using inverse probability weighted regression adjustment. J. Intell. Transp. Syst. Technol. Planning, Oper. doi:https://doi.org/10.1080/15472450.2025.2602132

Cameron, L., Chase, C., Haque, S., Joseph, G., Pinto, R., Wang, Q., 2021. Childhood stunting and cognitive effects of water and sanitation in Indonesia. Econ. Hum. Biol. 40, 100944. doi:https://doi.org/10.1016/j.ehb.2020.100944

Cao, A., Li, H., 2025. Leading change: The impact of female officials on the rural toilet revolution in China. Econ. Anal. Policy 85, 694–716. doi:https://doi.org/10.1016/j.eap.2024.12.029

Cheng, S., Li, Z., Uddin, S.M.N., Mang, H.P., Zhou, X., Zhang, J., Zheng, L., Zhang, L., 2018. Toilet revolution in China. J. Environ. Manage. 216, 347–356. doi:https://doi.org/10.1016/j.jenvman.2017.09.043

Chigusiwa, L., Kembo, G., Kairiza, T., 2023. Drought and social conflict in rural Zimbabwe: Does the burden fall on women and girls? Rev. Dev. Econ. 27, 178–197. doi:https://doi.org/10.1111/rode.12944

Dar, S.M., Vellakkal, S., 2025. Usage and Health Impact of Toilets: Evidence from a Nationwide Sanitation Program in India. Econ. Anal. Policy 88, 1652–1669. doi:https://doi.org/10.1016/j.eap.2025.10.048

dos Santos, P.S., Becker, K.L., de Oliveira, S. V., 2023. Race-based affirmative action for higher education in Brazil: Impact assessment on performance, time, and delay in completion*. Rev. Dev. Econ. 27, 247–267. doi:https://doi.org/10.1111/rode.12923

Dufhues, T., Möllers, J., Jantsch, A., Buchenrieder, G., Camfield, L., 2022. Don't Look Up! Individual Income Comparisons and Subjective Well-Being of Students in Thailand. J. Happiness Stud. 24, 477–503. doi:https://doi.org/10.1007/s10902-022-00604-4

Duflo, E., Greenstone, M., Guiteras, R.P., Clasen, T., 2015. Toilets can work: short and medium run health impacts of addressing complementarities and externalities in water and sanitation.

Eilers, L., Paloyo, A.R., Bechara, P., 2022. The effect of peer employment and neighborhood characteristics on individual employment. Empir. Econ. 62, 1885–1908. doi:https://doi.org/10.1007/s00181-021-02075-7

García-Rodríguez, N., Cachero-Martínez, S., González-Fidalgo, E., 2025. Sustainable Consumption for a Better Life: Consumer Well-Being—A Review and Research Agenda. Int. J. Consum. Stud. 49. doi:https://doi.org/10.1111/ijcs.70109

Hörner, D., Wollni, M., 2021. Integrated soil fertility management and household welfare in Ethiopia. Food Policy 100, 102022. doi:https://doi.org/10.1016/j.foodpol.2020.102022

Johnsson, I., Moon, H.R., 2021. Estimation of Peer Effects in Endogenous Social Networks: Control Function Approach. Rev. Econ. Stat. 103, 328–345. doi:https://doi.org/10.1162/rest_a_00870

Kunn, S., Palacios, J., Pestel, N., 2023. Indoor Air Quality and Strategic Decision Making. Manage. Sci. 69, 5354–5377. doi:https://doi.org/10.1287/mnsc.2022.4643

Li, J., 2025. Adoption of climate-smart agriculture practices and climate resilience in tea cultivation: micro-level evidence from Sri Lanka. China Agric. Econ. Rev. 1–22. doi:https://doi.org/10.1108/CAER-06-2025-0317

Li, J., Liu, X., Meng, X., Zhang, W., 2025. The Nexus Between Flush Toilet Use and Off-Farm Performance of Rural Households. Rev. Dev. Econ. 29, 1792–1807. doi:https://doi.org/10.1111/rode.13177

Li, J., Ma, W., Gong, B., 2023. Market participation and subjective well-being of maize farmers. Econ. Anal. Policy 80, 941–960. doi:https://doi.org/10.1016/j.eap.2023.09.037

Li, J., Vatsa, P., Ma, W., 2024. Flush toilet use and its impact on health and non-health expenditures. J. Int. Dev. 36, 2022–2046. doi:https://doi.org/10.1002/jid.3889

Ma, W., Li, J., Nnaji, A.P., Setsoafia, E.D., 2025. The role of agricultural cooperatives in improving mechanization levels: Differences between outsourcing machinery services and household-owned machines. Ann. Public Coop. Econ. 1–21. doi:https://doi.org/10.1111/apce.70011

Ma, W., Vatsa, P., Zheng, H., 2022. Cooking fuel choices and subjective well-being in rural China: Implications for a complete energy transition. Energy Policy 165, 112992. doi:https://doi.org/10.1016/j.enpol.2022.112992

Mallapragada, G., Chandukala, S.R., Liu, Q., 2016. Exploring the effects of "what" (product) and "where" (website) characteristics on online shopping behavior. J. Mark. 80, 21–38. doi:https://doi.org/10.1509/jm.15.0138

Minh, N.N., Anh, N.N., 2022. Social Capital, Income, and Subjective Well-Being in Developing Countries: Evidence from Vietnam. pp. 127–147. doi:https://doi.org/10.1007/978-981-19-0515-5_10

Mohetaer, Y., Han, C., Meng, L., Shangguan, Y., Liu, P., 2025. From Flush to Fulfillment: Unveiling the Influence of Upgraded Sanitation on Subjective Well-Being, Social Indicators Research. Springer Netherlands. doi:https://doi.org/10.1007/s11205-025-03589-8

Moore, K., O'Shea, E., Kenny, L., Barton, J., Tedesco, S., Sica, M., Crowe, C., Alamäki, A., Condell, J., Nordström, A., Timmons, S., 2021. Older Adults' Experiences With Using Wearable Devices: Qualitative Systematic Review and Meta-synthesis. JMIR mHealth uHealth 9, e23832. doi:https://doi.org/10.2196/23832

Ngamaba, K.H., Panagioti, M., Armitage, C.J., 2017. How strongly related are health status and subjective well-being? Systematic review and meta-analysis. Eur. J. Public Health 27, 879–885. doi:https://doi.org/10.1093/eurpub/ckx081

Nguyen, Trung Thanh, Nguyen, Thanh Tung, Do, M.H., Rahut, D., Nguyen, D.L., 2025. Remittances, sanitation and child malnutrition in middle-income countries: A case study from rural

Northeast Thailand and Central Vietnam. World Dev. 190, 106975. doi:https://doi.org/10.1016/j.worlddev.2025.106975

NHCC, 2022. China Health Statistics Yearbook. Peking Union Medical College Press, Beijing, China.

Nie, P., Li, Q., Sousa-Poza, A., 2021. Energy poverty and subjective well-being in China: New evidence from the China Family Panel Studies. Energy Econ. 103, 105548. doi:https://doi.org/10.1016/j.eneco.2021.105548

NSBC, 2023. Statistics Yearbook of China (2023). China Statistics Press, Beijing, China.

O'Connell, K.A., Nicholas, T.B., Palmer, M.H., 2023. Toileting behaviors, urinary cues, overactive bladder, and urinary incontinence in older women. Int. Urogynecol. J. 34, 707–716. doi:https://doi.org/10.1007/s00192-022-05228-z

Pakhtigian, E.L., Dickinson, K.L., Orgill-Meyer, J., Pattanayak, S.K., 2022. Sustaining latrine use: Peers, policies, and sanitation behaviors. J. Econ. Behav. Organ. 200, 223–242. doi:https://doi.org/10.1016/j.jebo.2022.05.024

Park, S. kyung, Lee, C.W., Park, D. Il, Woo, H.Y., Cheong, H.S., Shin, H.C., Ahn, K., Kwon, M.J., Joo, E.J., 2021. Detection of SARS-CoV-2 in Fecal Samples From Patients With Asymptomatic and Mild COVID-19 in Korea. Clin. Gastroenterol. Hepatol. 19, 1387-1394.e2. doi:https://doi.org/10.1016/j.cgh.2020.06.005

Pleeging, E., Burger, M., van Exel, J., 2021. Hope Mediates the Relation between Income and Subjective Well-Being. J. Happiness Stud. 22, 2075–2102. doi:https://doi.org/10.1007/s10902-020-00309-6

Rahman, M.S., Toiba, H., Nugroho, T.W., Hartono, R., Shaleh, M.I., Sugiono, S., Saeri, M., 2023. Does internet use make farmers happier? Evidence from Indonesia. Cogent Soc. Sci. 9. doi:https://doi.org/10.1080/23311886.2023.2243716

Sampson, G.S., Perry, E.D., 2019. The role of peer effects in natural resource appropriation - The case of groundwater. Am. J. Agric. Econ. 101, 154–171. doi:https://doi.org/10.1093/ajae/aay090

Schlossarek, M., Harmáček, J., Seidlová, A., Suchá, L., 2024. Inequalities and Social Capital as Factors of Subjective Well-Being: Case Study from Western Province, Zambia. J. Happiness Stud. 25, 1–24. doi:https://doi.org/10.1007/s10902-024-00778-z

Shen, B., Zheng, H., Rahut, D.B., 2025. Women's decision-making power and its impact on input use and economic returns: evidence from Sri Lanka's tea sector. China Agric. Econ. Rev. 1–16. doi:https://doi.org/10.1108/CAER-06-2025-0341

Smith, R., Ehrenberg, R., 2016. Modern Labor Economics, Modern Labor Economics. Pearson Education Asia LTD. doi:https://doi.org/10.4324/9781315510651

Stopnitzky, Y., 2017. No toilet no bride? Intrahousehold bargaining in male-skewed marriage markets in India. J. Dev. Econ. 127, 269–282. doi:https://doi.org/10.1016/j.jdeveco.2017.04.003

Tauseef, S., 2022. Can Money Buy Happiness? Subjective Wellbeing and Its Relationship with Income, Relative Income, Monetary and Non-monetary Poverty in Bangladesh. J. Happiness Stud. 23, 1073–1098. doi:https://doi.org/10.1007/s10902-021-00443-9

Tiwari, P., Tirumala, R.D., Shukla, J., 2022. Household choices of sanitation infrastructure and impact on disease in India. Environ. Plan. B Urban Anal. City Sci. 49, 2054–2071. doi:https://doi.org/10.1177/23998083221088293

Tong, H., Zhu, J., 2020. New peer effect-based approach for service matching in Cloud Manufacturing under uncertain preferences. Appl. Soft Comput. J. 94, 106444. doi:https://doi.org/10.1016/j.asoc.2020.106444

Vatsa, P., Ma, W., Zheng, H., Li, J., 2023. Climate-smart agricultural practices for promoting sustainable agrifood production: Yield impacts and implications for food security. Food Policy 121, 102551. doi:https://doi.org/10.1016/j.foodpol.2023.102551

Verma, R., Chiara, G.D., Goodchild, A., 2025. Does proximity matter in shopping behavior? Transp. Res. Part A Policy Pract. 196. doi:https://doi.org/10.1016/j.tra.2025.104471

Wang, D., Shen, Y., 2022. Sanitation and work time: Evidence from the toilet revolution in rural China. World Dev. 158, 105992. doi:https://doi.org/10.1016/j.worlddev.2022.105992

Wossen, T., Abdoulaye, T., Alene, A., Haile, M.G., Feleke, S., Olanrewaju, A., Manyong, V., 2017. Impacts of extension access and cooperative membership on technology adoption and household welfare. J. Rural Stud. 54, 223–233. doi:https://doi.org/10.1016/j.jrurstud.2017.06.022

Yamada, H., Vu, T.M., 2024. Do Toilets Save Young Children's Lives? Evidence from Cambodia. SSRN Electron. J. 1–25. doi:https://doi.org/10.2139/ssrn.4775478

Zhang, H., Ma, W., Li, J., Yang, W., 2023. Can citrus farmers earn more from selling online? Econ. Anal. Policy 80, 1549–1560. doi:https://doi.org/10.1016/j.eap.2023.10.026

Zhang, S., Li, Y., Zhang, Y., Lu, Z.N., Hao, Y., 2020. Does sanitation infrastructure in rural areas affect migrant workers' health? Empirical evidence from China. Environ. Geochem. Health 42, 625–646. doi:https://doi.org/10.1007/s10653-019-00396-2

Zhao, S., Ma, J., Li, W., 2025. Flushing away disease: A one health perspective on sanitation, pathogen transmission, and rural health in China. One Heal. 21. doi:https://doi.org/10.1016/j.onehlt.2025.101248

Zheng, H., Ma, W., 2021. Click it and buy happiness: does online shopping improve subjective well-being of rural residents in China? Appl. Econ. 53, 4192–4206. doi:https://doi.org/10.1080/00036846.2021.1897513

Zhou, L., Turvey, C.G., 2018. Drinking water and off-farm labour supply: between-gender and within-gender bias. Aust. J. Agric. Resour. Econ. 62, 103–120. doi:https://doi.org/10.1111/1467-8489.12239

Chapter 6
Mental Health and Life Satisfaction in Later Life: Evidence from Bangladesh

Alessia Destefanis, Dil B. Rahut, Tetsushi Sonobe, and Shafiun N. Shimul

6.1 Introduction

Since the 1960s, countries worldwide have experienced a significant decline in fertility and mortality rates, leading to an increasing proportion of elderly individuals within their populations. This demographic transition carries substantial implications for economies and societies alike, particularly in sectors such as healthcare, labor markets, and social welfare systems (Lutz et al. 2018).

Globally, the elderly population (defined as individuals aged 60 and older) numbered 1.2 billion in 2024 and is projected to rise to 2.1 billion by 2050 (United Nations 2024). This rapid expansion presents significant challenges for policy-makers, necessitating forward-looking strategies to mitigate the socio-economic consequences of an aging society. Against this global backdrop, the situation in Bangladesh presents a specific and urgent research problem. The number of people aged 60 and above is expected to increase from approximately 15 million in 2020 to 36 million by 2050 (Rahman 2020), highlighting the urgency of understanding and addressing the needs of this demographic. The urgency of this issue is underscored by recent national findings, which indicate alarmingly high rates of psychological

A. Destefanis (✉)
Paris School of Economics (PSE) & Université Paris 1 Panthéon-Sorbonne, Paris, France
e-mail: alessia.destefanis@psemail.eu

D. B. Rahut
Asian Development Bank Institute (ADBI), Tokyo, Japan
e-mail: drahut@adbi.org

T. Sonobe
National Graduate Institute for Policy Studies (GRIPS), Tokyo, Japan
e-mail: sonobete@grips.ac.jp

S. N. Shimul
Institute of Health Economics, University of Dhaka, Dhaka, Bangladesh
e-mail: shafiun.ihe@du.ac.bd

W. Ma et al. (eds.), *Beyond Income*, Contributions to Economics,
https://doi.org/10.1007/978-981-92-4957-2_6

distress, including a 58% prevalence of depression, among this growing demographic (Rahman et al. 2025).

Currently, Bangladesh is in an intermediate stage of population aging. It is anticipated that the advanced stage (where 25% of the population will be 65 or older) will be reached within the next three to four decades (Rahman 2020). This transition will exert pressure on the country's economic growth potential, public finances, and social insurance systems (Lutz et al. 2018). The aging process not only involves biological decline, such as increased susceptibility to age-related diseases and disabilities (Bowling and Dieppe 2018), but also encompasses critical socio-economic factors, including retirement, social exclusion, and evolving household structures.

The demographic shift poses challenges for developing economies in Asia, where traditional social safety nets are often informal and rooted in family structures. Historically, Asian societies have relied on intergenerational support systems and joint family arrangements to care for the elderly (Teerawichitchainan et al. 2015). However, these traditional norms are increasingly being disrupted by industrialization, urbanization, and globalization, which promote individualism, geographic mobility, and economic independence. As a result, nuclear family arrangements are becoming more common, particularly in South and Southeast Asia, and the role of elderly parents has become less central. In Bangladesh, this erosion of traditional family support has contributed to heightened vulnerability and declining mental well-being among older adults (Uddin 2023), though the precise pathways linking these structural changes to specific mental health outcomes require further empirical investigation.

While the mental well-being of elderly populations has been extensively studied in high-income countries, a relative dearth of research remains in low- and middle-income contexts, particularly in developing Asia (Rahman et al. 2020). This gap is especially pronounced regarding multidimensional assessments that integrate affective, cognitive, and quality-of-life dimensions. This study seeks to address this gap by focusing on Bangladesh. By identifying the key determinants of mental well-being among older adults, the study aims to inform policy design and contribute to broader discussions on how best to support aging populations in resource-constrained settings (Sultana et al. 2022). It is therefore motivated by the critical need for context-specific evidence, informed by a comprehensive conceptual framework of well-being.

To this end, the study utilizes data collected from a purpose-built survey conducted by the Asian Development Bank Institute (ADBI) in 2021. The survey includes responses from 400 individuals aged 60 and above, residing in both urban and rural regions of Bangladesh. These rich, primary data are used to investigate the socio-demographic, economic, and familial factors associated with mental well-being in later life. In addition, a rigorous econometric framework is employed to quantify the relationship between mental health indicators and subjective well-being outcomes (Sahu et al. 2012; Hawlader et al. 2021).

This study makes three primary contributions to the literature on aging in developing contexts. First, it provides novel empirical evidence from Bangladesh, a country undergoing rapid demographic transition, but where comprehensive, survey-based research on the mental well-being of the elderly remains scarce. Second, it adopts a multidimensional analytical approach by simultaneously employing three validated psychological scales (SWLS, CASP-19, CES-D) to capture distinct yet interrelated facets of well-being (life satisfaction, quality of life, and depression), offering a more nuanced picture than single-measure studies. Third, it identifies context-specific determinants, such as the protective role of higher education for quality of life.

The structure of the paper is as follows. Section 2 presents a literature review and the conceptual framework. Section 3 describes the survey design and data. Section 4 outlines the empirical methodology. Section 5 presents the main findings and their discussion. Section 6 concludes the paper by outlining policy implications and directions for future research.

6.2 Literature Review and Conceptual Framework

6.2.1 Mental Well-Being in Developing Asia and Bangladesh

Mental well-being encompasses an individual's emotional state, cognitive functioning, and capacity to manage the challenges of everyday life (WHO 2018). Among the elderly, feelings of happiness and gratitude are often closely tied to the quality of family relationships and living arrangements (Miao and Wu 2021). In many Asian societies, family structures have historically played a critical role in providing informal care and emotional support for older adults, particularly those unable to work due to illness or frailty. However, although financial transfers from adult children to aging parents remain common, emotional and physical support has declined considerably (Huda 2020). This trend is evident in both rural and urban settings, where decreasing rates of co-residence have led to altered living arrangements and heightened psychological vulnerability among older adults.

In Bangladesh, shifts in household composition have become increasingly pronounced since the 1990s, with a growing number of households comprising only elderly couples. This transformation has introduced new and often less supportive living environments, adversely impacting mental well-being. Quantitative evidence now confirms the severity of this trend; a large-scale 2025 study found that living without family is a key predictor of depression, which affects most elders (Rahman et al. 2025). Furthermore, the link between socio-economic vulnerability and poor mental health is robust, with factors like female gender, illiteracy, and poor self-rated health consistently associated with higher depression scores (Sultana et al. 2022; Imran et al. 2024). The empirical literature suggests that older individuals are increasingly reliant on phone calls and visits to mitigate feelings of abandonment. Factors such as declining independence, fear of death (Cassum et al. 2020), and pervasive experiences of loneliness, frailty, and anxiety contribute to diminished life satisfaction among the elderly.

Gender disparities further compound the mental health challenges faced by older individuals in Bangladesh. Elderly women face greater socio-economic vulnerabilities, often lacking personal income and depending on male relatives for financial support. Property rights and home ownership are also skewed in favor of men, despite some exceptions, such as Rahman et al. (1976), who found that, in the 1980s, over one-third of homes in rural Naogaon District were legally owned by women. Recent studies validate that these structural vulnerabilities translate into measurably worse outcomes, with elderly women reporting significantly poorer quality of life than their male counterparts (Imran et al. 2024). Nevertheless, housing conditions and access to basic amenities such as sanitation and clean water tend to be similar across genders in many rural areas (Barikdar et al. 2016b). This suggests that interventions must look beyond physical infrastructure to address deeper socio-economic inequities that shape mental well-being.

While household characteristics may reflect broader patterns of economic development rather than gender discrimination per se, access to secure housing and financial resources consistently influences mental well-being in later life (Tran and Vu Van 2017). As traditional co-residence patterns decline, elderly individuals increasingly prefer living in nuclear households with adequate accommodations and proximity to family members (Wei and Tsay 2024). In this context, understanding the social and tructural determinants of mental well-being is critical for designing effective, context-sensitive policy interventions in Bangladesh and similar settings. This context frames a key question for the present study: how do these evolving household structures, combined with socio-economic factors, differentially impact distinct dimensions of mental well-being, such as depression, life satisfaction, and quality of life?

6.2.2 *Intertwined Realities: Mental Health and Well-Being in Later Life*

Although conceptually distinct, mental well-being and mental health are deeply interconnected. Unaddressed declines in mental well-being can escalate into diagnosable conditions such as anxiety and depression, while living with a mental illness can, in turn, reduce day-to-day emotional and psychological well-being (Subramaniam et al. 2016). Recognizing this interdependence, recent studies have focused on identifying the drivers of depression and their subsequent effects on overall well-being among older populations. A clearer understanding of this relationship is foundational for the multidimensional assessment undertaken in this research.

Subramaniam et al. (2016) found that high levels of mental disability, low life satisfaction, and medical comorbidities were all negatively associated with both mental well-being and mental health outcomes. Sengupta and Benjamin (2015), analyzing data from India, reported higher rates of depression among elderly individuals who were female, over 80 years of age, urban residents, living alone or in nuclear families, without formal education, unemployed, or from poorer households.

Interestingly, their findings suggest that access to pensions did not substantially mitigate depressive symptoms, challenging common policy assumptions. The profound impact of social environment on mental health is further illustrated by research on Bangladesh's most vulnerable elders. Studies of institutionalized populations reveal extreme levels of cognitive impairment and severe depression, often in contexts with no mental health support (Akter et al. 2023), while research in Rohingya refugee camps highlights how extreme vulnerability and lack of formal education correlate with lower mental well-being (Anwar et al. 2024). However, a gap remains in understanding how these severe vulnerabilities manifest across a continuum of well-being outcomes in a general community-dwelling elderly population.

In Bangladesh, older women face especially acute mental health risks due to a combination of longer life expectancy and greater exposure to social and economic marginalization. These intersecting vulnerabilities underscore the need to address both immediate mental health needs and the broader social determinants of mental well-being. Understanding the bidirectional relationship between mental health and well-being is essential for developing holistic policy responses that address both prevention and treatment among aging populations.

6.2.3 Policies and Programs: Bangladesh's Response to Mental Health

Despite the growing needs of its aging population, Bangladesh has struggled to adequately protect the dignity and well-being of its elders. Barikdar et al. (2016a) attribute this failure to multiple structural and cultural factors, including the weakening of extended family systems, rising individualism, and increasing income inequality. These trends not only undermine traditional norms of respect and support for elders but also contradict constitutional commitments to social justice and basic welfare.

The Constitution of Bangladesh guarantees social security for older citizens, encompassing access to food, shelter, healthcare, and other necessities. In line with these principles, the government introduced the *Old Age Allowance program* in fiscal year 1997–1998. Aimed at promoting social inclusion and mental well-being, the program provides small pensions and support for Medicare and nutrition. However, this initiative currently remains limited in coverage and primarily benefits retired public sector employees. Its direct impact on psychological outcomes like depression or life satisfaction has not been rigorously evaluated.

More recently, the government has launched a broader *Program Implementation Plan* to improve healthcare access for the elderly. This initiative focuses on the development of sustainable health systems, enhanced management of healthcare delivery, and improved responsiveness of human resources. Contemporary research emphasizes that effective policy must look beyond clinical care. The concept of 'active aging,' influenced by factors such as autonomy, income, and physical activity (Afrin et al. 2025), and evidence on the positive impact of outdoor recreation on mental well-being (Tohan et al. 2024) point to the critical role of community-based psychosocial interventions. In parallel, various NGOs and social welfare organizations have initiated community-level efforts to engage elderly individuals and address their specific needs. Nevertheless, the scale of these interventions may remain inadequate given the magnitude of the challenge. Resource constraints, limited pension coverage, and fragmented service delivery may continue to hinder progress.

6.3 Survey Design and Data

6.3.1 ADBI Survey Design

The primary objective of the ADBI Bangladesh project is to collect comprehensive data on the well-being of elderly individuals in developing Asia, with a particular focus on the multidimensional aspects of their living conditions. This component of the project examines socio-economic, physical, and mental well-being among the elderly in Bangladesh, exploring how these dimensions interact and influence one another. The study was conducted in partnership with the Dhaka Institute of Health Economics.

Bangladesh, with a population exceeding 165 million across a land area of just 148,460 km^2, ranks as the eighth most populous country in the world and among the most densely populated. Administratively, the country is divided into eight divisions, which are further subdivided into districts (*zila*). For the purposes of this study, quantitative data were collected from two purposively selected districts representing distinct geographic and socio-economic contexts: Rangpur in the northwestern region and Narayanganj in central Bangladesh, part of the Dhaka Division.

To ensure a representative and diverse sample, the study employed a multi-stage sampling strategy. In the first stage, one subdistrict (*upazila*) was randomly selected from each of the two study districts. Within each selected upazila, two villages were then randomly chosen as the primary sampling units. Data collection began at the geographic center of each selected village; when no clear central point could be identified, prominent public locations (such as the main bazaar or the local school) served as alternative starting points. From the central point, eligible households (defined as those with at least one resident aged 60 years or older) were identified on either side of the landmark through systematic sampling. In each village, 50 eligible households were selected and interviewed, yielding a sample of 100 elderly individuals per village, and a total of 400 respondents across the four villages. This approach ensured the inclusion of elderly individuals from both rural (Rangpur) and peri-urban (Narayanganj) settings, strengthening the external validity of the findings.

Data were collected using a combination of structured face-to-face interviews, self-administered questionnaires, and physical measurements. Trained enumerators used a standardized questionnaire covering socio-economic status, physical health conditions, and mental well-being. Validated psychological instruments were incorporated to measure depression, anxiety, and life satisfaction. To ensure high data quality, a rigorous pre-testing phase, including a pilot study with a subset of elderly individuals, was conducted. Insights from the pilot informed the refinement of survey tools. Enumerators received comprehensive training on survey administration, ethical considerations, data confidentiality, and techniques for respecting and sensitively engaging with elderly respondents. The resulting dataset supports detailed empirical analysis of the relationships between socio-demographic factors and both physical and mental health outcomes among the elderly in Bangladesh. Analytical methods include multivariate regression models to estimate the impacts of key variables, as well as mediation and moderation analyses to assess indirect effects and contextual influences on overall well-being.

6.3.2 Descriptive Characteristics and Key Indicators

The demographic composition of the sample, summarized in Table 1, closely aligns with national patterns observed in prior research on the elderly in Bangladesh, thereby supporting the external validity and representativeness of the dataset.

The age distribution is concentrated in the younger-old age groups, with 38.01% of respondents aged 60–64 and 22.96% aged 65–69. Smaller proportions are aged 70–74 (15.05%) and 75+ (23.98%), capturing a reasonable spread across the senior age range. The sample demonstrates a relatively balanced gender composition, with 51.79% identifying as female and 48.21% as male.

In terms of religious affiliation, most participants (89.80%) identify as Muslim, with 10.20% reporting affiliation with non-Muslim religions. This ratio is based on national census estimates (Sahu et al. 2012), which reinforces the religious representativeness of the sample. Marital status data show that 64.19% of respondents are currently married, while 33.25% are widowed. Minor shares are separated (1.02%), unmarried (0.26%), or fall into the "other" category (1.28%).

Educational attainment in the sample is low, with 68.54% of individuals reporting no formal education. A further 20.72% completed primary education, 9.46% reached secondary level, and only 1.28% attained a college or university degree. These patterns reflect long-standing educational disparities, particularly among older cohorts, and underscore persistent barriers to formal learning opportunities during earlier life stages.

Employment history indicates that 73.85% of respondents have worked for at least 3 months, consistent with Rahman et al. (2020), who emphasized the economic activity of elderly populations, particularly in informal or agricultural sectors. Farming (37.85%) and casual non-farm labor (28.39%) represent the most common occupations, followed by salaried non-farm work (9.72%) and business (8.18%). Regarding current employment status, 47.83% are fully retired, 20.72% are partially retired, and 29.67% report not being retired at all; this highlights a notable share of elderly individuals who remain economically active, often out of necessity.

Health-related indicators further contextualize the sample's vulnerability. Age-related illnesses are prevalent, with 50.26% of respondents experiencing such conditions "*Sometimes*" and 34.62% reporting they experience them "*Always.*" Only 15.13% report no such conditions. Additional health variables include limited access to assistive devices (only 4.59% report using a hearing aid) and notable rates of Parkinsonian symptoms, with 32.30% experiencing hand tremors. Nutritional deficiencies are reported by 14.62% of the sample, reflecting continuing challenges in elderly nutrition and care.

It is important to note that the sample's geographical distribution is not nationally representative. Data were collected from four villages across two purposively selected districts (Rangpur and Narayanganj) to capture rural and peri-urban contexts. Yet, while not nationally representative, the sample's demographic profile is consistent with known national characteristics for this age cohort, supporting its relevance for analysis. These consistencies bolster the dataset's reliability and provide a strong empirical foundation for analyzing the well-being of older adults in Bangladesh.

Table 1 Summary statistics—demographics

Variable	Percentage (%)	Variable	Percentage (%)
Age group		**Current work status**	
60–64 years	38.01	Completely retired	47.83
65–69 years	22.96	Partially retired	20.72
70–74 years	15.05	Not retired at all	29.67
75+ years	23.98	Other	1.79
Gender		**Education level**	
Female	51.79	No education	68.54
Male	48.21	Primary education	20.72
Religion		Secondary education	9.46
Muslim	89.80	College/university	1.28
Non-Muslim	10.20	**Age-related diseases**	
Marital status		Never	15.13
Married	64.19	Sometimes	50.26
Unmarried	0.26	Always	34.62
Separated	1.02	**Uses hearing aid**	
Widowed	33.25	Yes	4.59
Other	1.28	No	95.41
Worked at least 3 months in life		**Nutritional diseases**	
Yes	73.85	Yes	14.62
No	26.15	No	85.38
Main occupation when young		**Parkinson symptoms**	

(continued)

Table 1 (continued)

Variable	Percentage (%)	Variable	Percentage (%)
Farming (self-employed, farm)	37.85	Yes	32.30
Business (self-employed, non-farm)	8.18	No	67.70
Wage labor (farm)	2.56		
Salaried (non-farm wage)	9.72		
Casual labor (single non-farm wage)	5.63		
Casual labor (multiple non-farm wages)	28.39		
Other	7.67		

Source Authors

6.4 Measuring Well-Being: Tools, Indicators, Specification

Well-being is inherently multidimensional and subjective, posing challenges for measurement and analysis. To address these challenges, this study employs a set of validated psychometric tools widely used across diverse contexts and populations. These instruments enable a nuanced understanding of subjective experiences, particularly regarding emotional health and life satisfaction among the elderly. The following scales are used in this study:

6.4.1 Satisfaction with Life: The SWLS Framework

To assess overall life satisfaction, the study uses the Satisfaction with Life Scale (SWLS) developed by Diener et al. (1985). This widely adopted scale captures individuals' global cognitive evaluations of their lives through five items: (1) In most ways my life is close to my ideal; (2) The conditions of my life are excellent; (3) I am satisfied with my life; (4) So far, I have gotten the important things I want in life; (5) If I could live my life over, I would change almost nothing.

Respondents indicate their level of agreement with each item on a 7-point Likert scale ranging from 1 (*strongly disagree*) to 7 (*strongly agree*). The SWLS has demonstrated strong psychometric reliability and validity across cultural and demographic contexts (Diener et al. 1985; Pavot and Diener 1993). For analysis, a composite SWLS index was created by summing the scores of the five items, yielding a total score ranging from 5 to 35, with higher scores indicating greater life satisfaction. This unweighted summation follows the standard scoring procedure for the scale (Pavot and Diener 1993).

Figure 1 displays histograms for each SWLS item and the overall composite index. Each panel corresponds to one item, showing the frequency distribution of responses across the 7-point scale. The composite index aggregates responses to provide a holistic measure of life satisfaction. Examining the distribution of responses, we observe that satisfaction scores are spread across the scale, with the highest frequency at level 2 (22.25%), indicating that a substantial proportion of the elderly population reports moderately low satisfaction. Levels 1 and 7 show relatively low frequencies, suggesting that extreme dissatisfaction or complete satisfaction are less common. Disaggregated responses to specific items provide further insight. For instance, 20.75% of respondents selected level 1 for the item My life is close to my ideal, indicating that many perceive a significant gap between their actual and ideal life circumstances. Similarly, responses to *the question "I have the important things I want in life"* vary considerably, reflecting differing levels of perceived material and emotional fulfillment. The item *I would change almost nothing in my life* offers a retrospective view on life satisfaction. Here too, responses are dispersed, highlighting the heterogeneity in how elderly individuals assess their life trajectories.

Overall, the results in Fig. 1 present a complex, layered picture of life satisfaction among older adults in Bangladesh. The composite SWLS index reinforces the finding that most respondents fall into moderate satisfaction categories, with relatively fewer reporting either extreme satisfaction or dissatisfaction. These insights underscore the importance of disaggregating well-being measures to understand the nuanced realities of aging populations.

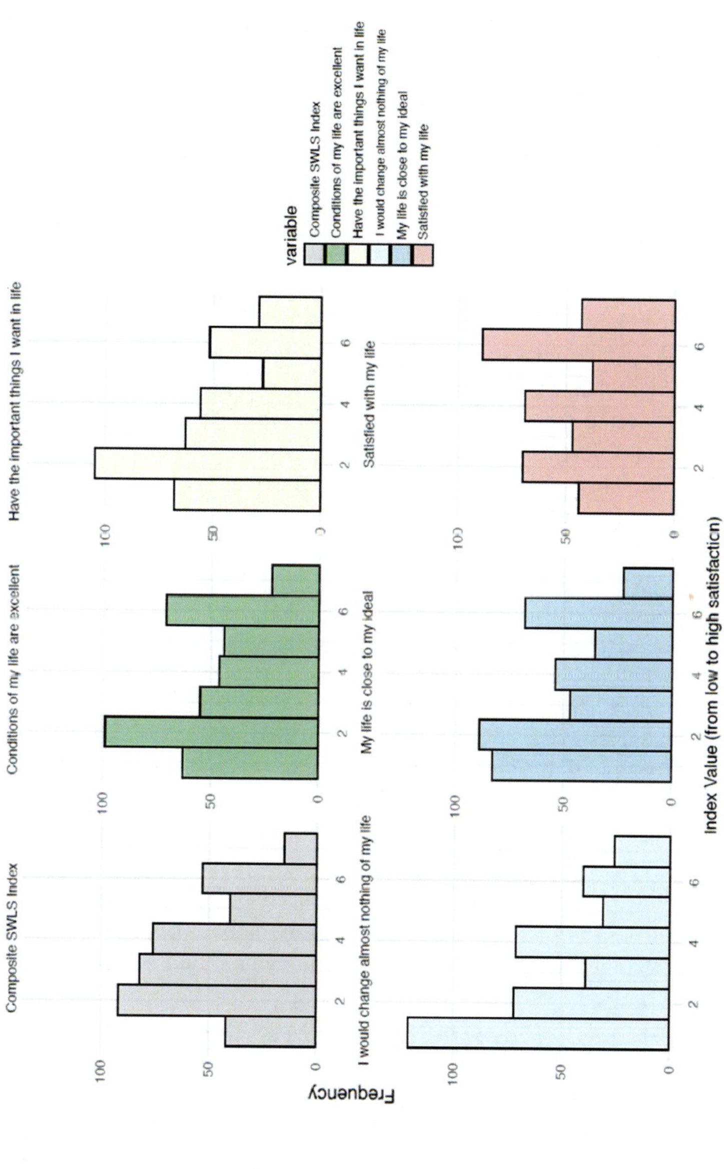

Fig. 1 Histograms of *satisfaction-with-life scale* (SWLS) indexes. *Source* Authors

6.4.2 Quality-of-Life Scale *(CASP-19)*

To assess quality of life among the elderly, this study employs the CASP-19 scale, developed by Hyde et al. (2003) at the Harvard School of Public Health. The scale is specifically designed for older adults and evaluates four essential domains: control, autonomy, self-realization, and pleasure.[1] Together, these dimensions provide a holistic understanding of the subjective quality of life in later years. The CASP-19 has been extensively validated and is recognized for its robust psychometric properties across various cultural contexts (Hyde et al. 2003).

Figure 2 displays the distribution of responses across the CASP-19 items. Each panel corresponds to one item on the scale, with bars representing the frequency of responses within four categories: *"Often"*, *"Sometimes"*, *"Not often"*, and *"Never"* (coded from 1 to 4). This format facilitates a detailed analysis of how the elderly perceive different aspects of their quality of life. A close inspection reveals that many older adults report frequent challenges in key domains. For instance, 59.50% of respondents agreed with the statement *My age prevents me from doing the things I would like to do,* indicating significant age-related constraints. Similarly, 61.50% of respondents reported that *Family responsibilities prevent them from doing the things they want to do, highlighting* the burdens placed on the elderly by familial obligations. Additionally, perceptions of limited agency are notable: 33.00% *often* felt that events were beyond their control, and 29.00% *often* felt left out of things.

While these findings suggest significant barriers to autonomy and social engagement, other responses were more moderate. For instance, the items *I feel free to plan for the future and can do the things I want to do received high frequencies in the "Sometimes" category (41.75% and 38.00%,* respectively), suggesting occasional rather than consistent autonomy. In contrast, items such as *"I feel that I can please myself with what I do" and "I feel that the future looks good for me"* showed relatively lower frequencies in the *"Not often"* category, indicating that such sentiments were less common among respondents. Notably, indicators of vitality and aspiration (such as *"I feel full of energy these days" and "I choose to do things I have never done before"*) had low frequencies in the *"Never"* category, highlighting a gap in experiences that typically enhance positive aging.

Collectively, the CASP-19 results offer a nuanced portrait of the constraints, aspirations, and lived realities of elderly individuals in Bangladesh. While many experience reduced autonomy and social inclusion, some retain a sense of control

[1] The CASP-19 comprises 19 items across four domains: -Control: *My age prevents me from doing the things I would like to do; I feel that what happens to me is out of my control; I feel free to plan for the future; I feel left out of things.* -Autonomy: *I can do the things I want to do; Family responsibilities prevent me from doing what I want to do; I feel that I can please myself what I can do; My health prevents me from doing things I want to do; Shortage of money stops me from doing things I want to do.* -Self-realization: *I look forward to each day; I feel that my life has meaning; I enjoy the things that I do; I enjoy being in the company of others; On balance, I look back on my life with a sense of happiness.* -Pleasure*: I feel full of energy these days; I choose to do things that I have never done before; I feel satisfied with the way my life has turned out; I feel that life is full of opportunities; I feel that the future looks good for me.*

and personal agency. These findings underscore the need for targeted social interventions that enhance quality of life by increasing freedom, social connection, and opportunities for self-expression.

6.4.3 Assessing Depression in the Elderly: The CES-D Tool

To evaluate depressive symptoms, the study uses the widely used CES-D (Center for Epidemiologic Studies Depression) scale, originally developed by Radloff (1977). The CES-D consists of 20 items designed to capture the frequency of depressive symptoms experienced in the past week, such as restlessness, poor appetite, loneliness, and sadness. Respondents indicate the frequency of these experiences using a four-point Likert scale: "*Rarely*" (less than 1 day*), "Some of the time*" (1–2 days), "*Occasionally*" (3–4 days), and "*Most of the time*" (5–7 days). The CES-D is recognized for its high reliability and has been validated in diverse populations, including older adults (Radloff 1977; Andresen et al. 1994).

Figure 3 presents histograms for each CES-D item, indicating the distribution of responses across the four frequency categories. This graphical representation enables a granular assessment of psychological well-being in the elderly population. The data suggest that several depressive symptoms occur at relatively low frequencies among the respondents. For example, 38.25% of participants reported "*Rarely*" being bothered by things that usually do not bother them, while 31.50% reported "Rarely" experiencing poor appetite. These findings suggest a degree of psychological resilience and relatively stable day-to-day functioning among many elderly individuals. However, several indicators raise concern. A substantial portion of respondents reported frequent symptoms of depression, including persistent sadness, low energy, and restlessness. For instance, although 36.50% reported "*Rarely*" feeling depressed, the remaining respondents were spread across higher-frequency categories, signaling notable mental distress. Likewise, symptoms such as *Everything I did was an effort*, *I felt fearful*, and *I had restless sleep* were reported with worrying frequency, highlighting the emotional and physical toll of aging in this context.

Notably, the frequency of positive emotions (such as feeling hopeful about the future, feeling happy, and enjoying life) was relatively low. Only 21% of respondents reported "*Rarely*" feeling that people disliked them, and just 33% indicated that they "*Rarely*" felt hopeful about the future. These figures suggest a deficit in positive effect and optimism among the surveyed population, which may reflect broader socio-economic and familial pressures. Taken together, the CES-D results underscore the high prevalence of depressive symptoms and the urgent need for mental health support systems tailored to the elderly in Bangladesh. The findings not only align with existing literature but also provide empirical grounding for policy and programmatic interventions to promote psychological well-being among aging populations.

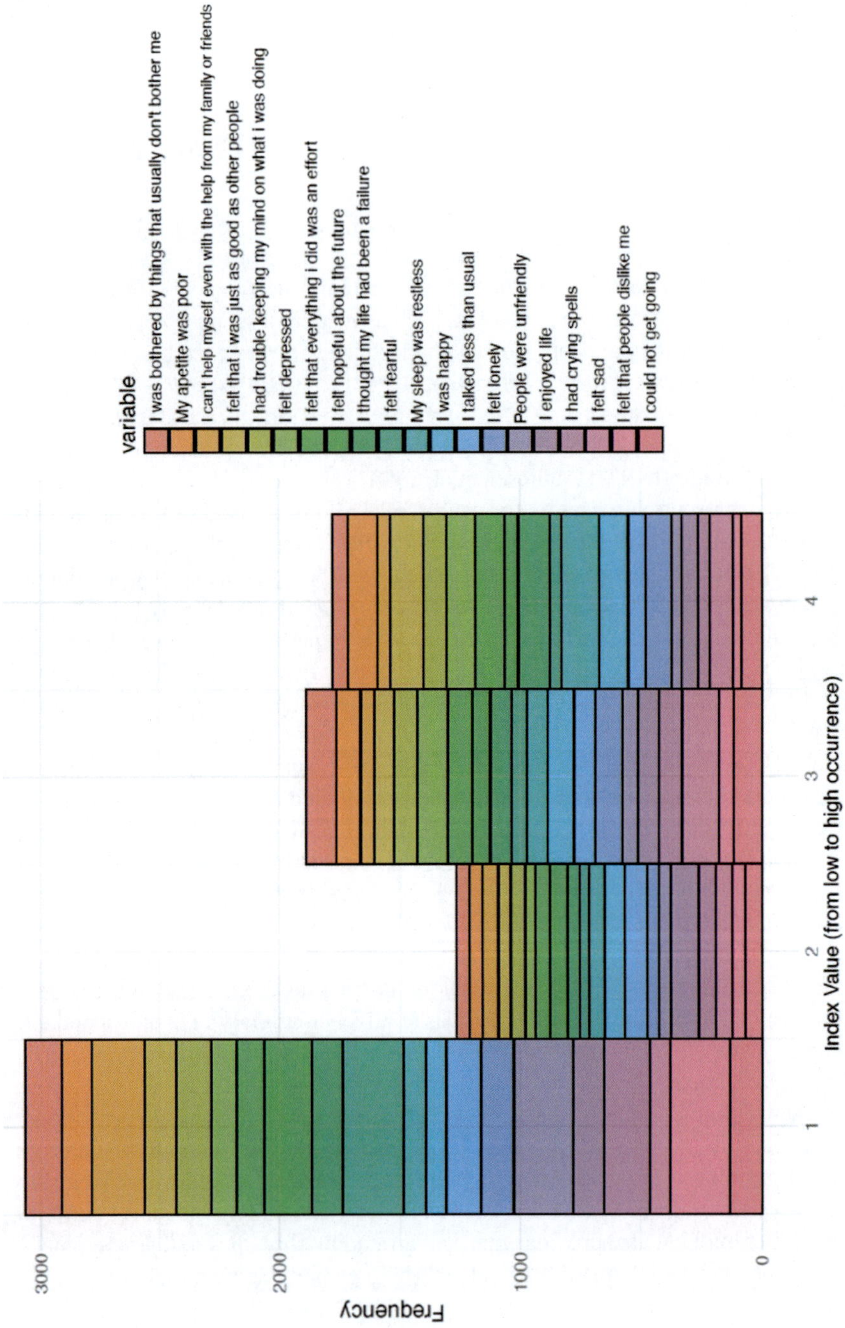

Fig. 2 Histogram of *quality-of-life scale* (CASP-19) indexes. *Source* authors

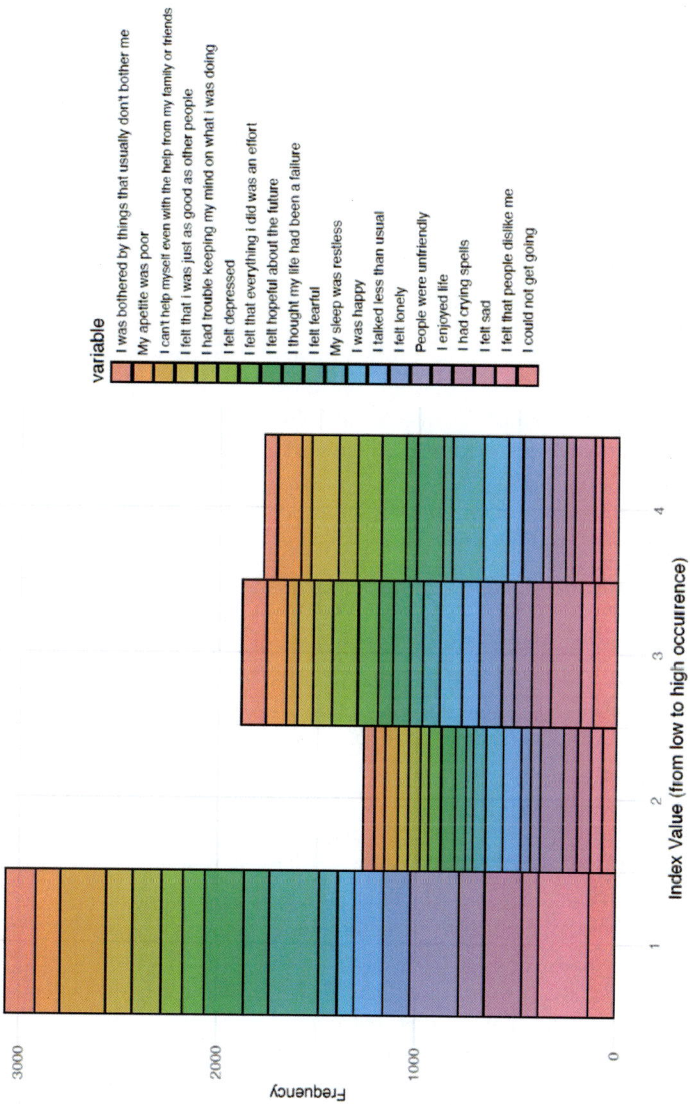

Fig. 3 Histogram of depression screening tool (CES-D) indexes. *Source* Authors

6.4.4 Econometric Approach: Ordered Probit Regression Models

To investigate the determinants of subjective well-being, this study employs an ordered probit regression model, which is particularly well-suited for analyzing ordinal outcome variables. In social and economic research, many outcome variables (such as life satisfaction) are measured on ordinal scales. These scales reflect ordered categories (e.g., from low to high satisfaction) without assuming equal distances between the categories. The *Satisfaction-with-Life Scale* (SWLS), for example, is an ordinal measure with multiple levels that capture the degree of satisfaction individuals feel with their lives.

The ordered probit model estimates the probability that an individual falls into one of these ordered categories, based on a set of explanatory variables. It assumes that an unobserved latent variable exists, representing the underlying level of satisfaction, which is mapped onto observed categories via estimated thresholds. This study uses the *polr* function in R, specifying the probit link to model the cumulative probability at each satisfaction level. The probit link assumes that the latent variable follows a standard normal distribution. It transforms the linear combination of predictors into cumulative probabilities, which are then used to estimate the likelihood that an observation falls into a particular satisfaction category. The estimated coefficients reflect the direction and strength of association between each independent variable and the probability of reporting higher or lower satisfaction.

To clearly disentangle these relationships, the models introduce control variables stepwise. This approach allows us to observe how the inclusion of different blocks of covariates alters the magnitude or significance of the key associations, thereby helping to identify potential confounding pathways. Model (1) does not include control variables. Model (2) adds a demographic block (age, gender, education, and work history) to capture baseline socio-demographic variation. Then, Model (3) adds controls for age-related illnesses, allowing us to isolate whether declines in subjective well-being are driven by health shocks rather than demographic factors alone. Finally, Model (4) adds detailed categorical variables that reflect both the intensity and quality of social engagement and intergenerational support, enabling a more nuanced understanding of social determinants.

The ordered probit specification simultaneously estimates the cut-points separating the ordinal satisfaction categories, appropriately accounting for the ordered but not equally spaced nature of the outcome. This leads to more precise modeling of the underlying latent well-being process than would be possible with linear or purely categorical methods. Overall, the stepwise modeling strategy and the ordered probit framework together provide a rigorous basis for identifying the socio-economic, health, and social factors most strongly associated with life satisfaction among Bangladesh's elderly population, while clarifying how these relationships change as additional sources of heterogeneity are accounted for.

6.5 Empirical Findings

This section presents the empirical findings from the analysis of life satisfaction and quality of life among the elderly population in Bangladesh. The primary objective is to identify key factors influencing well-being, as measured by two primary indices: the *Satisfaction-with-Life Scale* (SWLS) and the *Quality-of-Life Scale* (CASP-19). By examining the association between these well-being outcomes and a set of socio-demographic, economic, and health-related variables, we aim to gain a deeper understanding of the complex determinants of subjective well-being in later life.

The analysis employs ordered probit regression models, which allow for the estimation of relationships between ordinal outcome variables and a set of independent predictors. Four models are estimated, each incorporating a different combination of covariates to examine the robustness of the results and the relative importance of different factors. These include personal characteristics, indicators of mental health (particularly depression), physical health conditions, and variables related to social interaction and household structure. The results are expected to inform evidence-based policy recommendations to improve life satisfaction and overall quality of life among Bangladesh's aging population.

6.5.1 What Drives Life Satisfaction Among Elderly Bangladeshis?

Table 2 presents the results of a series of ordered probit regression models examining the relationship between life satisfaction and depressive symptoms among elderly individuals, with the Satisfaction-with-Life Scale (SWLS) as the dependent variable. The analysis sequentially introduces additional sets of covariates across the four models, allowing for a progressive assessment of the robustness of the association between depressive symptoms and subjective well-being.

The results demonstrate a strong negative relationship between depressive symptoms and life satisfaction. Individuals categorized as experiencing moderate depression consistently report significantly lower levels of satisfaction, with coefficients ranging from −0.927 in Model (1) to −0.507 in Model (4). These coefficients are statistically significant at the 1% or 5% level, indicating a robust and stable inverse association. High depressive symptoms are similarly associated with reduced life satisfaction in Models (1) through (3), with coefficients between −1.385 and −1.189. However, in Model (4), the coefficient for this category decreases in magnitude (−0.989) and loses statistical significance. This attenuation suggests that social and relational factors, such as participation in activities or the quality of familial relationships, may partially mediate the negative effect of severe depressive symptoms.

By contrast, the coefficients for the "slightly low" depressive symptoms category are not statistically significant in any model, implying that only moderate to severe

Table 2 Ordered probit regression models on satisfaction with life (SWLS index)

Variable	Model (1)	Model (2)	Model (3)	Model (4)
CESD index (depression)				
Slightly low	−0.153	−0.223	−0.057	0.057
	(0.176)	(0.183)	(0.195)	(0.204)
Moderate	−0.927***	−0.913***	−0.732***	−0.507**
	(0.194)	(0.202)	(0.214)	(0.232)
High	−1.332**	−1.385**	−1.189*	−0.989
	(0.646)	(0.664)	(0.676)	(0.842)
Included covariates				
Demographics	✗	✓	✓	✓
Age-related diseases	✗	✗	✓	✓
Activities	✗	✗	✗	✓
Satisfaction with children's relationship	✗	✗	✗	✓
Observations	379	374	366	358

Note Standard errors in parentheses. $*p < 0.1$; $**p < 0.05$; $***p < 0.01$
Source Authors

depression is substantively associated with lower subjective well-being among older adults. The inclusion of additional covariates in Models (3) and (4), detailed in Appendix Table 4, reveals several notable patterns. First, regarding marital status, unmarried individuals report significantly higher life satisfaction compared to other marital status groups. However, it is crucial to note that this category accounts for only 0.26% of the sample, making this estimate statistically unstable and unsuitable for substantive interpretation. This finding indeed diverges from much of the existing literature that associates marriage with enhanced well-being in old age. Second, regarding work history, Model (3) indicates that individuals who have never worked for at least 3 months report significantly higher life satisfaction. Though seemingly counterintuitive, this may reflect traditional household roles, particularly among women, where non-participation in the labor force coincided with strong family support structures. Third, while college or university education is positively associated with life satisfaction, the effect is not statistically significant. Primary and secondary education also do not exhibit meaningful associations, consistent with the paper's broader findings. Finally, concerning health status, Model (4) highlights the detrimental impact of chronic illness. Those experiencing age-related diseases, either "Sometimes" or "Always," report significantly lower life satisfaction. Additionally, individuals without hearing aids, even if they may need them, report significantly lower satisfaction, underscoring the importance of access to assistive health technologies. Other health conditions, such as nutritional disorders and Parkinsonian tremors, do not show significant effects in this specification.

6.5.2 Discussion: Life Satisfaction and Its Predictors

Regression analysis underscores depressive symptoms as a central determinant of life satisfaction among the elderly. A consistent and statistically significant negative association was found: as depressive symptoms intensify, self-reported life satisfaction decreases. This result is aligned with an extensive body of literature that documents the adverse impact of mental health conditions (particularly depression) on subjective well-being.

Interestingly, this paper finds a positive association between being unmarried and higher life satisfaction; an outcome that diverges from much of the existing literature in East Asian countries (Hori and Kamo 2018). This finding, however, requires cautious interpretation due to its extremely small sample size (0.26%). Hence, this result should not be interpreted as evidence of a general positive association between being unmarried and life satisfaction among the elderly in Bangladesh. The analysis also indicates that individuals who have never worked for at least three months report significantly higher life satisfaction. This result may reflect traditional household roles and reliance on family support structures.

Furthermore, the results point to the detrimental impact of chronic health conditions and the lack of assistive devices. Experiencing age-related diseases and not using hearing aids despite potential need are both associated with significantly lower life satisfaction. Control variables, such as education, employment history, and health, also exhibit expected patterns, although their significance varies across models, underscoring the multidimensional nature of life satisfaction.

6.5.3 Determinants of Quality of Life in Later Years

This section investigates the determinants of quality of life among the elderly population in Bangladesh, using the CASP-19 index as the primary outcome variable. Quality of life is a multidimensional concept encompassing individual well-being, autonomy, control, and life satisfaction, which are increasingly emphasized elements in economic and social research on aging. To evaluate how depressive symptoms and other relevant factors shape these dimensions, a series of ordered probit regression models is estimated. The analysis begins with a baseline specification that includes only depressive symptoms, measured via the CES-D index. Subsequently, it incorporates additional controls related to demographics, health status, education, and social relationships.

The results shown in Table 3 reveal a robust and consistent negative relationship between depressive symptoms and quality of life. Individuals experiencing moderate levels of depression report significantly lower CASP-19 scores across all four models. The estimated coefficients for this group range from −0.889 to −0.718 and are statistically significant at the 1% level, underscoring the persistent adverse impact of moderate depressive symptoms on well-being. For those with high depressive symptoms, the negative effect is even more pronounced in Models (1)

Table 3 Ordered probit regression models on quality of life (CASP index)

Variable	Model (1)	Model (2)	Model (3)	Model (4)
CESD index (depression)				
Slightly low	−0.104	−0.109	−0.039	−0.030
	(0.184)	(0.192)	(0.203)	(0.214)
Moderate	−0.889***	−0.882***	−0.799***	−0.718***
	(0.200)	(0.209)	(0.221)	(0.241)
High	−2.218***	−2.352***	−2.310***	−0.893
	(0.603)	(0.617)	(0.631)	(0.791)
Included covariates				
Demographics	✗	✓	✓	✓
Age-related diseases	✗	✗	✓	✓
Activities	✗	✗	✗	✓
Satisfaction with children relationship	✗	✗	✗	✓
Observations	379	374	366	358

Note Standard errors in parentheses. $*p < 0.1$; $**p < 0.05$; $***p < 0.01$
Source Authors

through (3), with coefficients exceeding −2.2, all statistically significant. However, in Model (4), which includes an expanded set of covariates (such as participation in activities and satisfaction with familial relationships), the coefficient decreases in magnitude (−0.893) and loses statistical significance. This attenuation suggests that social engagement and relational support may partially mediate the effects of severe depression on perceived quality of life.

By contrast, slightly low depressive symptoms do not show significant effects in any of the models, indicating that only moderate and severe forms of depression are meaningfully associated with reduced quality of life in this population. The stepwise inclusion of control variables also reveals important patterns, as controls do not notably alter the magnitude or significance of depressive symptom coefficients.

Additional evidence from Appendix Table 5 strengthens the interpretation of these findings. First, regarding education, college or university education is significantly and positively associated with quality of life across models. Secondary education also shows a positive and significant effect, whereas primary education does not. These findings align with international evidence linking higher educational attainment to improved resilience and subjective well-being in older age. Second, regarding social engagement, the variables "Going out once a week" and "Benefit of activities: sometimes" are both positively associated with quality of life. This suggests that moderate, consistent engagement in social activities has a meaningful impact on the psychological well-being of the elderly. Third, regarding family dynamics, most indicators of satisfaction with children's relationships and psychological support are not statistically significant. However, some intermediate satisfaction levels, such as being "neutral" or "slightly satisfied", show positive and significant coefficients, indicating that even modest familial harmony can contribute to improved well-being.

Taken together, these results highlight the significant impact of mental health, education, and social relationships on the quality of life among the elderly in Bangladesh. Notably, depressive symptoms (particularly moderate to severe) emerge as a consistent and significant detractor. The findings support the need for multi-dimensional policy approaches that integrate mental health services, educational interventions, and family-based or community support systems to promote healthy aging.

6.5.4 Discussion: Improving Quality of Life for the Elderly

Consistent with the findings on life satisfaction, the analysis confirms that depressive symptoms are significantly and negatively associated with quality of life, as measured by the CASP-19 index. The magnitude and significance of this association, particularly for moderate levels of depression, emphasize the psychological vulnerability of elderly individuals facing mental health challenges. This result is in line with prior studies, which find that depressive symptoms are among the strongest predictors of diminished quality of life in older populations.

The analysis further highlights the importance of education in promoting quality of life. College or university education shows a consistent, significant positive relationship with the CASP-19 index, and secondary education also shows a positive effect in several models. This aligns with international evidence linking higher educational attainment to improved resilience and subjective well-being in older age (Blanchflower and Oswald 2018), as well as with findings by Hasan et al. (2024) who used the latest World Values Survey (WVS) to examine the incidence, intensity, and determinants of well-being in Bangladesh.

In terms of social engagement, the results indicate that going out once a week and perceiving some benefit from activities are positively associated with quality of life. This suggests that even moderate social engagement can meaningfully contribute to well-being. Our finding on the protective role of social engagement is strongly supported by recent conceptual work. It aligns with the construct of "cognitive social capital" (i.e., the shared trust and reciprocity within a community), which has been shown to significantly lower the odds of depression among rural Bangladeshi elders (Islam et al. 2024). This suggests that interventions strengthening community bonds could be as vital as those targeting individual mental health.

Finally, regarding family dynamics, the analysis reveals that moderate levels of satisfaction with children's relationships (neutral or slight satisfaction) are associated with a higher quality of life, indicating that even modest familial harmony can be beneficial.

6.6 Conclusions and Policy Implications

6.6.1 Conclusion

This study provides a comprehensive examination of the well-being and living conditions of the elderly population in Bangladesh, with a specific focus on mental health, socio-demographic characteristics, and familial relationships. The empirical findings are largely consistent with existing literature, particularly in highlighting the negative relationship between depressive symptoms and both satisfaction with life and overall quality of life. However, the study also identifies context-specific findings, such as the statistically unstable positive association between the small, unmarried sample and life satisfaction. The beneficial link between higher educational attainment and quality of life also invites further exploration of local social dynamics and cultural expectations in later life. Such deviations underscore the need for localized policy design and for incorporating socio-cultural nuances in interpreting well-being outcomes.

Yet, limitations of this study should be considered when interpreting the findings. First, the cross-sectional design establishes associations but cannot determine causal directions. For instance, while we find depression is linked to lower well-being, it is plausible that poor life circumstances cause depressive symptoms, or that a reciprocal relationship exists. Second, the sampling strategy, while capturing important rural-urban variation, was not nationally random. The purposive selection of two districts may limit the generalizability of the findings to all regions of Bangladesh, particularly the coastal and eastern regions. Third, the reliance on self-reported data for key outcomes (life satisfaction, depression) and predictors (social engagement, health) may be subject to recall bias and social desirability effects. Fourth, despite the use of validated scales, residual confounding cannot be excluded. Unmeasured factors, such as personality traits, lifetime trauma, or the quality of the living environment beyond basic housing, could influence both mental health and reported well-being. Finally, the study's focus on broad socio-economic and familial correlates means that deeper qualitative dimensions (such as the nature of intergenerational conflict, experiences of dignity, or spiritual life) remain unexplored. Future research would benefit from longitudinal designs, nationally representative samples, and mixed-methods approaches to address these limitations and build a more dynamic and nuanced understanding of aging in Bangladesh.

Besides these limitations, our findings reveal critical challenges: a high prevalence of dissatisfaction, reduced quality of life, and elevated depressive symptoms among older adults. These patterns signal an urgent need for comprehensive, multidimensional policy interventions that aim to improve the mental and emotional well-being of the elderly. Globally, it is estimated that over 20% of individuals aged 60 and above suffer from mental or neurological disorders (Kadariya et al. 2019). In settings where institutional support systems are limited and traditional family structures are evolving, addressing the psychological impacts of aging becomes especially vital. Our results, contextualized by the latest national data showing most elders experience depressive symptoms (Rahman et al. 2025), indicate that this is not a marginal issue but a widespread public health priority. Strategies that promote mental health support, educational opportunities, social integration, and family harmony are crucial for mitigating depression and enhancing well-being in later life.

6.6.2 Policy Implications

From a policy perspective, the study recommends a coordinated approach that involves the government, healthcare institutions, and civil society. Specific recommendations stem directly from the empirical findings. First, the robust negative association between depressive symptoms and both life satisfaction and quality of life necessitates a primary policy focus on developing accessible, community-based mental health services tailored for the elderly. This includes integrating geriatric mental health screening into primary care systems and subsidizing first-line treatments. Such an intervention directly addresses a primary source of welfare loss identified in the ordered probit models, where moderate depression levels consistently predicted significantly lower well-being scores.

Second, the positive association between higher educational attainment (particularly college or university education) and quality of life suggests that policy should support lifelong learning and educational opportunities for older adults, thereby building resilience and improving well-being in later years.

Third, the findings regarding social engagement and family relationships indicate the need for a dual approach. The positive link between moderate social outings and perceived benefits from activities, as well as quality of life, supports the creation of accessible community hubs and social programs for the elderly. Concurrently, since even modest satisfaction with children's relationships is associated with better quality of life, policies should encourage and support intergenerational harmony and communication, while also respecting the diverse living arrangements that suit different elderly individuals.

Finally, the detrimental impact of unmet health needs, such as the lack of hearing aids and the presence of age-related diseases, underscores the importance of improving access to basic healthcare and assistive technologies for the elderly population. Fostering a supportive, inclusive, and mentally enriching environment for the elderly is essential to achieving healthy aging. This study contributes to that vision by offering empirical evidence and actionable insights that can guide both policy and future research in the Bangladeshi and broader South Asian contexts.

Acknowledgements We would like to express our sincere gratitude to the Asian Development Bank Institute, Tokyo for their invaluable support throughout this project. Additionally, we extend our heartfelt appreciation to the Institute of Health Economics at the University of Dhaka for their assistance and contributions. We also acknowledge with thanks that this work has benefited from the support of the Paris School of Economics and the *Agence Nationale de la Recherche* through the program *Investissements d'Avenir ANR-17-EURE-0001*. Their support has been instrumental in the successful completion of this research, and we are truly thankful to these institutions for their contributions.

Appendix

See Tables 4 and 5

Table 4 Ordered probit regression models on satisfaction with life (SWLS index)

Variable	(1)	(2)	(3)	(4)
CESD index (depr): Slightly low	−0.153 (0.176)	−0.223 (0.183)	−0.057 (0.195)	0.057 (0.204)
CESD index (depr): Moderate	−0.927*** (0.194)	−0.913*** (0.202)	−0.732*** (0.214)	−0.507** (0.232)
CESD index (depr): High	−1.332** (0.646)	−1.385** (0.664)	−1.189* (0.676)	−0.989 (0.842)
Age		−0.009 (0.054)	0.042 (0.055)	0.059 (0.059)
Male		0.177 (0.183)	0.090 (0.188)	0.069 (0.203)
Unmarried		6.146*** (0.000)	6.287*** (0.000)	5.692*** (0.000)
Separated		0.041 (0.667)	0.076 (0.680)	0.086 (0.700)
Widowed		−0.138 (0.159)	−0.178 (0.163)	−0.238 (0.177)
Other marital status		0.248 (0.674)	0.162 (0.678)	0.392 (0.697)
Not ever worked 3 months		0.638*** (0.219)	0.623*** (0.230)	0.532** (0.248)
Business (self in non-farm)		0.066 (0.232)	0.093 (0.235)	0.058 (0.248)
Wage in farm		−0.079 (0.411)	0.005 (0.415)	0.131 (0.454)
Wage in non-farm		−0.002 (0.217)	−0.023 (0.223)	−0.121 (0.237)
Casual labor in farm		0.488* (0.271)	0.539** (0.274)	0.355 (0.289)
Casual labor in non-farm		−0.068 (0.243)	−0.074 (0.251)	0.008 (0.269)
Other job position		0.036 (0.248)	0.160 (0.261)	0.159 (0.277)
Partly retired		−0.235 (0.156)	−0.261 (0.160)	−0.343* (0.175)
Not retired		−0.305** (0.147)	−0.334** (0.151)	−0.319** (0.161)
Other current job status		0.097 (0.438)	−0.321 (0.496)	−0.295 (0.512)
Primary education		0.097 (0.149)	0.142 (0.153)	0.072 (0.160)
Secondary education		0.180 (0.219)	0.170 (0.226)	−0.158 (0.240)

(continued)

Table 4 (continued)

Variable	(1)	(2)	(3)	(4)
College/university		0.972* (0.530)	0.869 (0.541)	0.429 (0.549)
Age disease: Sometimes			−0.421** (0.179)	−0.222 (0.189)
Age disease: Always			−0.436** (0.198)	−0.375* (0.208)
No hearing aid			−0.813*** (0.315)	−0.728** (0.330)
No nutritional disease			0.038 (0.175)	−0.117 (0.188)
No hands shaking (Parkinson)			0.305** (0.141)	0.353** (0.154)
Going out: Less than once a month				0.013 (0.472)
Going out: 1–3 times a month				−0.247 (0.422)
Going out: Once a week				−0.142 (0.516)
Going out: Few times a week				−0.724** (0.328)
Going out: Every day				−0.587** (0.282)
Benefit of activities: Rarely				−0.035 (0.402)
Benefit of activities: Sometimes				0.223 (0.336)
Benefit of activities: Often				0.385 (0.323)
Benefit of activities: Very often				0.598* (0.337)
Slightly unsatisfied w/ relationship w/ children				−0.124 (0.463)
Neutral satisfaction w/ relationship w/ children				0.719 (0.447)
Slightly satisfied w/ relationship w/ children				0.759* (0.416)
Satisfied w/ relationship w/ children				0.614 (0.436)
Children give psychological help: Rarely				−0.386 (0.395)
Children give psychological help: Sometimes				−0.292 (0.404)
Children give psychological help: Often				−0.262 (0.388)
Children give psychological help: Very often				0.346 (0.404)
Observations	379	374	366	358

Note Standard errors in parentheses. *p < 0.1; **p < 0.05; ***p < 0.01*
Source Authors

Table 5 Ordered probit regression models on quality of life (CASP index)

Variable	(1)	(2)	(3)	(4)
CESD index (depr): Slightly low	−0.104 (0.184)	−0.109 (0.192)	−0.039 (0.203)	−0.030 (0.214)
CESD index (depr): Moderate	−0.889*** (0.200)	−0.882*** (0.209)	−0.799*** (0.221)	−0.718*** (0.241)
CESD index (depr): High	−2.218*** (0.603)	−2.352*** (0.617)	−2.310*** (0.631)	−0.893 (0.791)
Age		−0.051 (0.054)	−0.019 (0.056)	−0.027 (0.060)
Male		0.082 (0.186)	0.054 (0.190)	0.189 (0.204)
Unmarried		4.475 (20.124)	4.429 (18.552)	4.508 (24.895)
Separated		1.299* (0.744)	1.273* (0.738)	1.325* (0.779)
Widowed		0.056 (0.162)	−0.007 (0.166)	0.194 (0.180)
Other marital status		0.546 (0.783)	0.508 (0.786)	0.189 (0.768)
Not ever worked 3 months		0.005 (0.217)	0.014 (0.227)	0.174 (0.248)
Business (self in non-farm)		−0.002 (0.234)	−0.005 (0.236)	−0.005 (0.250)
Wage in farm		0.529 (0.417)	0.547 (0.423)	0.526 (0.461)
Wage in non-farm		0.129 (0.220)	0.080 (0.224)	−0.009 (0.238)
Casual labor in farm		−0.164 (0.269)	−0.100 (0.271)	−0.148 (0.287)
Casual labor in non-farm		0.160 (0.239)	0.157 (0.245)	0.062 (0.264)
Other job position		0.269 (0.251)	0.358 (0.264)	0.188 (0.283)
Partly retired		0.194 (0.158)	0.177 (0.162)	0.168 (0.178)
Not retired		−0.085 (0.147)	−0.152 (0.151)	−0.220 (0.162)
Other current job status		0.045 (0.446)	0.077 (0.520)	0.161 (0.547)
Primary education		0.136 (0.152)	0.160 (0.156)	0.138 (0.164)
Secondary education		0.405* (0.227)	0.394* (0.234)	0.500** (0.253)
College/university		1.567** (0.679)	1.439** (0.673)	1.446** (0.669)

(continued)

Table 5 (continued)

Variable	(1)	(2)	(3)	(4)
Age disease: Sometimes			−0.110 (0.182)	−0.104 (0.193)
Age disease: Always			−0.133 (0.201)	−0.137 (0.212)
No hearing aid			−0.093 (0.303)	−0.103 (0.330)
No nutritional disease			0.166 (0.174)	−0.153 (0.189)
No hands shaking (Parkinson)			0.289** (0.141)	0.130 (0.154)
Going out: Less once a month				−0.276 (0.500)
Going out: 1–3 times a month				−0.066 (0.410)
Going out: Once a week				0.877* (0.514)
Going out: Few times a week				0.091 (0.329)
Going out: Every day				0.530* (0.285)
Benefit of activities: Rarely				0.272 (0.384)
Benefit of activities: Sometimes				0.974*** (0.332)
Benefit of activities: Often				0.576* (0.318)
Benefit of activities: Very often				1.028*** (0.333)
Slightly unsatisfied with relationship w/ children				0.372 (0.436)
Neutral satisfaction with relationship w/ children				0.833* (0.444)
Slightly satisfied with relationship w/ children				1.318*** (0.419)
Satisfied with relationship w/ children				1.152*** (0.437)
Children give psychological help: Rarely				−0.560 (0.397)
Children give psychological help: Sometimes				−0.473 (0.430)
Children give psychological help: Often				−0.787* (0.417)
Children give psychological help: Very often				−0.667 (0.427)
Observations	379	374	366	358

Note Standard errors in parentheses. *p < 0.1; **p < 0.05; **p < 0.01
Source Authors

References

Afrin, S., Khan, M. M. H., & Haque, M. A. (2025). Factors affecting the active aging situation in Bangladesh. *Frontiers in Public Health*, 13, 1517482.

Akter, N., Banu, B., Chowdhury, S. H., Islam, K. R., Tabassum, T. T., & Hossain, S. M. (2023). Astute exploration of collective mental health events among the residents of elderly care homes. *Heliyon*, 9(7).

Andresen, E. M., Malmgren, J. A., Carter, W. B., & Patrick, D. L. (1994). Screening for depression in well older adults: Evaluation of a short form of the CES-D (Center for Epidemiologic Studies Depression Scale). *American Journal of Preventive Medicine, 10*(2), 77–84.

Anwar, A., Akter, N., Yadav, U. N., Ghimire, S., Bhattacharjee, S., Eusufzai, S. Z., … & Mistry, S. K. (2024). Assessment of mental well-being and its socio-economic determinants among older adults in the Rohingya refugee camp of Bangladesh. *Scientific Reports*, 14(1), 17918.

Barikdar, A., Ahmed, T., & Lasker, S. P. (2016a). The situation of the elderly in Bangladesh. *Bangladesh Journal of Bioethics, 7*(1), 27–36.

Barikdar, A., Uddin, M. N., Islam, M. R., & Afrin, S. (2016b). Property rights of women and elderly in rural Bangladesh: Prevalence and predictors. *Journal of Social Science Studies, 3*(1), 42–59.

Blanchflower, D. G., & Oswald, A. J. (2018). Unhappiness and pain in modern America: A review essay, and further evidence, on Carol Graham's *Happiness for All? The Economic Journal, 128*(615), 412–435.

Bowling, A., & Dieppe, P. (2018). What is successful ageing and who should define it? *BMJ*, 331(7531), 1548-1551.

Cassum, L. A., Cash, K., Qidwai, W., & Vertejee, S. (2020). Exploring the experiences of the older adults who are brought to live in shelter homes in Karachi, Pakistan: A qualitative study. *BMC Geriatrics, 20*(1), 1–12.

Diener, E., Emmons, R. A., Larsen, R. J., & Griffin, S. (1985). The Satisfaction-with-Life Scale. *Journal of Personality Assessment, 49*, 71–75.

Hasan, M. R., Jayasinghe, M., & Selvanathan, E. A. (2024). New approach to measure well-being: A case study on Bangladesh. *Social Indicators Research*, 172(1), 283-311.

Hawlader, M. D. H., Rashid, M. U., Khan, M. A. S., Ara, T., Nabi, M. H., Haque, M. M. A., … & Rahman, M. L. (2021). Quality of life of COVID-19 recovered patients in Bangladesh. *PLoS One*, 16(10), e0257421.

Hori, M., & Kamo, Y. (2018). Gender differences in happiness: The effects of marriage, social roles, and social support in East Asia. *Applied Research in Quality of Life*, 13(4), 839-857.

Huda, C. E. (2020). Family transfers, coresidency, elderly labour supply and welfare perspective: Evidence from Indonesia. *Jurnal BPPK: Badan Pendidikan dan Pelatihan Keuangan, 13*(1), 47–63.

Hyde, M., Wiggins, R. D., Higgs, P., & Blane, D. B. (2003). A measure of quality of life in early old age: the theory, development and properties of a needs satisfaction model (CASP-19). *Aging & mental health*, 7(3), 186-194.

Imran, J. A., Mitra, A. K., Ria, M. A., Mitra, T., Konok, J. F., Shuchi, S. A., & Saha, P. K. (2024). Health-Related Quality of Life among Elderly Patients in Urban Bangladesh: A Cross-Sectional Study. *Diseases*, 12(9), 212.

Islam, M. Z., Prue, E., Farjana, S., Al Fidah, M. F., & Efa, S. S. (2024). Cognitive social capital and geriatric depression: A community-based case-control study among the rural elderly people of Bangladesh. *Cambridge Prisms: Global Mental Health*, 11, e89.

Kadariya, S., Gautam, R., & Aro, A. R. (2019). Physical activity, mental health, and well-being among older adults in South and Southeast Asia: a scoping review. *BioMed research international*, 2019(1), 6752182.

Lutz, W., Goujon, A., Kc, S., Stonawski, M., & Stilianakis, N. (2018). *Demographic and human capital scenarios for the 21st century: 2018 assessment for 201 countries.* Publications Office of the European Union.

Miao, J., & Wu, X. (2021). Subjective well-being of Chinese elderly: A comparative analysis among Hong Kong, Urban China and Taiwan. *Ageing & Society, 41*(3), 686–707.

Pavot, W., & Diener, E. (1993). Review of the Satisfaction-with-Life Scale. *Psychological Assessment, 5*(2), 164–172.

Radloff, L. S. (1977). The CES-D scale: A self-report depression scale for research in the general population. *Applied Psychological Measurement, 1*(3), 385–401.

Rahman, A. (2020, September 30). The increasing 'burden' of the elderly in Bangladesh. *The Daily Star*. https://www.thedailystar.net/opinion/news/the-increasing-burden-the-elderly-bangladesh-1970349

Rahman, M., Khan, M., Fattah, T., Tasnim, Z., Das, P. R., Prattay, K. M. R., … & Islam, M. R. (2025). Prevalence and associated risk factors for depression, anxiety, insomnia, and loneliness among the geriatric population in Bangladesh: a cross-sectional study. *BMC psychiatry*, 25(1), 1102.

Rahman, M. M., Tareque, M. I., & Rahman, K. M. (1976). Living arrangements and health status of the rural elderly of Naogaon district, Bangladesh. *Quarterly Journal Devoted to Research on Ageing*, 469, 411.

Rahman, M. S., Rahman, M. A., Ali, M., Rahman, M. S., Maniruzzaman, M., Yeasmin, M. A., … & Islam, S. M. S. (2020). Determinants of depressive symptoms among older people in Bangladesh. *Journal of affective disorders*, 264, 157–162.

Sahu, B., van Wissen, L. J. G., Hutter, I., & Bosch, A. (2012). Fertility differentials among religious minorities: Cross-national and regional evidence from India and Bangladesh. *Population, Space and Place*, 18(5), 503-515.

Sengupta, P., & Benjamin, A. I. (2015). Prevalence of depression and associated risk factors among the elderly in urban and rural field practice areas of a tertiary care institution in Ludhiana. *Indian Journal of Public Health, 59*(1), 3–8.

Subramaniam, M., Abdin, E., Sambasivam, R., Vaingankar, J. A., Picco, L., Pang, S., … & Chong, S. A. (2016). Prevalence of depression among older adults: Results from the Well-being of the Singapore Elderly Study. *Annals of the Academy of Medicine Singapore, 45*(4), 123–133.

Sultana, N., Nguyen, T. T. P., Hossain, A., Asaduzzaman, M., Nguyen, M. H., Jahan, I., Nguyen, K. T., & Duong, T. V. (2022). Psychometric Properties of the Short-Form Geriatric Depression Scale (GDS-SF) and Its Associated Factors among the Elderly in Bangladesh. *International Journal of Environmental Research and Public Health*, 19(13), 7935. doi:https://doi.org/10.3390/ijerph19137935

Teerawichitchainan, B., Knodel, J., & Pothisiri, W. (2015). What does living alone really mean for older persons? A comparative study of Myanmar, Vietnam, and Thailand. *Population Studies, 69*(2), 219–234.

Tohan, M. M., Ahmed, F., Juie, I. J., Kabir, A., & Rahman, M. A. (2024). Outdoor recreational activities and mental well-being of geriatric people in Bangladesh: structural equation modelling. *Discover Psychology*, 4(1), 33.

Tran, T., & Vu Van, H. (2017). *Housing and well-being among the Vietnamese elderly* (No. 2).

United Nations. (2024). World Population Prospects 2024: Summary of Results (UN DESA/POP/2024/TR/NO. 9). Department of Economic and Social Affairs, Population Division.

Wei, Y., & Tsay, W. J. (2024). Does distance make happiness? Geographic proximity of adult children and the well-being of older persons. *Journal of Aging & Social Policy*, 36(2), 222-240.

Uddin, M. A. (2023). Social support networks for older adults in Bangladesh: A systematic. *Journal of Noakhali Science and Technology University* (JNSTU), 7(1&2), 63-74.

World Health Organization (WHO). (2018). *Mental health: Strengthening our response*. https://www.who.int/news-room/fact-sheets/detail/mental-health-strengthening-our-response

Chapter 7
The Long-Term Impact of Adverse Childhood Experiences on Subjective Well-Being: Longitudinal Evidence from Rural China

Peng Nie and Xili Lin

7.1 Introduction

China has the world's largest aging population and is among the fastest-aging societies (Chen et al. 2022; Nie et al. 2021a). According to the most recent data from the National Bureau of Statistics (January 2025), China's population aged 60 and above was approximately 310.3 million in 2024 (22.0% of the total population), and is projected to increase to 491.5 million (36.5% of the total population) by 2050 (United Nations 2020). Notably, the issue of population aging in rural areas is more pronounced than in urban areas: The 2020 seventh population census revealed that 23.8% of the rural population was aged 60 or older—nearly 8 percentage points higher than in urban areas.

Subjective well-being (SWB) has emerged as a key indicator of quality of life among older adults. However, due to deteriorating physical functioning, low socioeconomic status (SES), and the outmigration of adult children, China's rural older adults may face a higher risk of poor SWB than their urban counterparts. In 2018, 37.1% of older adults aged 60 and above exhibited a higher degree of depressive symptoms, with a stark rural-urban disparity (41.5% vs. 27.7%) (Nie and Zhao 2023). Rural older adults also report significantly lower life satisfaction than their urban

P. Nie (✉) · X. Lin
School of Economics and Finance, Xi'an Jiaotong University, Xi'an, China
e-mail: niepeng2017@mail.xjtu.edu.cn

X. Lin
e-mail: linxili@stu.xjtu.edu.cn

P. Nie
Institute for Health Care & Public Management, Stuttgart, Germany

IZA@LISER, Belval, Luxembourg

W. Ma et al. (eds.), *Beyond Income*, Contributions to Economics,
https://doi.org/10.1007/978-981-92-4957-2_7

counterparts (44.1% vs. 54.6%) (Li et al. 2015). This contrast diverges from patterns observed in Western countries and other eastern Asian societies, where such differences in mental health are minimal. Thus, improving the psychological well-being of rural older adults has become an urgent public health priority in China.

While numerous studies have identified key determinants of SWB such as age (Bauer et al. 2017; Blanchflower and Oswald 2008b), gender (Inglehart 2002), income (Deaton 2008; Diener and Biswas-Diener 2002; Frijters et al. 2004), unemployment (Binder and Coad 2015), health (Gwozdz and Sousa-Poza 2010; Steptoe et al. 2015), social capital (Sarracino 2010), and religion (Diener and Diener 2009), a growing body of literature from developed nations highlights the lasting impact of adverse childhood experiences (ACEs) on subjective well-being (SWB) in adolescents (Houtepen et al. 2020; Moore and Ramirez 2016) and young adults (Corcoran and McNulty 2018; Wilson-Genderson et al. 2022). However, evidence from China - particularly in rural areas - remains scarce. The generalizability of Western findings is limited by key cultural differences: certain harsh disciplinary practices or family conflicts that are clearly defined as ACEs in the West may be culturally normalized in rural China due to norms emphasizing parental authority and child obedience. These differences influence both the incidence and perceptions of ACEs. Furthermore, existing studies are predominantly cross-sectional, seldom address endogeneity concerns and offer limited insight into the underlying pathways linking ACEs to later-life SWB.

To fill these gaps, this study leverages longitudinal data from the 2011–2020 waves of the China Health and Retirement Longitudinal Study (CHARLS), linked with the 2014 CHARLS Life History Survey, to investigate the long-term effects of ACEs on SWB among middle-aged and older adults in rural China. This study contributes to the literature on the ACEs-SWB relationship in several important ways. First, it extends the ACEs-SWB literature beyond Western settings to rural China, providing empirical evidence from an East Asian cultural context where the incidence and perception of ACEs differ substantially. Methodologically, we leverage nationally representative longitudinal data from CHARLS, which strengthens causal inference by accounting for time-invariant heterogeneity, improves measurement accuracy, and mitigates attrition bias. Furthermore, we employ an instrumental variable approach to address potential endogeneity in the ACEs-SWB relationship. Finally, we explore the mechanisms underlying the ACEs-SWB relationship, thereby deepening understanding of how early-life experiences shape long-term well-being.

The remainder of this study is structured as follows: Sect. 2 reviews the relevant literature on the ACEs-SWB relationship and documents possible heuristic mechanisms underlying the ACEs' impact on SWB. Section 3 describes the data and empirical strategy. Section 4 reports the results, and Sect. 5 concludes with a discussion of key findings and their implications for policy.

7.2 Prior Literature and Underlying Mechanisms

7.2.1 Prior Literature

The existing literature on the ACEs-SWB relationship has predominantly focused on adolescents and young adults in developed countries, while middle-aged and older adults have received relatively limited attention. For instance, Oshio et al. (2013) analyze survey data from municipalities in the Tokyo metropolitan area and demonstrate that childhood adversity significantly reduces SWB in adulthood, with social support and socioeconomic status (SES) partially mediating this effect. Similarly, Corcoran and McNulty (2018) find that ACEs diminish SWB through insecure attachment in a sample of 190 Irish university students - a pattern observed among Spanish university students (Bartolomé-Valenzuela et al. 2024). Recent evidence further confirms a negative association between ACEs and psychological well-being among Saudi Arabian university students, with emotional intelligence partially buffering this relationship (Irshad and Lone 2025). In addition, benevolent childhood experiences have been shown to attenuate the negative association between ACEs and mental health outcomes (Nahar et al. 2025). Furthermore, Rzeszutek et al. (2025) find that specific ACEs are associated with a higher risk of Polish adult post-traumatic stress disorder (PTSD) and lower SWB.

Several studies have begun to document the long-term consequences of ACEs for SWB in midlife and older adulthood. Using longitudinal data from the National Survey of Midlife Development in the United States (MIDUS), Mosley-Johnson et al. (2019) show that ACEs are significantly associated with lower life satisfaction, psychological well-being, and social well-being, particularly among individuals with histories of childhood abuse and household dysfunction. Similarly, drawing on MIDUS data, Potter et al. (2025) further find that cumulative ACEs are associated with poorer SWB among middle-aged and older adults, with those facing higher levels of ACEs exhibiting stronger negative affect in response to physical health stressors. Cross-national evidence reinforces the persistence of childhood adversity effects into later life: Blanchflower and Bryson (2024) leverage the UK's National Child Development Study (NCDS) to demonstrate that childhood bullying at ages 7 and 11 negatively affects SWB from adolescence into middle age (ages 16–62). A recent study on low-income Korean immigrant older adults reveals that ACEs are indirectly associated with depressive symptoms via self-perceptions of aging (Park et al. 2026).

In contrast, evidence from China remains limited. Zhang et al. (2020), using cross-sectional data from 1019 high-school graduates, identify a negative association between ACE exposure and psychological well-being. Similarly, Chang et al. (2019) analyze a sample of 1501 rural residents aged 18–59 and find that higher ACE scores correlate with elevated risks of depression and PTSD in adulthood. Additional studies have explored mediating mechanisms: Wu et al. (2022) show that self-esteem mediates the ACEs-SWB link among Chinese college students, while Fu and Chen (2023) find that elder abuse mediates this association among older adults.

Interestingly, gratitude and resilience (Ho et al. 2021), and mindfulness (Huang et al. 2021) have been found to buffer the negative effects of ACEs. Based on a sample of 1871 university students, Huang et al. (2021) further report that childhood emotional neglect and abuse reduce happiness during the COVID-19 pandemic.

Overall, several aspects of previous research are worth highlighting. First, most studies focus on developed countries, with limited research on rural China, where distinct cultural, political, and social contexts may shape the prevalence and consequences of ACEs. Thus, findings from Western contexts may not generalize to rural China, as traditional cultural norms such as strict child-rearing practices emphasizing parental authority, filial obedience, and family harmony (Xu et al. 2024; Zhang et al. 2020) may heighten vulnerability to ACEs. Second, previous literature predominantly relies on cross-sectional designs, with only a few studies employing short-term longitudinal data. Third, endogeneity concerns in the ACEs–SWB relationship are rarely rigorously addressed. Fourth, the mechanisms underlying the link between ACEs and later-life SWB remain underexplored in rural China. To address these research gaps, this study makes four key contributions to the literature. First, leveraging longitudinal data from the 2011–2020 waves of the CHARLS linked with the 2014 CHARLS Life History Survey, we examine the long-term effects of ACEs on SWB among middle-aged and older adults in rural China. The use of longitudinal data provides three main advantages: it allows us to control for time-invariant unobserved heterogeneity, thereby strengthening causal inference; it tracks changes in SWB and covariates over time, yielding more accurate measurements less susceptible to temporary shocks; and CHARLS's high inter-wave tracking rates[1] preserve sample representativeness and mitigate biases from selective attrition. Second, unlike prior literature, we employ both positive (life satisfaction) and negative (depression) SWB measures to provide a more nuanced understanding of the ACEs-SWB nexus. Third, we apply IV estimation to address potential endogeneity issues of ACEs. Finally, beyond examining the impact of ACEs on SWB, we explore the underlying pathways through which ACEs affect SWB.

7.2.2 Underlying Mechanisms

ACEs may influence later-life SWB through three primary pathways: (i) health status, (ii) health-related behaviors, and (iii) social participation.

Health status. Extensive evidence links ACEs to adverse adult health outcomes, including poor self-rated health, obesity, and chronic conditions such as hypertension and diabetes (Almuneef et al. 2014; Chang et al. 2019; Houtepen et al., 2020). The toxic stress framework posits that early-life adversity—without buffering from

[1] The CHARLS exhibits exceptionally high tracking rates. Retention has remained above 86% in every follow-up wave, with approximately 87% of the original baseline households still participating in the most recent wave (2020) (Zhao et al. 2023). This consistently high retention rate critically ensures the long-term representativeness of the sample and substantially mitigates concerns about bias from selective attrition.

safe, stable relationships—can lead to the prolonged activation of the body's stress response systems (Shonkoff et al. 2012). This chronic stress becomes biologically embedded, disrupting the development of nervous, endocrine, and immune systems. Over the life course, such physiological dysregulation accumulates as allostatic load, increasing vulnerability to long-term health deterioration (Ho et al. 2021; Wilson-Genderson et al. 2022). Given that health is a well-established fundamental determinant of SWB, this physiological pathway represents a primary mechanism through which ACEs reduce late-life SWB (Gwozdz and Sousa-Poza 2010; Steptoe et al. 2015).

Health-related behaviors. ACEs are also strongly associated with an increased likelihood of engaging in unhealthy behaviors, including smoking, excessive alcohol consumption, and substance use (Houtepen et al. 2020; Morton and Ferraro 2018). Neurobiological and developmental theories converge to explain this link: ACEs impair emotion regulation capacities, leading individuals to adopt maladaptive coping strategies (e.g., health-risk behaviors) to manage persistent emotional distress (Avalos and Johnson 2025). These behaviors directly undermine SWB. Although correlated, health status and health-related behaviors represent distinct pathways: the former captures the accumulated physiological and psychological burden across the life course, while the latter reflects behavioral adaptations to early-life adversity. Prior research confirms these are complementary (not interchangeable) pathways linking ACEs and SWB (Zhao and Li 2022; Zheng et al. 2021).

Social participation. Adults with ACEs face persistent barriers to meaningful social participation. For instance, ACE exposure is linked to higher rates of emotional insecurity and dysregulation, leading to maladaptive interpersonal strategies that hinder the formation and maintenance of trusting relationships (Tzouvara et al. 2023). Consequently, individuals with ACEs experience significantly greater loneliness and objective social isolation across the life course. These interpersonal deficits also reduce access to emotional support from family and peers, reinforcing social marginalization (Green Jr et al. 2012). Additionally, ACE-related outcomes such as substance abuse and infectious diseases can erode social trust and limit access to social resources, thereby creating negative feedback loops (Green Jr et al. 2012; Morton and Ferraro 2018). Furthermore, social engagement is a well-documented determinant of SWB (Sarracino 2010). Figure 1 illustrates a simple heuristic for possible mechanisms for the ACEs-SWB linkage.

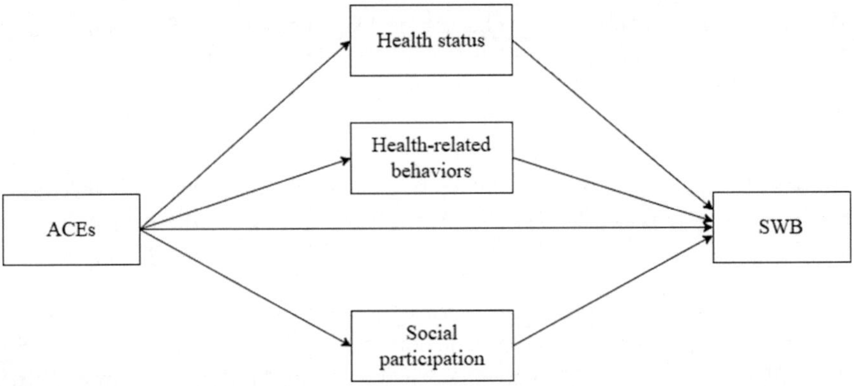

Fig. 1 Underlying mechanisms of the impact of ACEs on SWB among rural adults aged 45+ *Notes* ACEs = adverse childhood experiences; SWB = subjective well-being. *Source* Authors

7.3 Data and Method

7.3.1 Data

This study employs data from the China Health and Retirement Longitudinal Study (CHARLS), a nationally representative longitudinal survey conducted by the National School of Development at Peking University. CHARLS focuses on individuals aged 45 and above, with the baseline survey conducted in 2011 and follow-up waves conducted in 2013, 2015, 2018, and 2020.[2] The sample construction process is summarized in Fig. 2. We began with a pooled rural subsample from the 2011, 2013, 2015, 2018, and 2020 CHARLS waves, which we matched to the 2014 Life History Survey to obtain retrospective ACEs data. For each wave, we applied the following exclusion criteria sequentially (see Fig. 2): We first removed observations with missing data on ACEs or SWB. Then we removed observations with missing data on basic control variables. This procedure yields a final analytic sample of 17,265 participants. The wave-specific sample sizes are as follows: 3046 (2011), 3263 (2013), 2509 (2015), 4421 (2018), and 4026 (2020).

7.3.2 Subjective Well-Being (SWB)

The dependent variables include life satisfaction (measured on a 5-point scale, 1 = not at all satisfied to 5 = completely satisfied) and the Center for Epidemiologic Studies Depression (CES-D) score (measured on a 10-item scale). Life satisfaction

[2] A detailed introduction of CHARLS's sampling design is available in Zhao et al. (2014).

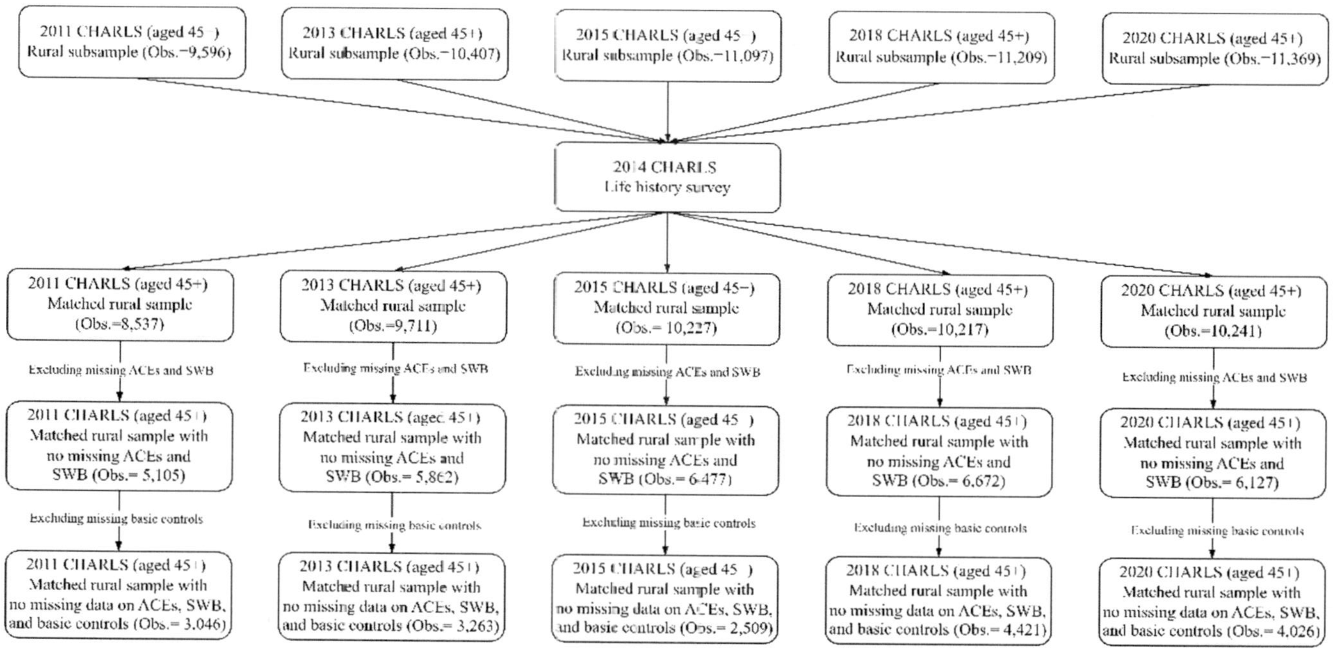

Fig. 2 Flow chart of the study sample. N*otes:* CHARLS = China Health and Retirement Longitudinal Study; Obs. = number of observations. ACEs = adverse childhood experiences; SWB = subjective well-being. Source: Authors

was selected as a core measure of SWB because it represents a stable, cognitive-judgmental evaluation of one's life as a whole. As a long-term self-assessment, it is less susceptible to transient emotional states and better reflects the enduring impact of life experiences (Pénard et al., 2013; Nie et al. 2021b). This makes it particularly well-suited for capturing the sustained consequences of childhood adversity. For CES-D, each item assesses the frequency of specific emotions experienced during the past week, rated on a 4-point scale (0 = rarely to 3 = most of the time). Negative items are scored directly, while positive items are reverse-coded. The total CES-D score ranges from 0 to 30, with higher scores indicating a greater likelihood of depression. As a robustness check, we also introduce a binary indicator of depressive symptoms (1 = CES-D score $\geq$ 10; 0 = CES-D score < 10).

7.3.3 ACEs

The three ACE domains—peer bullying, physical abuse, and emotional neglect—were chosen to capture significant adversity both within and outside the family environment, all of which are established as highly impactful on long-term SWB (Hughes et al. 2017; Ge et al. 2024). To construct a comprehensive measure, each ACE item is assessed on a four-point scale (0–3). These scores are then summed to yield a cumulative ACE score, with higher scores indicating greater exposure to adverse experiences. For robustness checks, we also examine each item separately. This approach is standard practice because it effectively captures both the multi-dimensional nature and the intensity of adverse experiences. The cumulative score reflects the well-documented finding that greater frequency and co-occurrence of ACEs indicate more chronic exposure to stress, which is disproportionately detrimental to long-term psychological well-being (Kovacic and Orso 2022; Xu et al. 2024).

Peer bullying is measured by two questions: "When you were a child, how often were you picked on by kids at school/in the neighborhood?", with four responses ranging from 0 (never) to 3 (often) for each question. The total score ranges from 0 to 6, with a higher score indicating greater exposure to bullying.

Physical abuse is assessed using three questions: "When you were growing up, did your female/male guardian or sibling ever hit you?", with responses coded on a 4-point scale ranging from 0 (never) to 3 (often). A total score (0–9) is calculated, with higher scores indicating more severe physical abuse.

Emotional neglect is measured by six questions, including "How much love and affection did your female guardian give you while you were growing up?", "How much effort did your female guardian put into watching over you?", "How strict was your female/male guardian with her/his rules for you?", and "Did your female/male guardian treat your siblings better than you when you were growing up?". Responses are similarly scored from 0 (never) to 3 (often), yielding a total score (0–18), where higher scores reflect greater emotional neglect.

7.3.4 Controls

Following previous SWB research (Deaton 2008; Nie et al. 2021b), covariates include individual and household characteristics. Individual characteristics encompass age and its squared term, gender (1 = male, 0 = female), educational level (low = primary school or below, medium = middle/high school, and high = vocational school or above), and marital status (1 = married/living together, 0 = separated/divorced/widowed/single). Household characteristics include total household income (logged) and household size.

7.3.5 Mechanism Variables

To explore potential mechanisms through which ACEs influence SWB, we consider three categories of hypothesized mediators: (i) health status, (ii) health-related behaviors, and (iii) social activity participation. Specifically, health status is assessed using four measures, including self-reported health (SRH, 1 = poor/very poor, 0 = very good/good/fair), number of chronic diseases, number of functional limitations in activities of daily living (ADLs: dressing, bathing, eating, getting in or out of bed, toileting, and continence), and instrumental activities of daily living (IADLs: housework, cooking, shopping, taking medications, and managing money). Health-related behaviors include physical inactivity (1 = no mild, moderate, or vigorous activity >10 min/week, 0 otherwise), sleep deprivation (1 = sleeps <7 h/night, 0 = otherwise), smoking (1 = yes, 0 = no), and alcohol use (1 = yes, 0 = no). Social participation is measured by engagement in social activities (1 = participation in social activities in the previous month; 0 = otherwise) and by the number of different types of activities.

7.3.6 Estimation Strategies

First, we employ standard OLS to examine the relationship between ACEs and SWB. Then, considering the potential endogeneity of ACEs, we introduce the two-stage least squares (2SLS) estimator to investigate the causal relationship between ACEs and SWB.

7.3.6.1 Ordinary Least Squares (OLS) Regressions

Although the 5-point scaling of our life satisfaction measure may suggest that a latent-variable estimation method would be most appropriate, the bias introduced by an OLS analysis is relatively small (Ferrer-i-Carbonell and Frijters 2004). Therefore, we adopt the standard OLS regression method applied in the majority of SWB studies

(Blanchflower and Oswald 2008a; Nie et al. 2021b). More specifically, we apply an OLS estimation based on the following model:

$$SWB_{it} = \beta_0 + \beta_1 ACE_i + \beta_2 X_{it} + \rho_c + \delta_t + \mu_{it} \quad (1)$$

where SWB_{it} denotes the SWB of individual i in terms of life satisfaction and CES-D score, and ACE_i denotes ACEs suffered by individual i. X_{it} involves individual and household characteristics. ρ_c denotes community fixed effects, δ_t represents year fixed effects, and μ_{it} is a random error term.

7.3.6.2 Two-Stage Least Squares (2SLS)

The use of OLS estimation raises concerns about potential endogeneity in ACEs. While reverse causality is likely less problematic in our context, omitted-variable bias remains a significant source of endogeneity, as both ACEs and SWB may be simultaneously affected by unobserved family and individual factors. For instance, parents experiencing financial distress may create more adverse family environments, thereby increasing children's exposure to ACEs and independently impairing their SWB in adulthood. Similarly, heritable parental traits—such as low emotional stability or poor impulse control—may simultaneously increase a child's risk of ACEs and, through genetic pathways, directly lower their SWB later in life. To identify the causal effect of ACEs on SWB, we employ a two-stage instrumental variable (IV) approach. Our primary IV, childhood neighborhood, measures mutual assistance among neighbors during childhood. This variable is derived from the 2014 CHARLS Life History Survey question: "Were the neighbors of the place where you lived as a child willing to help each other out?", coded on a 4-point scale from 0 (not willing at all) to 3 (very willing). For robustness, we also construct an alternative IV, neighborhood harmony, based on the question: "Were the neighbors of the place where you lived as a child very close-knit?" (0 = not close-knit at all, 1 = not very close-knit, 2 = somewhat close-knit, 3 = very close-knit).

Our IV satisfies two key IV assumptions. First, childhood neighborhood cohesion buffers family-level stressors, reducing ACEs such as abuse, neglect, and family dysfunction (Mosley-Johnson et al. 2019; Zhao and Li 2022). This suggests our IV meets the relevance assumption. Second, for our cohort (rural Chinese adults aged 45 and above), childhood neighborhood exposure was exogenously determined. Their childhoods (1930s–1970s) coincided with a period of limited mobility and land-based livelihoods, leaving families with no discretion in selecting their neighborhood. Additionally, we include community fixed effects to control for time-invariant community-level confounders (e.g., local culture, long-run economic development, and social capital) that may link childhood neighborhood cohesion to adult SWB. Our identification thus relies on within-community variation in childhood neighborhood experiences, which we argue influences later-life well-being primarily by shaping exposure to ACEs. Thus, our IV also meets the exclusion restriction assumption. Specifically, we estimate the following second-stage equation of the IV model:

$$SWB_{it} = \alpha_0 + \alpha_1 ACE_i^* + \alpha_2 X_{it} + \lambda_c + \gamma_t + \varepsilon_{it} \quad (2)$$

where ACE_i^* denotes the predicted value of the potentially endogenous variable of individual ACEs, λ_c denotes community fixed effects, γ_t represents year fixed effects, and ε_{it} is an error term. To obtain ACE_i^*, we estimate the first-stage equation using a linear regression model as follows:

$$ACE_i = \varphi_0 + \varphi_1 Z_i + \varphi_2 X_{it} + \theta_c + \tau_t + \omega_{it} \quad (3)$$

Z_i represents the IV, proxied by childhood neighbor relationships within a community. The definitions of other variables are the same as those in Eq. (2).

7.4 Results

7.4.1 Descriptive Statistics

As shown in Table 1, the mean values for respondents' life satisfaction and CES-D score are 3.2 and 8.57, respectively. The average number of ACEs reported by respondents is 7.67. The sample has a mean age of approximately 59.7 years, with 58% female participants and 90% currently married or cohabiting. Education is predominantly low (68%), followed by medium (30%) and high (2%) levels.

7.4.2 *Effect of ACEs on SWB*

Table 2 presents the results from the OLS and 2SLS estimates examining the impact of ACEs on SWB. Columns (1) and (2) show OLS results, indicating that ACEs are significantly and positively associated with CES-D scores and negatively associated with life satisfaction, suggesting that childhood adversity is linked with poorer SWB in adulthood. The first-stage results of IV estimation demonstrate that our instrument (neighborhood help) is significantly and negatively correlated with ACEs (columns 3 and 5). This supports our assumption that individuals who grow up in more supportive neighborhood environments are less likely to experience childhood adversity. The first-stage F-test results (F-statistic = 108.230 and 102.208) reject the null hypothesis of a weak instrument. Columns (4) and (6) present the second-stage results of IV estimates and show that ACEs significantly increase CES-D scores and reduce life satisfaction. Notably, the effect sizes are larger in the IV estimates than in the OLS estimates, suggesting that OLS estimation is likely subject to attenuation bias. The results for the control variables align with established patterns in the well-being literature. Higher education levels and household income are consistently associated with better SWB outcomes, the latter confirming the important role of economic

Table 1 Summary statistics

Variable	N	Mean	SD	Min	Max
Subjective Well-being					
Life satisfaction	16,982	3.200	0.750	1	5
CES-D score	17,265	8.570	6.220	0	30
Explanatory variables					
ACEs	17,265	7.670	4.200	0	30
Emotional neglect	17,265	5.210	2.820	0	18
Physical abuse	17,265	1.730	1.720	0	9
Peer bullying	17,265	0.740	1.290	0	6
Control variables					
Age (in years)	17,265	59.70	8.840	45	96
Gender (1 = male; 0 = female)	17,265	0.580	0.490	0	1
Education:					
Low	17,265	0.680	0.470	0	1
Medium	17,265	0.300	0.460	0	1
High	17,265	0.0200	0.130	0	1
Marital status (1 = married/living together; 0 = separated/divorced/widowed/single)	17,265	0.900	0.300	0	1
Household size	17,265	3.090	1.580	1	14
Logged household income	17,265	9.300	1.580	4.650	15.50
Instrumental variable					
Neighborhood help (0–3)	17,127	2.360	0.740	0	3
Mechanism variables					
Health					
Self-reported health (0 = very good/good/fair; 1 = poor/very poor)	13,234	0.730	0.440	0	1
Chronic diseases	17,265	1.800	1.690	0	13
ADL	17,265	0.340	0.920	0	6
IADL	17,265	0.370	0.910	0	5
Health-related behavior					
Smoking (1 = yes; 0 = no)	15,401	0.440	0.500	0	1
Alcohol use (1 = yes; 0 = no)	13,232	0.510	0.500	0	1
Physical inactivity (1 = yes; 0 = no)	12,170	0.0900	0.290	0	1
Sleep deprivation (1 = sleeps <7 h/day; 0 = otherwise)	17,152	0.540	0.500	0	1
Social activity participation	17,263	0.460	0.500	0	1

(continued)

Table 1 (continued)

Variable	N	Mean	SD	Min	Max
Engagement in social activities	17,263	0.810	0.990	0	8
Number of social activities	15,401	0.440	0.500	0	1

Notes ACEs = adverse childhood experiences. ACEs include three domains: peer bullying, assessed by two items capturing the frequency of being bullied or picked on by other children at school or in the neighborhood (a 4-point scale ranging from 0 = never to 3 = often); physical abuse, measured by three items asking whether a parent, guardian, or sibling ever hit the respondent (a 4-point scale ranging from 0 = never to 3 = often); and emotional neglect, measured by six items evaluating the frequency of experiences related to a lack of love, care, supervision, as well as perceptions of excessive strictness or differential treatment from guardians (a 4-point scale ranging from 0 = never to 3 = often). The scores for all items across the three domains are summed to create a cumulative total ACEs score. Education: low (primary school or below), medium (middle/high school), high (vocational school or above).*Source* Authors

resources in the Chinese context (Nie et al. 2021b). Similarly, married individuals report significantly lower depression and higher life satisfaction, a finding consistently documented in high-income countries and echoed in rural China by Knight et al. (2009). These results confirm the overall validity of our model.

7.4.3 Effects of Different Types of ACEs on SWB

Table 3 presents the IV estimates examining how distinct ACE types - peer bullying, physical abuse, and emotional neglect (capturing extra-familial and intra-familial adversity)-affect SWB differently.[3] Two key findings are worth highlighting: First, all three types of ACEs are significantly associated with poorer SWB outcomes, irrespective of life satisfaction or depression. Second, while the magnitudes of estimated coefficients vary, the consistency and significance of all three types suggest that both physical and emotional maltreatment-whether originating in household or community settings - exert long-term negative effects across different SWB dimensions.

7.4.4 Potential Mechanisms

To elucidate the pathways linking ACEs to SWB, we employ IV estimations to examine the effects of ACEs on three key mediators: health status, health-related behaviors, and social activity participation.[4] Table 4 reveals several key findings: First, ACEs significantly increase the likelihood of reporting poor health, the number

[3] The full results are available in Appendix Table 12.

[4] The full results are available in Appendix Table 13.

Table 2 OLS and IV estimates of the impacts of ACEs on SWB

	OLS		2SLS			
	CES-D score	Life satisfaction	ACEs	CES-D score	ACEs	Life satisfaction
	(1)	(2)	(3)	(4)	(5)	(6)
ACEs	0.158*** (0.012)	−0.014*** (0.001)		1.232*** (0.171)		−0.176*** (0.024)
Neighborhood help			−0.468*** (0.045)		−0.460*** (0.046)	
Age	0.431*** (0.061)	−0.0004 (0.008)	−0.020 (0.043)	0.458*** (0.076)	−0.022 (0.043)	−0.005 (0.011)
Age squared	−0.003*** (0.001)	0.00004 (0.0001)	−0.001 (0.0003)	−0.003*** (0.001)	−0.001 (0.0004)	−0.00003 (0.0001)
Male	−2.274*** (0.097)	0.047*** (0.012)	1.242*** (0.064)	−3.603*** (0.244)	1.257*** (0.064)	0.248*** (0.034)
Education: Medium	−0.613*** (0.103)	−0.026** (0.013)	−0.104 (0.072)	−0.501*** (0.129)	−0.115 (0.072)	−0.045*** (0.017)
Education: High	−1.684*** (0.291)	0.002 (0.040)	0.224 (0.224)	−1.930*** (0.369)	0.210 (0.226)	0.039 (0.053)
Marital status	−1.718*** (0.172)	0.099*** (0.022)	−0.358*** (0.104)	−1.323*** (0.211)	−0.360*** (0.106)	0.044 (0.029)
Household size	0.042 (0.033)	0.003 (0.004)	0.019 (0.022)	0.025 (0.041)	0.020 (0.023)	0.005 (0.006)
Household income	−0.366*** (0.033)	0.031*** (0.004)	0.008 (0.022)	−0.363*** (0.041)	0.008 (0.023)	0.031*** (0.006)
Community fixed effects	Yes	Yes	Yes	Yes	Yes	Yes
Year fixed effects	Yes	Yes	Yes	Yes	Yes	Yes
Kleibergen-Paap rk Wald F statistic			108.230		102.208	
N	17,265	16,982	17,127	17,127	16,845	16,845

Notes Robust standard errors in parentheses. *** $p < 0.01$, ** $p < 0.05$, * $p < 0.1$. Education: low (primary school or below), medium (middle/high school), high (vocational school or above). *Source* Authors

of chronic diseases, ADLs, and IADLs (columns 1–4, Panel A), corroborating Liu et al. (2022)'s findings on ACEs' health consequences in China. Second, ACEs are associated with a higher risk of sleep deprivation and physical inactivity (columns 3–4, Panel B) - both are well-established determinants of lower SWB (Steptoe and Fancourt, 2019). However, they show no significant association with smoking or alcohol use (columns 1–2, Panel B). This null finding may reflect China's distinct cultural context, in which tobacco/alcohol use is more strongly influenced by social

Table 3 IV estimates of the effects of different types of ACEs on SWB

	Life satisfaction			CES-D score		
	(1)	(2)	(3)	(4)	(5)	(6)
Peer bullying	−0.386*** (0.047)			2.717*** (0.339)		
Physical abuse		−0.732*** (0.139)			5.086*** (0.960)	
Emotional neglect			−0.576*** (0.139)			4.044*** (0.962)
Community fixed effects	Yes	Yes	Yes	Yes	Yes	Yes
Year fixed effects	Yes	Yes	Yes	Yes	Yes	Yes
Kleibergen-Paap rk Wald F statistic	185.338	36.094	19.946	194.475	38.978	20.991
N	16,845	16,845	16,845	17,127	17,127	17,127

Notes The explanatory variables are different types of ACEs. ***, **, * indicate significance at the levels of 1%, 5%, and 10%, respectively. Robust standard errors are in parentheses. *Source* Authors

customs than by childhood adversity (Huang and Grol-Prokopczyk, 2022). Third, ACEs are significantly associated with reduced social engagement, decreasing both the likelihood of participation and the diversity of activities (columns 1–2, Panel C), suggesting social disengagement as a potential channel.

7.4.5 Robustness Checks

To assess the reliability of our primary findings, we perform several robustness checks, including the use of alternative models and IVs, an alternative SWB measure, potential confounding from the COVID-19 pandemic, birth-cohort fixed effects, and adulthood and parental characteristics.

7.4.5.1 Alternative Models and IVs

To ensure the robustness of our findings, we have estimated two alternative models: an ordered probit and an IV ordered probit. The results, presented in Table 5, are in line with our main analysis. Once again, ACEs have a consistently positive and significant effect on CES-D score and a significantly negative effect on life satisfaction.

To assess the robustness and validity of the IV estimation, we examine its sensitivity to alternative specifications by testing additional IVs. First, we substitute our primary IV (neighborhood help) with neighborhood harmony. The estimates

Table 4 Mechanism analysis

Panel A: Health status	SRH	Chronic diseases	ADLs	IADLs
	(1)	(2)	(3)	(4)
ACEs	0.066*** (0.012)	0.155*** (0.038)	0.114*** (0.025)	0.140*** (0.026)
Community fixed effects	Yes	Yes	Yes	Yes
Year fixed effects	Yes	Yes	Yes	Yes
Kleibergen-Paap rk Wald F statistic	108.281	108.230	108.230	108.230
N	17,123	17,127	17,127	17,127
Panel B: Health-related behaviors	Smoking	Alcohol use	Physical inactivity	Sleep deprivation
ACEs	0.013 (0.008)	−0.010 (0.011)	0.022** (0.010)	0.039*** (0.012)
Community fixed effects	Yes	Yes	Yes	Yes
Year fixed effects	Yes	Yes	Yes	Yes
Kleibergen-Paap rk Wald F statistic	105.062	84.071	63.689	108.087
N	15,272	13,128	12,072	17,018
Panel C: Social activity participation	Engagement in social activities	Number of social activities		
ACEs	−0.058***	−0.127***		
	(0.012)	(0.025)		
Community fixed effects	Yes	Yes		
Year fixed effects	Yes	Yes		
Kleibergen-Paap rk Wald F statistic	108.106	108.106		
N	17,125	17,125		

Notes: Robust standard errors in parentheses. *** $p < 0.01$, ** $p < 0.05$, * $p < 0.1$. *Source* Authors

(columns 1–2, Table 6) are similar to our baseline results. Second, we use both neighborhood help and neighborhood harmony as instruments and conduct an overidentification test. The IV estimates (columns 3–6, Table 6) are also similar to our baseline results, and the Hansen J tests yield *p*-values above 0.1 across all specifications, failing to reject the null hypothesis that our instruments are valid.

Table 5 Robustness checks: alternative models

	Ordered probit		IV ordered probit	
	Life satisfaction	CES-D score	Life satisfaction	CES-D score
	(1)	(2)	(3)	(4)
ACEs	−0.022*** (0.002)	0.027*** (0.002)	−0.193*** (0.013)	0.123*** (0.014)
Community fixed effects	Yes	Yes	Yes	Yes
Year fixed effects	Yes	Yes	Yes	Yes
N	16,982	17,265	16,845	17,265

Notes Robust standard errors in parentheses. *** $p < 0.01$, ** $p < 0.05$, * $p < 0.1$. *Source* Authors

Table 6 Robustness checks: assessing IV's validity

	Using neighbor harmony		Using both neighborhood help and harmony			
	Life satisfaction	CES-D score	ACEs	CES-D score	ACEs	Life satisfaction
	(1)	(2)	(3)	(4)	(5)	(6)
ACEs	−0.158*** (0.017)	0.947*** (0.118)		1.042*** (0.167)		−0.163*** (0.024)
Neighborhood help			−0.221** (0.089)		−0.207*** (0.089)	
Neighborhood harmony			−0.637*** (0.109)		−0.646*** (0.109)	
Community fixed effects	Yes	Yes	Yes	Yes	Yes	Yes
Year fixed effects	Yes	Yes	Yes	Yes	Yes	Yes
Hansen J statistic (p value)				1.906 (0.1674)		0.414 (0.5198)
Kleibergen-Paap rk Wald F statistic	193.640	195.783		36.886		36.715
N	16,927	17,210	17,097	17,097	16,815	16,815

Notes Robust standard errors in parentheses. *** $p < 0.01$, ** $p < 0.05$, * $p < 0.1$. *Source* Authors

Furthermore, we employ the imperfect instrumental variable approach of Nevo and Rosen (2012), which provides consistent estimates even if the exclusion restriction is partially violated. As shown in Table 7, the 95% confidence intervals for these estimates exclude zero and encompass our baseline 2SLS results. This indicates that the significant negative effect of ACEs on later-life SWB persists even after accounting for potential imperfections in our instruments.

Table 7 Bounds of estimates with weakly endogenous instrumental variable

	CES-D score	Life satisfaction
	(1)	(2)
Lower bound	0.1969	−0.2120
Upper bound	1.3166	−0.0230

Notes Model specifications of panels A and B are the same as those in columns 2 and 4 of Table 5, respectively. The upper and lower bounds are calculated following Nevo and Rosen's (2012) approach. *Source* Authors

Table 8 Robustness checks: alternative SWB measure, samples, and specifications

	Alternative SWB measure	Excluding the 2020 wave		Birth cohort fixed effects	
	Depressive symptom	Life satisfaction	CES-D score	Life satisfaction	CES-D score
	(1)	(2)	(3)	(4)	(5)
ACEs	0.080*** (0.013)	−0.168*** (0.027)	1.226*** (0.193)	−0.174*** (0.023)	1.257*** (0.168)
Community fixed effects	Yes	Yes	Yes	Yes	Yes
Year fixed effects	Yes	Yes	Yes	Yes	Yes
Kleibergen-Paap rk Wald F statistic	108.230	78.456	84.275	108.062	113.687
N	17,127	12,853	13,135	16,845	17,127

Notes Robust standard errors in parentheses. *** $p < 0.01$, ** $p < 0.05$, * $p < 0.1$ *Source* Authors

7.4.5.2 Alternative SWB Measure

As a robustness check, we use a binary measure (1 = CES-D score $\geq$ 10; 0 = otherwise) as a proxy for depressive symptoms and rerun the IV estimate. Results in column (1) of Table 8 confirm the robustness of our main results.

7.4.5.3 Considering the Impact of COVID-19

Given the COVID-19 pandemic's unique stressors (e.g., social isolation, fear of infection, and service disruptions), which may confound ACEs-SWB relationships, we exclude the 2020 wave. The results confirm the robustness of our main findings from Table 2, showing that ACEs significantly increase CES-D scores and reduce life satisfaction (columns 2–3, Table 8).

7.4.5.4 Birth Cohort Fixed Effects

To address potential generational differences in ACE exposure and SWB trajectories shaped by historical events or policy changes, we incorporate birth-cohort fixed effects, and our main results remain robust (columns 4 and 5, Table 8).

7.4.5.5 Controlling for Adulthood and Parental Characteristics

To further address potential confounding factors and confirm the robustness of our findings, we control for a set of adulthood characteristics that could influence SWB, including medical insurance coverage (1 = yes, 0 = no), pension benefits (1 = yes, 0 = no), and type of last job (1 = non-farming, 0 = farming), social connectedness (proxied by frequency of in-person meetings and remote communications (phone, text, mail, or email) with children, measured on a nine-point scale ranging from 0 = less than once a year to 8 = almost every day). For respondents with multiple children, we use the median frequency across all children. As shown in Table 9, including these variables does not alter the estimated ACE-SWB relationship, confirming the robustness of our main results.

To further account for the potential confounding influence of parental characteristics, we conduct an additional robustness check controlling for key parental characteristics: both mother's and father's education (illiterate vs. literate) and occupation (non-farming vs. farming). As shown in Table 10, the estimated effect of ACEs on SWB remains statistically significant and stable after controlling for these factors, reinforcing the robustness of our primary findings.

7.4.6 Heterogeneity Analysis

To identify the most vulnerable groups and deepen our understanding of the impact of ACEs on SWB, we examine heterogeneity across various sociodemographic characteristics. The negative effect of ACEs is more pronounced among individuals with middle school or higher education than among those with primary school or less. This difference is statistically significant based on a Wald test (Panel A, Table 11), likely because elevated life expectations amplify the perceived impact of early-life adversity on well-being (Clark et al., 2008). Regionally, rural residents in eastern China experience a larger ACEs-SWB penalty than those in central/western regions (Panel B, Table 11), possibly reflecting stronger comparative pressures in economically developed areas (Knight and Gunatilaka, 2010). However, the difference is insignificant for depression. Gender differences emerge but lack statistical significance: females show marginally greater ACEs on life satisfaction, while males exhibit slightly stronger associations with depression.

Table 9 Robustness checks: controlling for adulthood characteristics

	Life satisfaction	CES-D score
	(1)	(2)
ACEs	−0.166***	1.122***
	(0.029)	(0.203)
Age	−0.008	0.519***
	(0.015)	(0.105)
Age squared	0.00001	−0.003***
	(0.0001)	(0.001)
Male	0.235***	−3.624***
	(0.039)	(0.271)
Education: Medium	−0.057**	−0.439***
	(0.023)	(0.169)
Education: High	−0.038	−1.490***
	(0.063)	(0.438)
Marital status	0.034	−1.026***
	(0.033)	(0.240)
Household size	0.006	0.003
	(0.008)	(0.057)
Logged household income	0.033***	−0.362***
	(0.008)	(0.056)
Pension benefit	−0.015	0.112
	(0.028)	(0.207)
Medical insurance	0.040	0.287
	(0.063)	(0.401)
Frequency of meeting with children	−0.0003	−0.091**
	(0.006)	(0.042)
Frequency of connecting with children	0.017***	−0.147***
	(0.006)	(0.041)
Last job	0.066***	−0.709***
	(0.025)	(0.181)
Community fixed effects	Yes	Yes
Year fixed effects	Yes	Yes
Kleibergen-Paap rk Wald F statistic	67.738	72.875
N	9479	9604

Notes Robust standard errors in parentheses. *** $p < 0.01$, ** $p < 0.05$, * $p < 0.1$. Education: low (primary school or below), medium (middle/high school), high (vocational school or above). *Source* Authors

Table 10 Robustness checks: controlling for parental characteristics

	Life satisfaction	CES-D score
	(1)	(2)
ACEs	−0.180***	1.168***
	(0.025)	(0.173)
Age	−0.001	0.413***
	(0.011)	(0.078)
Age squared	−0.00007	−0.002***
	(0.00009)	(0.001)
Male	0.251***	−3.565***
	(0.037)	(0.255)
Education: Medium	−0.032*	−0.486***
	(0.018)	(0.132)
Education: High	0.039	−1.754***
	(0.057)	(0.382)
Marital status	0.025	−1.278***
	(0.030)	(0.216)
Household size	0.010*	0.005
	(0.006)	(0.042)
Logged household income	0.028***	−0.332***
	(0.006)	(0.042)
Mother's education	0.013	−0.433**
	(0.026)	(0.182)
Father's education	−0.003	−0.220*
	(0.017)	(0.125)
Mother's occupation	0.040	1.123**
	(0.077)	(0.557)
Father's occupation	0.019	−0.290
	(0.026)	(0.182)
Community fixed effects	Yes	Yes
Year fixed effects	Yes	Yes
Kleibergen-Paap rk Wald F statistic	99.3553	104.1120
N	15,475	15,739

Notes Robust standard errors in parentheses. *** $p < 0.01$, ** $p < 0.05$, * $p < 0.1$. Education: low (primary school or below), medium (middle/high school), high (vocational school or above). *Source* Authors

Table 11 IV estimates for the effect of ACEs on SWB by various sociodemographic characteristics

	Life satisfaction		CES-D score	
	(1)	(2)	(3)	(4)
Panel A: By education	Middle school or above	Primary school or below	Middle school or above	Primary school or below
ACEs	−0.246*** (0.059)	−0.154*** (0.026)	2.473*** (0.554)	0.940*** (0.176)
Controls	Yes	Yes	Yes	Yes
Kleibergen-Paap rk Wald F statistic	23.055	79.160	23.042	85.701
N	5383	11,462	5440	11,687
Wald test P-value	0.068		0.002	
Panel B: By region	Central and west	East	Central and west	East
ACEs	−0.143*** (0.027)	−0.241*** (0.050)	1.158*** (0.206)	1.393*** (0.316)
Controls	Yes	Yes	Yes	Yes
Kleibergen-Paap rk Wald F statistic	67.354	33.845	73.591	33.619
N	10,545	6300	10,742	6385
Wald test P-value	0.036		0.304	
Panel C: By gender	Male	Female	Male	Female
ACEs	−0.158*** (0.031)	−0.192*** (0.035)	1.340*** (0.244)	1.049*** (0.227)
Controls	Yes	Yes	Yes	Yes
Kleibergen-Paap rk Wald F statistic	53.390	54.091	55.361	58.545
N	9803	7042	9961	7166
Wald test P-value	0.242		0.204	

Notes Robust standard errors in parentheses. *** $p < 0.01$, ** $p < 0.05$, * $p < 0.1$ *Source* Authors

7.5 Conclusion and Implications

Using nationally representative longitudinal data from the 2011–2020 CHARLS, this study investigates the relationship between ACEs and SWB among rural Chinese adults aged 45 and above. Our findings confirm that ACEs significantly reduce later-life SWB, manifesting as higher depressive symptoms and lower life satisfaction. These negative effects are more pronounced among highly educated individuals and those residing in rural eastern China, possibly due to higher life expectations and greater socioeconomic pressures. Mechanism analyses reveal that ACEs impair SWB by worsening health, promoting unhealthy behaviors (e.g., poor sleep and physical inactivity), and reducing social participation.

Our findings have several important policy implications. First, given the high prevalence of ACEs in rural areas, policymakers urgently need to strengthen the rural child welfare system. This includes expanding family support programs (e.g., parenting training and financial subsidies for low-income families) to alleviate parenting stress and reduce the risk of child maltreatment (Almuneef et al. 2014; Ho et al. 2021). Additionally, establishing a multi-level early warning system integrating village committees, rural schools, and health clinics to accurately identify at-risk children early and provide timely psychological counseling and temporary care. Especially for rural eastern China, tailored programs are needed to address region-specific stressors (e.g., migration-related parent-child separation) by supporting left-behind children through community-based care centers and digital parenting support tools. Second, to disrupt the "long arm" of ACEs, policymakers should target the identified mediating pathways. This involves expanding access to affordable basic health services (e.g., mobile clinics, telemedicine platforms) to effectively manage chronic conditions and psychological issues linked to ACEs. For unhealthy behaviors, delivering community-based health education programs tailored to rural populations. To boost social participation, invest in rural community infrastructure (e.g., community centers) and group activities (e.g., hobby clubs, volunteer programs) that foster social connections, particularly for highly-educated rural residents who may face greater social isolation due to unmet expectations. Third, strengthening mental health support systems to address deficits in SWB. It is essential to launch public awareness campaigns (via rural radio, community meetings) to normalize discussions of mental health, reduce stigma, and raise awareness of ACE-related psychological impacts. Additionally, expanding the rural mental health workforce by training primary care providers, village doctors, and community workers in basic mental health screening and counseling.

This study has several notable strengths, including the use of nationally representative longitudinal data, a comprehensive assessment of SWB incorporating both positive and negative dimensions, the application of IV estimation to address endogeneity, and an in-depth exploration of the underlying mechanisms.

This study, however, is subject to three primary limitations. First, the retrospective measure of ACEs may be susceptible to recall and social desirability biases. Future research should employ prospective longitudinal designs and techniques like randomized response methods to improve measurement reliability. Second, while our instrumental variable approach helps address endogeneity, the exclusion restriction could be challenged by unobserved confounders. Employing quasi-natural experiments offers a promising avenue for future research to further solidify causal inferences. Third, while self-esteem is a theoretically important mechanism linking ACEs to later-life well-being, we are unable to test this pathway because relevant data are unavailable. When such data become available, examining the mediating role of self-esteem should be a priority for future research.

Acknowledgments The authors would like to thank the National School of Development, together with the Institute for Social Science Survey at Peking University, for providing the CHARLS data. We also thank the editor and two anonymous reviewers for their helpful comments.

Funding This work was supported by the National Natural Science Foundation of China (grant number 71804142). The findings, interpretations, and conclusions expressed in this paper are entirely those of the authors, and all errors are our own.

Data availability
Data will be made available on request.

Competing Interests
The authors declare no competing interests.

Appendix

(See Tables 12 and 13).

Table 12 IV estimates of the effects of different types of ACEs on SWB

	Life satisfaction	Life satisfaction	Life satisfaction	CES-D score	CES-D score	CES-D score
	(1)	(2)	(3)	(4)	(5)	(6)
Peer bullying	−0.386*** (0.047)			2.717*** (0.339)		
Physical abuse		−0.732*** (0.139)			5.086*** (0.960)	
Emotional neglect			−0.576*** (0.139)			4.044*** (0.962)
Age	−0.017* (0.010)	−0.009 (0.015)	0.016 (0.019)	0.540*** (0.070)	0.480*** (0.102)	0.317** (0.134)
Age squared	0.0001 (0.0001)	−0.00003 (0.0001)	−0.0003 (0.0002)	−0.004*** (0.001)	−0.002*** (0.001)	−0.001 (0.001)
Male	0.087*** (0.016)	0.561*** (0.104)	0.244*** (0.059)	−2.489*** (0.118)	−5.742*** (0.714)	−3.561*** (0.403)
Education: Medium	−0.043*** (0.015)	−0.074*** (0.026)	−0.024 (0.030)	−0.501*** (0.115)	−0.294 (0.184)	−0.665*** (0.216)
Education: High	0.114** (0.050)	0.044 (0.084)	−0.076 (0.094)	−2.438*** (0.347)	−1.944*** (0.591)	−1.162* (0.643)
Marital status	0.097*** (0.024)	0.042 (0.039)	−0.035 (0.059)	−1.705*** (0.181)	−1.316*** (0.273)	−0.759* (0.417)
Household size	−0.001 (0.005)	0.010 (0.008)	0.010 (0.010)	0.067* (0.037)	−0.011 (0.056)	−0.008 (0.071)
Logged household income	0.029*** (0.005)	0.039*** (0.008)	0.028*** (0.010)	−0.345*** (0.037)	−0.413*** (0.055)	−0.350*** (0.069)
Community fixed effects	Yes	Yes	Yes	Yes	Yes	Yes
Year fixed effects	Yes	Yes	Yes	Yes	Yes	Yes
Kleibergen-Paap rk Wald F statistic	185.338	36.094	19.946	194.475	38.978	20.991
N	16,845	16,845	16,845	17,127	17,127	17,127

Notes The explanatory variables are different types of ACEs. ***, **, * indicate significance at the levels of 1%, 5%, and 10%, respectively. Robust standard errors are in parentheses. Education: low (primary school or below), medium (middle/high school), high (vocational school or above). *Source* Authors

Table 13 Mechanism analysis

Panel A: Health status	SRH	Chronic diseases	ADLs	IADLs
	(1)	(2)	(3)	(4)
ACEs	0.066*** (0.012)	0.155*** (0.038)	0.114*** (0.025)	0.140*** (0.026)
Age	0.020*** (0.005)	0.188*** (0.017)	0.017 (0.011)	0.005 (0.012)
Age squared	−0.0001* (0.00004)	−0.001*** (0.0002)	0.0001 (0.0001)	0.0002 0.0001
Male	−0.141*** (0.016)	−0.398*** (0.054)	−0.262*** (0.035)	−0.350*** (0.036)
Education: Medium	−0.022*** (0.009)	−0.007 (0.029)	−0.043** (0.017)	−0.076*** (0.017)
Education: High	−0.119*** (0.024)	0.221** (0.101)	−0.254*** (0.041)	−0.237*** (0.048)
Marital status	0.017 (0.014)	−0.077 (0.048)	0.013 (0.031)	0.026 (0.032)
Household size	0.004 (0.003)	−0.005 (0.009)	0.016*** (0.006)	0.028*** (0.006)
Logged household income	−0.024*** (0.003)	−0.023** (0.009)	−0.023*** (0.005)	−0.036*** (0.006)
Community fixed effects	Yes	Yes	Yes	Yes
Year fixed effects	Yes	Yes	Yes	Yes
Kleibergen-Paap rk Wald F statistic	108.281	108.230	108.230	108.230
N	17,123	17,127	17,127	17,127
Panel B: Health-related behaviors	Smoking	Alcohol use	Physical inactivity	Sleep deprivation
ACEs	0.013 (0.008)	−0.010 (0.011)	0.022** (0.010)	0.039*** (0.012)
Age	0.026*** (0.004)	0.009* (0.005)	−0.016*** (0.004)	0.030*** (0.006)
Age squared	−0.0002*** (0.00003)	−0.0001** (0.00004)	0.0002*** (0.00004)	−0.0002*** (0.0001)
Male	0.642*** (0.011)	0.539*** (0.016)	−0.034** (0.013)	−0.116*** (0.017)
Education: Medium	−0.017*** (0.006)	−0.010 (0.009)	−0.013** (0.006)	0.00002 (0.009)
Education: High	−0.117*** (0.028)	−0.019 (0.029)	−0.031 (0.021)	−0.051* (0.031)

(continued)

Table 13 (continued)

Panel A: Health status	SRH	Chronic diseases	ADLs	IADLs
Marital status	−0.034*** (0.010)	−0.014 (0.014)	−0.005 (0.011)	−0.039*** (0.014)
Household size	−0.003 (0.002)	−0.008*** (0.003)	−0.001 (0.002)	−0.0004 (0.003)
Logged household income	0.001 (0.002)	0.014*** (0.003)	−0.006*** (0.002)	0.001 (0.003)
Community fixed effects	Yes	Yes	Yes	Yes
Year fixed effects	Yes	Yes	Yes	Yes
Kleibergen-Paap rk Wald F statistic	105.062	84.071	63.689	108.087
N	15,272	13,128	12,072	17,018
Panel C: Social activity participation	Social participation	Number of social activities		
ACEs	−0.058*** (0.012)	−0.127*** (0.025)		
Age	−0.011* (0.006)	−0.043*** (0.011)		
Age squared	0.00002 (0.0001)	0.0001 (0.0001)		
Male	0.062*** (0.018)	0.223*** (0.035)		
Education: Medium	0.029*** (0.010)	0.089*** (0.021)		
Education: High	0.210*** (0.031)	0.499*** (0.080)		
Marital status	−0.084*** (0.015)	−0.118*** (0.029)		
Household size	−0.013*** (0.003)	−0.037*** (0.006)		
Logged household income	0.024*** (0.003)	0.064*** (0.006)		
Community fixed effects	Yes	Yes		
Year fixed effects	Yes	Yes		
Kleibergen-Paap rk Wald F statistic	108.106	108.106		
N	17,125	17,125		

Notes Robust standard errors in parentheses. *** $p < 0.01$, ** $p < 0.05$, * $p < 0.1$. Education: low (primary school or below), medium (middle/high school), high (vocational school or above) *Source* Authors

References

Almuneef, M., Qayad, M., Aleissa, M., & Albuhairan, F. (2014). Adverse childhood experiences, chronic diseases, and risky health behaviors in Saudi Arabian adults: a pilot study. *Child Abuse & Neglect, 38*(11), 1787-1793.

Avalos, I. F., & Johnson, P. S. (2025). Childhood trauma and risky sexual behaviors: Comparing positive and negative emotion-related processes. *Child Abuse & Neglect, 170*, 107804.

Bartolomé-Valenzuela, M., Pereda, N., & Guilera, G. (2024). Patterns of adverse childhood experiences and associations with lower mental well-being among university students. *Child Abuse & Neglect, 152*, 106770.

Bauer, J. M., Levin, V., Munoz Boudet, A. M., Nie, P., & Sousa-Poza, A. (2017). Subjective well-being across the lifespan in Europe and Central Asia. *Journal of Population Ageing, 10*, 125-158.

Binder, M., & Coad, A. (2015). Heterogeneity in the relationship between unemployment and subjective wellbeing: A quantile approach. *Economica, 82*(328), 865-891.

Blanchflower, D. G., & Bryson, A. (2024). The adult consequences of being bullied in childhood. *Social Science & Medicine, 345*, 116690.

Blanchflower, D. G., & Oswald, A. J. (2008a). Hypertension and happiness across nations. *Journal of Health Economics, 27*(2), 218-233.

Blanchflower, D. G., & Oswald, A. J. (2008b). Is well-being U-shaped over the life cycle? *Social Science & Medicine, 66*(8), 1733-1749.

Chang, X., Jiang, X., Mkandarwire, T., & Shen, M. (2019). Associations between adverse childhood experiences and health outcomes in adults aged 18–59 years. *Plos One, 14*(2), e0211850.

Chen, X., Giles, J., Yao, Y., Yip, W., Meng, Q., Berkman, L., Chen, H., Chen, X., Feng, J., & Feng, Z. (2022). The path to healthy ageing in China: a Peking University–Lancet Commission. *The Lancet, 400*(10367), 1967-2006.

Clark, A. E., Frijters, P., & Shields, M. A. (2008). Relative income, happiness, and utility: An explanation for the Easterlin paradox and other puzzles. *Journal of Economic Literature, 46*(1), 95-144.

Corcoran, M., & McNulty, M. (2018). Examining the role of attachment in the relationship between childhood adversity, psychological distress and subjective well-being. *Child Abuse & Neglect, 76*, 297-309.

Deaton, A. (2008). Income, health, and well-being around the world: Evidence from the Gallup World Poll. *Journal of Economic Perspectives, 22*(2), 53-72.

Diener, E., & Biswas-Diener, R. (2002). Will money increase subjective well-being? *Social Indicators Research, 57*, 119-169.

Diener, E., & Diener, M. (2009). Cross-cultural correlates of life satisfaction and self-esteem. In E. Diener (Ed.), *Culture and Well-Being: The Collected Works of Ed Diener* (pp. 71–91): Springer Netherlands.

Ferrer-i-Carbonell, A., & Frijters, P. (2004). How important is methodology for the estimates of the determinants of happiness? *The Economic Journal, 114*(497), 641-659.

Frijters, P., Haisken-DeNew, J. P., & Shields, M. A. (2004). Money does matter! Evidence from increasing real income and life satisfaction in East Germany following reunification. *American Economic Review, 94*(3), 730-740.

Fu, Y., & Chen, M. (2023). Long-term effects of childhood adversity on the subjective well-being of older adults in urban China: The mediating effect of elder abuse. *Aging & Mental Health, 27*(3), 621-629.

Ge, T., Liu, Y., Han, Q., Cheng, X., & Jiang, Q. (2024). Childhood intra-and extra-familial maltreatment and later-life trajectories of depressive symptoms: evidence from China. *BMC Geriatrics, 24*(1), 598.

Green Jr, H. D., Tucker, J. S., Wenzel, S. L., Golinelli, D., Kennedy, D. P., Ryan, G. W., & Zhou, A. J. (2012). Association of childhood abuse with homeless women's social networks. *Child Abuse & Neglect, 36*(1), 21-31.

Gwozdz, W., & Sousa-Poza, A. (2010). Ageing, health and life satisfaction of the oldest old: An analysis for Germany. *Social Indicators Research, 97*, 397-417.

Ho, G. W., Chan, A., Shevlin, M., Karatzias, T., Chan, P., & Leung, D. (2021). Childhood adversity, resilience, and mental health: A sequential mixed-methods study of Chinese young adults. *Journal of Interpersonal Violence, 36*(19-20), NP10345-NP10370.

Houtepen, L. C., Heron, J., Suderman, M. J., Fraser, A., Chittleborough, C. R., & Howe, L. D. (2020). Associations of adverse childhood experiences with educational attainment and adolescent health and the role of family and socioeconomic factors: a prospective cohort study in the UK. *PLOS Medicine, 17*(3), e1003031.

Huang, C. C., Chen, Y., Cheung, S., Hu, H., & Wang, E. (2021). Adverse childhood experiences, mindfulness and happiness in Chinese college students during the COVID-19 pandemic. *Child & Family Social Work, 26*(4), 677-686.

Huang, R., & Grol-Prokopczyk, H. (2022). Health and health behaviors in China: anomalies in the SES-health gradient? *SSM-Population Health, 17*, 101069.

Hughes, K., Bellis, M. A., Hardcastle, K. A., Sethi, D., Butchart, A., Mikton, C., Jones, L., & Dunne, M. P. (2017). The effect of multiple adverse childhood experiences on health: a systematic review and meta-analysis. *The Lancet Public Health*, 2(8), e356-e366.

Inglehart, R. (2002). Gender, aging, and subjective well-being. *International Journal of Comparative Sociology, 43*(3-5), 391-408.

Irshad, S., & Lone, A. (2025). Adverse childhood experiences and their influence on psychological well-being and emotional intelligence among university students. *BMC psychology*, 13(1), 255.

Knight, J., & Gunatilaka, R. (2010). The rural–urban divide in China: Income but not happiness? *The Journal of Development Studies, 46*(3), 506-534.

Knight, J., Lina, S. O. N. G., & Gunatilaka, R. (2009). Subjective well-being and its determinants in rural China. *China Economic Review*, 20(4), 635-649.

Kovacic, M., & Orso, C. E. (2022). Trends in inequality of opportunity in health over the life cycle: The role of early-life conditions. *Journal of Economic Behavior & Organization, 201*, 60-82.

Li, C., Chi, I., Zhang, X., Cheng, Z., Zhang, L., & Chen, G. (2015). Urban and rural factors associated with life satisfaction among older Chinese adults. *Aging & Mental Health, 19*(10), 947-954.

Liu, H., Ackert, L. F., Chang, F., Oyelere, R. U., Qi, L., & Shi, Y. (2022). Childhood trauma among Chinese inmates. *China Economic Review, 73*, 101794.

Moore, K. A., & N. Ramirez, A. (2016). Adverse childhood experience and adolescent well-being: Do protective factors matter? *Child Indicators Research, 9*, 299-316.

Morton, P. M., & Ferraro, K. F. (2018). Does early-life misfortune increase the likelihood of psychotropic medication use in later life? *Research on Aging, 40*(6), 558-579.

Mosley-Johnson, E., Garacci, E., Wagner, N., Mendez, C., Williams, J. S., & Egede, L. E. (2019). Assessing the relationship between adverse childhood experiences and life satisfaction, psychological well-being, and social well-being: United States Longitudinal Cohort 1995–2014. *Quality of Life Research, 28*, 907-914.

Nahar, K., Mousum, S., Salwa, M., Fatema, K., Chowdhury, T., Tasnim, A., Khan, M. M. H., & Haque, M. A. (2025). Childhood echoes: How benevolent and adverse childhood experiences shape adult mental well-being. *Child Abuse & Neglect*, 163, 107308.

Nevo, A., & Rosen, A. M. (2012). Identification with imperfect instruments. *Review of Economics and Statistics*, 94(3), 659-671.

Nie, P., Li, Y., Zhang, N., Sun, X., Xin, B., & Wang, Y. (2021a). The change and correlates of healthy ageing among Chinese older adults: findings from the China health and retirement longitudinal study. *BMC Geriatrics, 21*, 1-13.

Nie, P., Ma, W., & Sousa-Poza, A. (2021b). The relationship between smartphone use and subjective well-being in rural China. *Electronic Commerce Research, 21*(4), 983-1009.

Nie, P., & Zhao, Y. (2023). Aging in China. In D. E. Bloom, Sousa-Poza, A., and Sunde, U. (Ed.), *Routledge Handbook on the Economics of Ageing* (pp. 691–712). London: Routledge.

Oshio, T., Umeda, M., & Kawakami, N. (2013). Childhood adversity and adulthood subjective well-being: Evidence from Japan. *Journal of Happiness Studies, 14*, 843-860.

Park, J., Lee, H., Chung, S., & Jang, Y. (2026). The impact of adverse childhood experiences on depressive symptoms in later life: Mediating role of self-perceptions of aging in low-income older Korean immigrants. *Journal of Gerontological Social Work*, 69(1), 79-90.

Pénard, T., Poussing, N., & Suire, R. (2013). Does the Internet make people happier? *The Journal of Socio-Economics*, 46, 105-116.

Potter, S., Bridger, E., & Drewelies, J. (2025). Daily health and well-being in adulthood and old age: The role of adverse childhood experiences. *Applied Psychology: Health and Well-Being*, 17(1), e12637.

Rzeszutek, M., Grabowska, M., Dragan, M., Lis-Turlejska, M., Schier, K., Kowalkowska, J., Styśko-Kunkowska, M., Malinowska, E., Osiński, T., Bargiel-Matusiewicz, K., Sosińska, B., Ibisz, M., Almazova, S., Bagiński, M., & Szumiał, S. (2025). Negative and positive childhood experiences with regard to PTSD and subjective well-being in the national sample of Poles. *Scientific Reports*, 15(1), 38825.

Sarracino, F. (2010). Social capital and subjective well-being trends: Comparing 11 western European countries. *The Journal of Socio-Economics, 39*(4), 482-517.

Shonkoff, J. P., Garner, A. S., Committee on Psychosocial Aspects of Child and Family Health, Committee on Early Childhood, Adoption, and Dependent Care, and Section on Developmental and Behavioral Pediatrics, Siegel, B. S., Dobbins, M. I., Earls, M. F., Garner, A. S., McGuinn, L., Pascoe, J., & Wood, D. L. (2012). The lifelong effects of early childhood adversity and toxic stress. *Pediatrics, 129*(1), e232-e246.

Steptoe, A., Deaton, A., & Stone, A. A. (2015). Subjective wellbeing, health, and ageing. *The Lancet, 385*(9968), 640-648.

Steptoe, A., & Fancourt, D. (2019). Leading a meaningful life at older ages and its relationship with social engagement, prosperity, health, biology, and time use. *Proceedings of the National Academy of Sciences, 116*(4), 1207-1212.

Tzouvara, V., Kupdere, P., Wilson, K., Matthews, L., Simpson, A., & Foye, U. (2023). Adverse childhood experiences, mental health, and social functioning: A scoping review of the literature. *Child Abuse & Neglect, 139*, 106092.

United Nations. (2020). *World population ageing 2019* (ST/ESA/SER.A/444). Retrieved from New York: https://digitallibrary.un.org/record/3846855?v=pdf

Wilson-Genderson, M., Heid, A. R., Cartwright, F., & Pruchno, R. (2022). Adverse childhood experiences, adult trauma, and depressive symptom trajectories. *Aging & Mental Health, 26*(11), 2170-2178.

Wu, Q., Cao, H., Lin, X., Zhou, N., & Chi, P. (2022). Child maltreatment and subjective well-being in Chinese emerging adults: a process model involving self-esteem and self-compassion. *Journal of Interpersonal Violence, 37*(15-16), NP13685-NP13706.

Xu, P., Liu, Z., Xu, Y., Li, T., Xu, G., Xu, X., Wang, L., Yan, Y., Xiao, S., & Li, L. (2024). The prevalence and profiles of adverse childhood experiences and their associations with adult mental health outcomes in China: a cross-sectional study. *The Lancet Regional Health-Western Pacific, 53*.

Zhang, L., Mersky, J. P., & Topitzes, J. (2020). Adverse childhood experiences and psychological well-being in a rural sample of Chinese young adults. *Child Abuse & Neglect, 108*, 104658.

Zhao, Y., Chen, X., Wang, Y., Meng, Q., Bo, H., Chen, C., Chen, Y., Gong, J., Jia, Y., Wang, G., Wu, X., Yan, L., Yang, P., & Zhou, H. (2023). China Health and retirement longitudinal study wave 5 (2020) user guide. Beijing: National School of Development at Peking University.

Zhao, C., & Li, X. (2022). Living under the shadow: Adverse childhood experiences and entrepreneurial behaviors in Chinese adults. *Journal of Business Research, 138*, 239-255.

Zhao, Y., Hu, Y., Smith, J. P., Strauss, J., & Yang, G. (2014). Cohort profile: the China health and retirement longitudinal study (CHARLS). *International Journal of Epidemiology, 43*(1), 61-68.

Zheng, X., Shangguan, S., Fang, Z., & Fang, X. (2021). Early-life exposure to parental mental distress and adulthood depression among middle-aged and elderly Chinese. *Economics & Human Biology*, *41*, 100994.